CAPTURING THE **Beat** MOMENT

CAPTURING THE Beat MOMENT

Cultural Politics and the Poetics of Presence

Erik Mortenson

Southern Illinois University Press
Carbondale and Edwardsville

14   13   12   11   4   3   2   1

Library of Congress Cataloging-in-Publication Data

Mortenson, Erik, 1970–
    Capturing the beat moment : cultural politics and
the poetics of presence / Erik Mortenson.
        p.   cm.
    Includes bibliographical references and index.
    ISBN-13: 978-0-8093-3013-3 (alk. paper)
    ISBN-10: 0-8093-3013-X (alk. paper)
    ISBN-13: 978-0-8093-8613-0 (ebook)
    ISBN-10: 0-8093-8613-5 (ebook)
    1. Beat generation. 2. American literature—20th
century—History and criticism. I. Title.
PS228.B6M66 2010
810.9'0054—dc22   2010010658

To my parents,
and to Lia

When work is done as sacred work, unselfishly, with a peaceful mind, without lust or hate, with no desire for reward, then the work is pure.

—*The Bhagavad Gita*

Contents

Acknowledgments

This book could not have been completed without the sustained support of colleagues, friends, and family. I sincerely thank Barrett Watten for his unflagging support of the manuscript from start to finish. He set a style of mentorship that I strive to attain in my own career, remaining critical yet supportive, all the while allowing my own thoughts and ideas to develop. Thanks goes to Carla Harryman for always offering a fresh perspective. I also owe a deep gratitude to Charles Stivale. His personal mentorship, along with the profitable debates and dialogues from our Deleuze Humanities group, pushed my thinking in new and invigorating directions. Michael Davidson was gracious enough to read the manuscript at an early stage. Jerry Herron and Henry Golemba also provided valuable comments throughout the manuscript stages. I thank Ryan Clendenin, whose late-night, coffee-fueled discussions always challenged me to not lose focus on the personal throughout the project. Christopher Kramer offered the same advice and was always a source of inspiration when spirits were flagging. I wish to thank Mark Huston for always challenging me with the philosophical, and Heidi Eichbauer for reminding me of the spiritual. I am grateful to Lia McCoskey for her critical eye that caught many errors throughout the revision process and for always encouraging me to stay with the project even when times were tough. Tony Trigilio provided invaluable comments, and his insightful suggestions produced a better manuscript. The same goes for Kurt Hemmer, a tireless supporter of Beat Studies and a true colleague.

I also thank Karl Kageff for believing in this book and to everyone at Southern Illinois University Press who contributed their time at all stages of the project. I also thank Molly Schwartzburg and the staff at the Harry Ransom Humanities Research Center. Thanks goes out to the editors at *College Literature* and the *Chicago Review*, both of whom have previously published sections of this work, as well as to John-Whalen Bridge, who, along with Gary Storhoff, edited *The Emergence of Buddhist American Literature*, from which a portion of this book was taken. For permission to use Ginsberg's photos, I thank Peter Hale at the Allen Ginsberg Trust. I am grateful for Andres Serrano's permission to use his artwork and for

Robert La Vigne's permission to use his. Thanks to the Wylie Agency for the use of Ginsberg's poem "Kral Majales" and to Corbis for permission to reprint Andy Warhol's "Double Elvis." I thank the estate of Lenore Kandel for permission to use the cover to her book and to the people at New Directions for allowing me to reprint the cover of Gregory Corso's volume. Dean Sami Gülgöz at Koç University has likewise been supportive of this project, and I thank him.

Finally, I thank my parents, Art and Ellen Mortenson, for their love and support throughout my life, without which this book would not have been possible.

My apologies to anyone I might have forgotten. Although this book is ultimately mine and any mistakes or shortcomings my own, it would not have been possible without the support of innumerable people, and I thank them all here.

Introduction
Rethinking the Beats

> *God is a parking meter.*
> —*Bob Kaufman*

"Seize the moment." "Be present." "Live in the now." This volume examines the ideological and cultural assumptions that underpin a supposedly natural return to the evanescent present in Beat Generation writings. For the Beats, capturing true immediacy involves focusing attention on desire and action as they spontaneously respond to the material conditions of each passing moment. This attention allows the Beats to establish an authentic connection to the world that forms the basis for a poetics of presence—a writing that transcribes the flux of experience as it wells up in each successive instant. In order to achieve this relationship to the moment, the Beats oftentimes challenged cultural norms, earning for themselves the title of rebels or outsiders. However, contextualizing the Beats within an early-postmodern rubric that reinscribes Beat writings within the divide between the modern and postmodern reveals that they were very much a product of their time. While the passing moment may appear to offer an unexplored territory awaiting discovery, the Beats arrive in each new present with a burden of history (both individual and social) that complicates the ways in which they attempt to utilize the present. This is not to claim that the Beat quest for the ephemeral moment is misguided. On the contrary, the Beats' desire to "capture immediacy" offers valuable insights into how meaning is constantly produced. This book ultimately argues that the Beats' relationship to the moment is a productive one; examining the motivations that the Beats necessarily bring to their project can produce better understanding of both the successes and failures of the Beat desire to live and write the present as it continually unfolds through space and time.

The epigraph that heads this introduction, taken from Bob Kaufman's broadside "Second April," demonstrates the multiple forces at play in Beat writing. What makes Kaufman's line so effective is that it forces a second glance at two concepts normally taken for granted. The parking meter enacts a particular structural relationship to the world, and by equating this instrument with the concept of God, Kaufman pulls back the veil to expose a nexus of possible relationships. Placing two highly charged images alongside one another, Kaufman produces myriad meanings in the gap between. The term "God" connotes transcendental authority, a power higher than humankind who acts as arbiter and judge. The term "parking meter" is a device that distributes both time and space in a pecuniary manner. Much like a clock, the parking meter measures temporality. But unlike the ubiquity of clock time, the parking meter is situated in space. And as a rented space, Kaufman's image becomes inextricably linked to capitalism—one must pay to leave one's car there.

Just how do these two images fit together? Kaufman is commenting on God itself—our metaphysical deity demarcates the space of our bodies and the time they may exist upon the earth, and we pay for this service in tithes, devotion, and supplication. Once our meter is up, we must vacate our spot, so another can take our place. Or perhaps we have turned our parking meters into God. Here Kaufman calls us to task for installing a regime of temporal and spatial surveillance that we must constantly feed in order to remain in place. In a burgeoning postwar consumer economy, everything is for sale, including time and space. But it is also the ambiguity between potential readings that Kaufman is capturing with his line. The inability to finally know which reading is "correct" is a reflection of the social condition that Americans found themselves in during the 1950s. Unable to accept a position wholesale after the atrocities of World War II, Americans nevertheless sought a comforting stability in an otherwise unstable world. Kaufman's line offers an existential choice that jars the reader into understanding—choose a meaning or live in a world devoid of one.

The choice of Kaufman here is not arbitrary. Kaufman's position as a half-Jewish, half–African American writer encapsulates the cultural tensions of the postwar era. In challenging the conformist paradigms of the time, the Beats often reproduced many of the social assumptions at work in the very culture they critiqued. This double-edged nature of Beat discourse makes it the perfect vehicle for exploring the tensions and changes occurring in American literature and culture during the postwar period. This current critique is necessarily revisionist—through an expanded Beat canon, it offers an account of Beat practices that reveal how gender and race affect Beat politics of the moment.[1] Opening the Beat canon to women writers such as Diane di Prima, Janine Pommy Vega, and Joyce Johnson as well as to African American authors like Bob Kaufman and LeRoi Jones / Amiri Baraka allows for a much-richer understanding of the Beats and the possibilities that their thinking creates. Because of their marginalized position within society, these writers provide Beat thinking on the moment with a social valence unavailable to their more recognized colleagues. Placing these groups into dialogue not only helps us to locate the shortcomings of more privileged and accepted Beat conceptions of the moment but simultaneously offers novel conceptions of immediacy that foreground the ways in which the social impinges on the moment's seeming neutrality. The Beat moment is a construct and can only be understood through a broadened canon.

In addition to exploring writers outside the Jack Kerouac–Allen Ginsberg–William S. Burroughs triumvirate, this study is also informed by a range of philosophical conceptions—existentialism, marxism, poststructuralism—that elucidate and challenge Beat thinking on the moment. Taking their cue from the Beats themselves, many critics tend to dismiss the relevance of theory for Beat scholarship. The anti-academe, anti-intellectual Beats, so the story goes, were not interested in dense philosophical arguments that abstracted one out of concrete experience. Yet, what this trend misses is that Beat thinking is highly theoretical, even if it is not overtly couched in philosophical terms. The Beats discussed ideas with philosophical currency, and to ignore their formulations of the moment is to do a disservice to the range and depth of their thinking. Again, recent Beat scholarship marks a shift towards utilizing theory to explicate their texts, and this volume follows in this burgeoning tradition.[2] The idea is not to simply overlay a theoretical formulation onto Beat writing in order to make it conform to the strictures of a particular "ism." Rather, theoretical conceptualizations need to be placed next to Beat ones in order to arrive at a "third space" between. Juxtaposing literary writing and philosophical discourse allows each component to elucidate the other. Confronting Beat writing with the philosophical provides a necessary critique of the construction and effectiveness of Beat conceptions of the moment, thus giving their work the intellectual rigor it demands and deserves.

Beat thinking about the moment, however, does not occur in a vacuum. The Beats occupied an important period in American literary and cultural history when the modern was giving way to what is now termed the postmodern. The use of the term "moment" in this work's title thus has a double meaning. Exploring the Beats' desire to live life fully within each successive present, *Capturing the Beat Moment* seeks to explain the factors that inhibit this return, what this moment might look like, and the possibilities it offers for personal discovery and social change. Yet, "moment" also stands for the social, political, and cultural position in which the Beats find themselves. As difficult as the terms "modernism" and "postmodernism" are to define, they are indispensable to an understanding of the Beats' liminal position in postwar America. The 1950s saw many changes: demographic shifts in population, a change from a hot to a cold war, and a shift from an industrial to a consumer economy. Exploring this pivotal moment allows insight into how cultural events impacted Beat thinking and how the Beats themselves left their mark on the American landscape. Sandwiched between an age of industry and an age of technology, between a culture of presence and one of mediated images, between modernity and postmodernity, the Beats occupy an important moment in the cultural history of America.

The postwar decade had a profound impact on Beat thinking. As Daniel Belgrad claims, this "culture of spontaneity" was "balanced on the cusp between a modernist exploration of individual consciousness and a postmodern exploration of cultural conventions; and between a modernist quest for universal values and a postmodern insistence on the contextuality of meaning" (263). If modernism is rightly described as encompassing a desire for totality, and postmodernism the challenge to such creation of meaning in the form of the discrete, the displaced, and the constructed, then Belgrad is arguing that a special place be allotted for this postwar culture. The Beats' exploration of individual consciousness certainly aligns them with modernism. And their "modernist quest for universal values" leads the Beats on a search for truth, value, and reality in a constantly changing world.[3] Yet, the Beats also presage the postmodern turn. Despite such desires for totality, the Beats are continually in flux, ceaselessly exploring new avenues to personal and social alterations and testing the limits of subjectivity, agency, representation, and collectivity.

A second clue to the Beats' exemplary status in the twentieth century comes from the journal *Boundary 2*. Writing from within the transition from the modern to the postmodern, critics in this journal posited a postmodernism that looks strikingly different from the subsequent version that has emerged. Looking back upon this propitious moment, editor Paul Bové terms this period "early postmodernism," and it is this designation that I apply to the Beats to make sense of a writing that falls somewhere between modernist and postmodernist. For these critics, there is still the possibility of meaning, but it is always contingent—"a" truth, not "the" truth. As discussed throughout this book, a few Beat scholars have remarked on the relevance of the modern or postmodern as rubrics for understanding the Beat canon; still, none has explored this topic in systematic depth.[4] An examination of the Beats' liminal position as early postmodern, however, is essential in coming to terms with the challenges they pose to modernist thought and the possibilities they offer to rethink the current "high" postmodern condition.

One way to understand the early postmodern is to explore how its conception of the moment differs from that of modernism and postmodernism. Peter Osborne observes in *The Politics of Time* that the very notion of modernity is filled with anxiety. Each new present threatens all that has come before it, leaving modernism with the difficult problem of making sense of a constantly changing world. From within this viewpoint there is no foreseeable end to modern innovation; perhaps for the first time in history, there is a sense that humankind is now destined to live in a world that must constantly re-create itself with each passing moment. Modernist writers court this condition, living on history's perpetually unfolding edge. Although modernists may follow Ezra Pound's dictum "make it new," this declaration creates an originality that enters into tradition with a cumulative effect. This is how T. S. Eliot, in "Tradition and the Individual Talent," can claim that as new works are created, they cause a ripple effect in a canon that remains generally stable across time. "Modernity is that which is ephemeral, fugitive, contingent upon the occasion; it is half of art, whose other half is the eternal and unchangeable," describes Charles Baudelaire (37). Modernity pushes the artist to address the contingent upon the occasion, which is always fleeting and always new. But this is only half of Baudelaire's equation. The other half is the eternal and unchangeable, a vast repository of elements that remain fixed across time. The world might be constantly changing, but responses to that flux still partake of constancy that defeats time.

Postmodernism has reacted strongly to these grand narratives used by modernists to countermand the flux of temporality, instead positing notions of distanciation, deferral, and absence as correctives to what it sees as modernism's reliance on a dubious historical justification for discrete events. Such stability, Jacques Derrida demonstrates, is simply a desire for wholeness bereft of epistemological underpinnings. Rather than corral moments under a rubric that seeks to give them meaning, postmodernism instead opts to revel in the instant as a singular event in time. Postmodernism likewise relies on the new. In *A Singular Modernity*, Fredric Jameson claims that postmodernism "seems utterly unable to divest itself of this final requirement of originality" (152). But there is a difference in this postmodern moment—though original, it is not employed in the service of totality.

Early postmodernism attempts to reside between these two tendencies. For the Beats, life is seen as an existential project and thus forms a sort of totality—each lived moment aggregates into a larger entity. This is the Beats' modernism, a desire to make sense of lived experience that is constantly undergoing change and flux. History is not just another arbitrarily assigned grand narrative but a legacy of choices and conditions that can be utilized to do work in the future. But within the moment itself, wholeness is quickly discarded, even discouraged. Here, grand narratives do become inhibitory, and the goal of the Beats is to allow themselves the widest possible range of encounters with the newness that stands outside their particular being. The Beats' postmodernism resides in their desire to repeatedly break free from any constraining rubric that thwarts the ability to expand the range of experience. Such experimentation goes beyond the desire simply to "make it new." Rather, it seeks to alter the categories of subject, body, and language in a manner that transcends their modernist predecessors. Modernist totality grounds the Beats; postmodernist differentiation lets them experiment and explore.

Take, for instance, the question of subjectivity. Modernism is generally seen as championing an individualized human subject making sense (or attempting to) of ever-changing conditions. The modernist hero-writer transcribes the chaos into literary form, while the bourgeois subject either fights valiantly against a stifling social system or succumbs to its logic or temptations. In either case, it is a fight for the individual to reclaim a more authentic sense of self in a world torn with confusion and falsities. Postmodernism, so the story goes, heralds the death of the subject. As yet another grand narrative, the subject is ripe for extermination, based as it is on so many untenable assumptions of autonomy and cohesion. Jameson, again in *A Singular Modernity*, makes the claim that these two positions are really not that far apart. Modernism desires a "new and deeper, richer subjectivity," while poststructuralist attacks on "centered subjects" might actually "constitute a liberation" (136, 34). Although constructing a new self and doing away with the notion of self both underscore dissatisfaction with existing conceptions of subjectivity, these two approaches lead down divergent paths. The former offers the possibility for a version of subjectivity superior to that which preceded it, while the latter takes issue with the notion that a stable self could be had at all.

Unsurprisingly, the Beats utilize both poles to craft a subjectivity stable enough to endure across time but porous enough to absorb the outside. The Beats are certainly looking for a new subjectivity to replace the subject positions foisted on them by a cold-war mentality of suspicion, fear, and hatred of the other. Yet, they do not simply create a new subjectivity to replace the old but ceaselessly explore possibilities in an effort to constantly break down fixed conceptions of the subject. Once again, modernist notions of stable subject positions provide a ground so that experiments into the more postmodern realm of decenteredness can have a place to return home. For the early-postmodern Beats, the subject is neither rigid nor dead but alternately both.

This same elasticity informs Beat thinking on language. In the modernist framework, language evidences a sort of wholeness—the world can indeed be represented. Although an individual subject may feel alienated, for instance, there is still a sense in which this alienation can be described to the reader. The modernist text contains a latent meaning, inscribed by the author-creator, that awaits discovery. Postmodernism has rightly taken issue with this viewpoint, instead positing a conception of language that involves deferral and indeterminateness. In Michel Foucault's terms, it is not that the subject speaks through the medium of language but that language speaks through the medium of the subject. Power relations are embedded in discourse, so any user of language is in some degree the passive recipient of a world preconstructed.

Early postmodernism takes issue with both of these positions. Appealing to the body itself, the Beats base their poetics on a conception of language derived from the corporeal. From lungs that breathe to hearts that beat, language is intimately connected with a body that is continually fluctuating across space and time. Such a conception avoids the modern view of language as a static vessel for meaning since the body is constantly changing. At the same time, there is a sense in this early-postmodern period that although language may not contain one single meaning, it can still contain "a" meaning that is contingent on time, place, and the reader. As theorists such as Maurice Merleau-Ponty (a French existentialist thinker familiar with Heidegger) and Gilles Deleuze make clear, writing done "through the body" allows both writer and reader to enter a flow that is simultaneously governed by the body and open to individual interpretation. This return to the body allows early postmodernism to avoid the stasis associated with modernism as well as the relativism (which is just stasis in another form) of the postmodern.

The early-postmodern position of the Beats provides a perfect opportunity for discussing the large-scale changes that were occurring in postwar America during the 1950s and 1960s. Although the Beats were not always self-conscious of this liminal position, their work nevertheless captures a moment when modernism began shifting over to a later postmodernism. What is so important about the Beats in particular is that they attempt a fusion of both periodizing concepts that, at its best, provides insights into the remaining uses of modernism's grand narratives and offers novel ways to rethink postmodernism's insistence on the discrete instant. The Beats combine the best of both concepts in order to craft a notion of the moment that allows for both agency and openness to the outside. Thus, the Beats are involved in a delicate balancing act. Utilizing modernism's grand narratives to provide a basis for their project, they then attempt to incorporate a postmodern decenteredness of being in order to reach new realms of experience. At the same time, recourse to modernist totality keeps their postmodern project from slipping into the relativism so characteristic of the current postmodern condition. Too much wholeness and the experiment fails, too little and there is no method for incorporating the experiences acquired back into quotidian existence. Riding the cusp of the modern-postmodern split, the Beats opt for the best of both agency and chaos, accumulating meaning in the midst of constant experimentation.

Beat scholarship can be divided into three main types: the single-author study, the thematic treatment, and the cultural inquiry. Most works on the Beats seek to understand a single author through a combination of close textual analysis and recourse to biographical and other extraliterary details. Such classic studies include Tim Hunt's *Kerouac's Crooked Road* and Regina Weinreich's *Spontaneous Poetics of Jack Kerouac,* both of which offer insightful explorations into Kerouac's writerly decisions. Other single-author studies such as Timothy S. Murphy's *Wising Up the Marks* or Tony Trigilio's book *Allen Ginsberg's Buddhist Poetics* view a Beat author through a particular topic or concern. Murphy, for example, draws on the work of Deleuze to discuss power in Burroughs's work, while

Trigilio examines Buddhism in Ginsberg's corpus. There is no dearth of scholarship on the Beats, and many more, worthwhile studies could be named. The Beat desire to capture the moment means that many of these studies discuss the role of spontaneity, especially as it pertains to Beat writing. Unfortunately, however, no single-author study addresses this book's topic of the moment exclusively.

Thematic treatments of the Beats engage multiple authors in order to examine larger trends in the Beat canon. While such studies are obviously too broad to attain the sort of depth characteristic of single-author works, they do have the advantage of being able to place Beat authors in a productive tension that helps to reveal trends within the Beat canon that might not be noticeable when examining a single author. Excluding studies such as Gregory Stephenson's *Daybreak Boys* that collect various Beat authors by assigning them each a separate chapter, the paradigmatic model for such multiauthor works is Michael Davidson's *San Francisco Renaissance*. Employing a concept of poetic community flexible enough to accommodate the disparate thinking within his San Francisco Renaissance, Davidson is able to trace the fecund exchanges and congruities that generate larger concepts across the Beat canon.

Capturing the Beat Moment follows in this tradition. There is a burgeoning desire in Beat studies to do away with the rubric of "Beat" altogether. Many critics feel that the term does not do justice to the myriad authors underneath its banner. Like any categorizing principle, essential differences are unfortunately elided. I would like to retain the concept of "Beat." One obvious reason is that it still enjoys currency—in the *Beat Reader* and the Beat Studies Association, for example. But more important, there are payoffs to studying authors as a group rather than as individuals. This method allows an understanding of how a concept, current in the culture at large, gets reworked by a specific group with specific interests. The Beats did not think alike, but they were united in their interest in the moment and its possibilities for living and writing. The solutions they proposed thus deserve closer scrutiny.

In addition to single-author and thematic treatments of the Beats, there is a growing trend towards utilizing Beat texts in the service of larger, cross-disciplinary cultural inquiries. Emblematic of this move are works such as Belgrad's *Culture of Spontaneity*, W. T. Lhamon's *Deliberate Speed*, and David Savran's *Taking It Like a Man*. All of these follow in the tradition of Barbara Ehrenreich's older, yet still influential, *Hearts of Men*. What unites these scholarly works is these authors' use of the Beats as a means to disclose larger trends in postwar culture. Belgrad, for instance, is concerned with the turn towards spontaneity in the postwar moment, and thus the Beats are important for the ways in which their writing practice elucidates this concept. For Savran, the Beats are useful as a means for discussing how the white male has come to be seen as a victim in American society. For this volume's purposes, these cultural analyses provide a starting point for thinking through Beat concepts. Cultural context is essential for a full understanding of the conceptualizations that the Beats developed, but to end with the social is to ignore that these formulations have efficacy that exceeds their particular social milieu. A recovery of the social, political, and cultural contexts of the postwar period in an effort to better comprehend the Beats' relationship to the fifties and sixties is crucial—without it, we run the risks of not only misrepresenting Beat reactions to their contemporaneous society but likewise miss the fruitful intersections that shed light on our own current situation.

As one of the first multiauthor studies that engages an expanded Beat canon critically, this volume marks a departure from previous Beat scholarship. The method employed here is one of triangulation—the personal and the theoretical are placed in tension with Beat texts in order to produce meaning in the interstices. All three points of this triangle are indispensable. The Beats are not chosen arbitrarily—their work constitutes a storehouse of concepts, ideas, and experiments that form the base material for discussion. The Beats actually lived these conceptions of the moment, and thus their writings are not just pieces of literature but documents of experimentation that provide invaluable evidence for evaluating the efficacy and relevance of their thinking. But as useful as the Beats are in disclosing possible avenues for exploration, their work often lacks the reflexivity necessary to adequately evaluate the concepts they created. The introduction of philosophy and literary theory provides a means to question Beat formulations, leading to a deeper understanding of their conception of the present. Here, the idea is not simply to use theory to explain the Beats or to use the Beats as evidence of the success of a particular theory but to place the two in tension so that a new, better conception can emerge. And into this heady mix comes the personal. This project represents a working through of how to encounter the moment on a personal level as well, inviting the reader who may not share in exactly the same feelings as the author to at least join him in questioning (and hopefully integrating) the gains made in this study on the existential level. The hope is that this method of triangulation will not only yield a better understanding of the Beat moment and its place in postwar literary and cultural history but will likewise allow for a more fruitful conception of how Beat thinking on the moment might be utilized for everyday, lived existence.

The first task, then, is to locate the Beats within their specific cultural milieu. The opening chapter explores Beat attempts to break free from constrictive notions of space and time that prevailed in the 1950s in order to reach a more primal realm of spontaneous experience. During this period, the Beats combated repressive spatial and temporal limitations derived from the workplace, the suburb, and the cold war with an insistence on spontaneous, lived experience that sought to redefine space-time as a fluid, personal conception. In order to theorize these concerns, I argue for existentialism and marxism as lenses for understanding the Beat project. Scholars such as Stephenson and John Lardas call on the Beats' anti-intellectual bent in order to dismiss the relevancy of these two movements, but a closer inspection of Beat letters, journals, biographies, and writing reveals that they were influenced by the intellectual currents that formed a cultural backdrop to their work. Drawing on marxists such as Georg Lukács to theorize the "reification" of society and on existential phenomenologists like Merleau-Ponty and Martin Heidegger to explain authentic attempts to combat it, this chapter addresses the societal pressures that inhibit the Beat return to the moment.

The textual site for this inquiry is Kerouac's novel *On the Road*. Supplemented with his other travel narratives, Kerouac's work provides a model for the type of authenticity that the Beats champion in their quest for the moment. Here, returning to the moment entails a strict attention to immediate desires and conditions, and freedom requires spontaneous action as each successive moment unfolds. Such unconstrained behavior challenged the fifties' status quo; in Beat scholarship, it is lauded as a major contribution to personal emancipation from repressive institutions and social structures. Yet, what are the implications of gender and race for this model? This first chapter explores discussions of domesticity and child rearing in Beat women writers such as di Prima to interrogate conceptions of spontaneous temporality derived from male Beat writers such as Kerouac. The work of African Americans such as Baraka likewise provide an implicit critique of Kerouac's expansive spatial program. The point here is that access to a liberatory temporality and spatiality is not equally available to all, at least not in the same form as it is to white, male Beats. This does not invalidate Kerouac's claims or lessen his achievements—it nuances his discussion of authentic space-time in order to arrive at an expanded understanding of Beat thinking and its applicability across cultural moments and embodied conditions.

Chapter 2 explores an important key to understanding the Beat moment—personal vision. In a 1948 Harlem apartment, Ginsberg saw "heaven in a cornice" and realized the interconnectedness of the personal and the social that would become a hallmark of his work. This conflation of the exalted with the quotidian is emblematic of a Beat desire to infuse spirituality into everyday existence. Visionary moments like Ginsberg's allow one to break free from normal, everyday conceptions of lived experience in order to conceptualize how space and time might be lived differently. But visions do more than provide a window to the outside—they simultaneously call into question basic assumptions about subjectivity. For the Beats, epiphanic experience requires that the visionary be willing to undergo a drastic change in his or her very self. Only by remaining open to the world can the vision occur, and, thus, this second chapter not only explores how the Beats attain such openness but likewise situates Beat conceptions of subjectivity within an early-postmodern framework. The Beats are neither modern nor postmodern—their work incorporates both in order to craft a conception of subjectivity that grounds the individual in the world and allows him or her to constantly mutate and adapt.

The heightened moment might abstract the Beats out of time, but that does not mean that the relationships among past, present, and future are elided. Ginsberg's cornice became heavenly, but it also retained a particular history that continued to exist long after he left his apartment. To theorize the place of history in the visionary moment, I draw extensively on the work of Heidegger and Walter Benjamin. Reading the Beats between these theorists' conceptions of how the past might be used in the visionary present demonstrates the dangers inherent in historicizing the moment. In order to problematize their accounts further, I turn to Baraka's work on the "changing same" to inject the issue of race into the discussion. For Baraka, the visionary moment is necessarily historical and raises the vexed issue of political commitment. Thus, Baraka's work prompts the question, What is the vision's relationship to the future? Buddhist thought, exemplified by the work of Shunryu Suzuki, provides an answer. Ginsberg and Kerouac turn to Buddhist thinking in an effort to discover a means of tying past, present, and future together in such a manner that the gains from past visions become available for future moments. Although both these writers engage Buddhism differently, they remain united in their belief that the vision must have a *use*.

Privileging the moment as a means to challenge fixed conceptions of both self and society requires that the Beats pay close attention to the physical. Thus, I address embodiment in the third chapter, which is organized around the trope of sexual orgasm. The orgasmic moment has the advantage of raising several issues simultaneously: the role of the body in the moment of ecstasy, historical conceptions of sexuality, and the politics of gender. The chapter begins with a critique of the figure that stands behind Beat thinking on orgasm—Wilhelm Reich. For Reich, the act of orgasm is instrumental for returning to an authentic body that has been corrupted by the inauthenticities of society. While male Beats certainly pay homage to Reich's views, they more often employ orgasm in the service of transcendence outside the body. Thus, the chapter turns to Deleuze and Felix Guattari's discussion of the "body without organs" to theorize Beat attempts at using the body for experimentation. The Beats' liminal early-postmodern position places them squarely between these two extremes— they need a modern body to ground them in the world, but a postmodern conception of corporeality affords them the opportunity to transcend their embodied condition.

Rather than viewing Beat sexual exploration as inherently liberatory, however, I challenge this account through appeals to female Beat authors such as Vega, Johnson, di Prima, and Lenore Kandel. These female Beat authors provide a check on their male Beat counterparts by challenging masculine notions of orgasmic transcendence and by proffering their own versions of the sexual. The debate revolves around the form and significance of orgasm for women. Reading these women Beats through a psychoanalytic register derived primarily from Sigmund Freud, Luce Irigaray, and Reich reveals that female Beat writers' conceptions of orgasm stress immanence, not transcendence. While care must be taken to avoid the specter of essentialism, Beat women craft a notion of orgasm less concerned with jettisoning the body than with getting back into it. In order for Beat thinking on orgasm to yield results, both male and female, transcendent and immanent, must be brought into dialogue.

The Beats may find value in a highly spiritualized moment, but as writers, they still run into the crucial problem of representing their idiosyncratic experience. The fourth chapter plunges into what Jameson terms the "representation debates" that help to define both the modern and the postmodern. The uneasy alliance the Beats have with respect to the photographic image provides a useful site for discussing what it means to capture the moment. Here, the Beats are interested in the gaps among reality, image, and caption that the photograph creates. How does one re-present that which has already slipped into the past? This question leads directly into the conception of the sublime as it appears in Immanuel Kant, Edmund Burke, and their recent commentator Jean-François Lyotard. For Ginsberg, the goal is to utilize this gap in the service of transcendence. The wedge that time drives between representations creates not a limit but an opportunity—a flash illumination that catapults the reader into a new level of consciousness.

The photographic image, though it arrests a moment in time, becomes burdened with meanings as it circulates within a wider social field. For postmodern thinkers, the use value of the photo becomes of paramount importance, as the image exceeds the frame of representation and spills out into the world. The Beats have a much more sacramental notion of the photograph as index to the real, and although they do not seek to pin down its multifarious levels of signification, they do hope to guide views towards a subset of possible readings. Fear of endless, postmodern proliferation thus urges Kerouac to posit his own narratives for photos and points to the Beats' early-postmodern desire for a meaning that is nevertheless constantly in flux. Setting the notion of "becoming" found in the philosophical work of Deleuze and Guattari in dialogue with Kerouac's critique of the photograph's representational porousness, the fourth chapter argues that by writing through the body, Beats such as Kerouac seek to portray not the event itself but its affect. Rather than objectify experience into static representation, the Beats are striving to capture a flow that knows no one distinct meaning.

Capturing such intense moments with a bodily impact ultimately rests on a claim of intersubjectivity. As discussed throughout this book, past scholarship tends to view the Beats as apolitical—they were more concerned with consciousness-raising on the personal level than with wholesale social change. Recent Beat scholarship challenges this view, claiming that the cultural work done by Beat texts retains a political agency that seeps into the social field. The final chapter goes a step further, exploring Beat social formations that are self-consciously designed to offer alternatives to existing social and political structures. Although predicated on individual spatial and temporal experiences, Beat works theorize alternative social structures that are simultaneously individuated, fleeting, and total. Instead of building a rigid utopia that is spatially and temporally contained, the Beats instead opt for what Foucault terms a "heterotopia." Like a circus tent, a Beat heterotopia exists only temporarily, and when its usefulness is finished, it is disassembled. Heterotopia locates the Beat social project squarely within the early-postmodern framework of this study. From the modern, the Beats draw on the rationalized notion of planned utopia to provide a structure for their social formations. There must be some measure of totality, otherwise the group cannot be formed. A postmodern insistence on the discrete and antirational, however, keeps such homogeneity from becoming too rigid and exclusionary. By drawing on a modern past and anticipating a postmodern future, Beat heterotopia builds a temporary, flexible community that nevertheless retains the force necessary to achieve its goals.

In order to bring Beat thinking into the social, this chapter analyzes concrete instantiations of Beat heterotopias, beginning with Burroughs's final trilogy of novels. In them, Burroughs is concerned with theorizing heterotopia in the form of the gang or band—a loose affiliation of like-minded individuals who share a common purpose. Despite Burroughs's successes, however, his social constructions rely on a strict adherence to "the law" that ultimately creates an exclusionary social contract guaranteed by the threat of violence. The sixties' counterculture, epitomized by groups such as the Diggers, Ken Kesey and his Merry Pranksters, and various communal-living projects, illustrate the opposite tendency. Rather than constraining their heterotopias through a strict application of the law, these groups err on the side of heterogeneity, constructing heterotopias too loosely bound to remain effective. Ginsberg, with his practice of mantra chanting, produces a more viable alternative. Focusing participants around an egalitarian notion of the body, the chanting of om creates a heterotopian moment in which individuals join together to form an effective group unit, all the while maintaining the heterogeneity and diversity that are the hallmark of the Beat project.

However distanced today may be from mid-twentieth-century America, the insights into the moment that the Beats gleaned from their inquiries have not lost their timeliness. The current social situation is in many ways merely an intensification of the beliefs and constructs developed in the postwar era that serve to cut everyone off from truly experiencing the world. The Beats developed a relationship with the ephemeral present that society as a whole chose to disregard. Returning to this watershed moment in American culture allows us to salvage productive Beat formulations while jettisoning what we can now see as exclusionary or misguided. An inquiry into the Beat attempt to live, write, and build community within the passing moment provides both a richer comprehension of the Beat canon as a whole and illuminates possible solutions to our overly mediated social condition. For the enduring power of Beat writing is located in one not-so-simple question that is as applicable today as it was when the Beats first posed it—How does one capture an immediacy to a world that is constantly slipping away?

1. Being Present
Authenticity in Postwar America

During a visit to Jack Kerouac's hometown of Lowell, Massachusetts, I had the opportunity to take a guided tour of the town conducted by the National Park Service. One of the more famous landmarks was the gigantic clock that rises above City Hall. This clock finds its way into *Doctor Sax* and numerous other Kerouac works, always standing as an imposing symbol of time. But for a mill town such as Lowell, the City Hall clock represents something much less abstract. The park ranger explained that the mill workers were in constant fear that the shop clock was off: that they were starting earlier and finishing later than was required. Thus, the City Hall clock was conceived—not only to alert the entire town to the exact time but to ensure that mill time, too, was kept honest. This clock has come to stand for many things. For a young Kerouac, it was an imposing feature of city life; for an older Kerouac, it was a symbol of life's continual passing. For the mill workers, it probably stood for both security as well as a reminder to what extent their lives revolved around a clock. For this scholar, it is a landmark, a piece of literature made real in stone. And towering above all these conceptions, figuratively and literally, the City Hall clock remains rigidly itself—dispensing time across public space and private lives alike.

Lowell is an excellent place to begin thinking about Kerouac and the Beat revolution that he helped to inaugurate because what is at stake here is a question of control over space and time, a battle over who gets to determine where and when any given set of activities will occur. It is a fight over the moment. A National Park guidebook describes what life working for a Lowell mill was like: "The factory bells dominated daily life. They woke the workers at 4:30 *A.M.* on summer mornings, called them into the mills at 4:50, rang them out for breakfast and back in, out and in for dinner, out again at 7 *P.M.* at the day's close. At 10 the bells rang the curfew. The mills had identical schedules and set their bells to ring in unison" (United States 51). The mill owned time—and the activities that took place within it. Workers arose not when they were rested but when a bell demanded it. Basic human activities such as eating were strictly regulated, leading to a system governed by the clock instead of the body. According to Richard Edwards in *Contested Terrain*, the mills owned space as well: "In the early shops the spinners and weavers needed to move around, to obtain materials or to dispose of finished goods. . . . But in the new power-driven mills all machines operated together, and the operative had neither any cause nor any right to move about the mill. Instead, the worker became nearly as much locked in place as the machine" (114). As with time, the mills controlled space, telling workers where exactly they will be at any given moment in the day. The Lowell mills present a changing of the guard, a transition from an older tradition of individual craftsmanship and control over the product to a new industrial society highly controlled and rationalized.

Kerouac never worked in the mills, but when he was a resident of Lowell, they were never far from his mind or his body. As much as he loved his hometown, Kerouac still wanted out. He knew that the mills were a dead end, and the life of the mill worker one of repetitious drudgery. Although he may not have had the Lowell mills specifically in mind, Kerouac recoiled from the rigid timetables and spatial itineraries that the mills demanded. The Beat rebellion that he helped to champion saw these temporal and spatial constraints as a fundamental barrier to discovering a truer, more "authentic" version of oneself. Yet, Kerouac could not escape simply by leaving Lowell. Millwork was representative of all the forces throughout fifties' society that sought to control and delimit—the need to work, the assumption of marriage and household, or the fear of the atomic bomb. As difficult as it was to achieve, what the Beats were after was a return to a moment overflowing with personal freedom and spontaneous action. Time ruled not by the clock but by desire and circumstance. Space governed not by boundaries but by openness and mobility. The factory floor and the mindset associated with it jarred one out of the present, and the Beats felt it was imperative to get back to the moment if life was to be lived to its fullest.

Existentialism and the Beats

Existentialism, popularized in America during the postwar period, offers a parallel critique of society that helps us to understand the Beat desire for the lived moment. Although the connection between the Beats and existentialism has received scant attention, it is crucial for several reasons.

Existentialism launches an attack on postwar culture that provides a means of understanding the sort of "inauthenticities" that kept people from experiencing the moment. Although care must be taken to avoid hasty generalizations about an entire decade, the postwar years were characterized by pressure to conform to social and cultural standards. Existentialism provides a vocabulary to discuss these pressures and thus helps to illuminate and explain the Beat desire to challenge social norms. Moreover, a direct historical connection between the Beats and existentialism has mainly gone unexplored. The Beats read existentialist texts, and although it would be a mistake to claim that the Beats were existentialists, they nevertheless were influenced by the encounter. Uncovering this buried connection is thus an important first step in understanding why the Beats wanted to capture the moment and the obstacles that were placed in their path.

Postwar America was predicated on the notion of conformity—to be a good citizen, one had to play by society's rules. Americans were expected to work hard and consume harder in order to contribute to a successful economy and to hate the communists, who threatened to take it all away with an atomic bomb. And all the while, one had to make time for one's spouse, family, and personal interests—nobody wanted to appear one-sided. Existentialism views these social niceties as a means of distraction. According to David E. Cooper, rather than face reality directly, existentialism believes that "people suppress a sense of alienation from the world by becoming 'absorbed' in or 'tranquilized' by the comforting, ready-made schemes of beliefs and values which prevail in their societies" (33). The Beats did not just read the existentialists, they agreed with them. Life was being covered up with ready-made schemes, and unless people were willing to admit that they were being tranquilized, the country was destined to remain in a world of make-believe. Thus, existentialism not only faced the same postwar situation as the Beats but also offered the same solution— a direct encounter with the reality of the moment was the only way to counter an increasingly distracted and preoccupied world.

Existentialism sought to break free from the alienating aspects of society to achieve a more direct relationship with the world. According to Daniel Belgrad in *The Culture of Spontaneity*, "Existentialists struggled to live 'authentically,' open to the possibilities of existence, and to avoid enslavement to the dictates of conceptual structures and social norms" (107). Millwork may represent the most egregious affront to personal freedom, but society is littered with conceptual structures and social norms that keep the individual from achieving a true self. Overt temporal and spatial repression was replaced with a more insidious form of normalization that existentialist thinkers labeled "inauthentic." Thus, Belgrad observes, "Existentialism encouraged defiance against the conformity of Cold War anti-Communism and the regimented work culture of corporate liberalism" (112). With attention focused on either the deadly threat of communism abroad or the pleasures afforded by a consumer economy at home, the 1950s' American was unable to fully engage with the actual, material situations that surrounded him or her. Beat writers and existentialists, by contrast, were united in their belief that this authentic world was worth striving towards and that common notions of patriotism, the work ethic, and the American dream were actually hindrances to achieving this truer relationship to the world.

What makes existentialism so relevant to an understanding of the Beats' early-postmodern position is that both groups found themselves in a postwar social situation in which systems building had irrevocably broken down. In *The Age of Doubt*, William Graebner explains that the "contingency" of postwar America "was characterized by the growing sense that it was now more difficult than ever before to ground one's conduct in a stable system of values" (19). Here is the beginning of the postmodern period, where the "grand narratives" of modernity are starting to fail. Into this void created by a world war and an atomic bomb came competing theories that attempted to make sense of the postwar condition. The Beats rejected culturally defined notions of country, workplace, and home as possible means of understanding their lives, instead opting for a more personalized, spiritual response to the uncertainty that the postwar generated.

Existentialism is not just another codified movement offered for their perusal but an identical stance toward the world. Graebner claims that existentialism "assumed the impossibility of reconciling contradictions . . . against this condition of continual uncertainty and doubt. . . . [O]ne could assert only the primacy of the struggle, the value of waging the good fight" (147). Both the Beats and the existentialists attempted to discover meaning in a supposedly meaningless world. Rather than settling for a comfortably stable conception that would guide their thinking, both groups challenged postwar contingency by striving to find value in their lives. In the end, meaning is contained in the search itself—a belief that through constant struggle, the world will eventually be made to yield sense and understanding to the searcher.

Norman Mailer outlines this connection in his essay "The White Negro." Equating the "white Negro" with the "existential hipster," Mailer writes that for this "American existentialist," life must have a purpose: "A life which is directed by one's faith in the necessity of action is a life committed to the notion that the substratum of existence is the search, the end meaningful but mysterious" (341). The hipster rebels against a postwar world of conformity, seeking a larger meaning than the ones offered to him. And what gives this search its urgency is the specter of death always lurking in the background. Mailer reasons that if "our collective condition is to live with instant death by atomic war," then the only recourse is to "explore that domain of experience where security is boredom and therefore sickness, and one exists in the present" (339). For Mailer, this journey involves being mentally and, more important, physically aware of each passing moment. Ideally, such attention culminates in an "apocalyptic orgasm" (347) that Mailer sees as the end of the search (more on this in chapter 3). Regardless of the destination, the Beats share with the existentialists the idea that there is meaning in the world, even if that meaning is difficult to attain and perhaps ultimately "mysterious."

Mailer's essay, however, is problematic in its recourse to African American experience as the basis for hipster rebellion. What draws Mailer to "the Negro" as the "source of Hip" (340) is that African Americans have been forced to exist on the margins of society. Because of the prevalence of racism in America, "the Negro has the simplest of alternatives: live a life of constant humility or ever-threatening danger" (341). As this chapter later shows, this characterization is accurate. But the conclusions Mailer draws from this are unsettling. In such a situation, Mailer writes, "the Negro had stayed alive and begun to grow by following the need of his body. . . . [H]e kept for his survival the art of the primitive, he lived in the enormous present" (341). It is not that Mailer fails to recognize the predicament that African Americans were in during the mid-twentieth century. On the contrary, this limited choice is what gives them a deeper understanding of America. The problem in Mailer's formulation is that he reduces African American experience to the physical. In a contemporaneous reaction to Mailer's article, Ned Polsky claims, "The White Negro accepts the real Negro not as a human being in his totality, but as the bringer of a highly specified and restricted 'cultural dowry,' to use Mailer's phrase" ("2. Ned Polsky," 369). Mailer contains African American identity, limiting it to a subset of representations ("cultural dowry") that he uses to extricate whiteness from cold-war containment. African American experience simply becomes jazz, drugs, and the argot they spawned, "Saturday Night Kicks" (341), and most important, the quest for orgasm—all of which provide the White Negro with the tools he needs to rebel.

The insistence on individual meaning-creation runs directly counter to the postwar demand for conformity to the social order. In *Containment Culture*, Alan Nadel argues for a notion of postwar America based on the atomic bomb. This trope creates a set of narratives that run throughout the culture, ordering the ways in which events are understood and containing deviant action. Nadel writes that "it was a period, as many prominent studies have indicated, when 'conformity' became a positive value in and of itself. The virtue of conformity—to some idea of religion, to 'middle-class' values, to distinct gender roles and rigid courtship rituals—became a form of public knowledge" (4). Yet, this conformity also produced anxiety for those unwilling or unable to live within its tenets, and the Beats were one such group. In his poem "Howl," for example, Ginsberg's "best minds of my generation" are those who have been pushed to the periphery by the demands placed on them by society (*Collected Poems* 126). Existentialist thought shares such disdain for ready-made modes of living. In *The Culture of Spontaneity*, Belgrad notes that "existentialism and the aesthetic of spontaneity were most similar in their shared condemnation of the way fixed conceptual structures truncated and falsified reality" (107). Although Belgrad ultimately downplays the role of existentialism in Beat thought, both groups agree on the need to challenge existing social structures in order to attain a more primal engagement with the world.

Unfortunately, the connection between these two groups has become tangled. The Beat reception of existentialism and the critical understanding of that reception are marred by misunderstanding, distrust, and suspicion. Despite these difficulties, the Beat relationship to existentialism can be understood by disentangling existentialist thought from its initial reception.[1] Existentialism saw a postwar vogue in France. In *Irrational Man*, William Barrett explains, "French Existentialism was a kind of Bohemian ferment in Paris; it had, as a garnish for the philosophy, the cult its younger devotees had made of night-club hangouts, American jazz, special hairdos, and style of dress" (7–8). The faddishness of such display led to the belief that existentialism was more style than substance. It was more important to be seen as an existentialist than to apply philosophical insights to one's own life. Such conformist behavior runs directly counter to existentialism's demand for personal authenticity. Unfortunately, this cult eventually found its way to America after the occupation, further complicating American receptions of existentialist thought proper. As Ann Fulton writes in her study *Apostles of Sartre*, "Sartre's philosophy was popular among a small group of intellectuals and writers. Sometimes attracted as much to Sartre's identification with Parisian bohemian life as by his philosophical doctrines, these Americans reproduced Sartre's popularity in France on a smaller scale" (27). Rather than engaging the philosophical texts themselves, devotees often settled for existentialism as a sort of lifestyle choice. Ironically, existentialism came to signify what the term "Beatnik" would signify a decade later: a black-sweatered bohemian smoking a cigarette at a cafe table.

Such faddishness was anathema to a Beat movement struggling to free itself from the conformity of the postwar years. Why trade one set of social conventions for another? But existentialism's popular appeal was not the only reason for the Beats' hesitancy to embrace the movement. In America, existentialism was characterized as a pessimistic philosophy. Fulton relates some of the titles that magazines like *Harper's* and *Life* deployed when introducing Americans to this nascent movement: "French and American Pessimism" and "Existentialism: Postwar Paris Enthrones a Bleak Philosophy of Pessimism" (29).[2] Buoyed by a sense of triumph and economic success, postwar America relegated such pessimism to a war-torn Europe that was struggling to come to terms with a sense of guilt and disillusionment. As Fulton remarks, it would not be until "the ideological strife of the Cold War intensified after 1947 and concerns about loss of individuality escalated" (34) that America would be ready for the sort of concerns Sartre and others were raising.

The Beats were not immune to such stereotypes, and both these charges of faddishness and pessimism combine when existentialism is overtly addressed in their texts. Kerouac's attacks on this movement coalesce around the New School for Social Research (a progressive, New York institution that provided a safe haven for many threatened scholars in Europe), which he attended from 1948 until 1949. Quoting the Yale philosopher Maurice Natanson, Fulton describes the New School during the late 1940s as a "'kind of Garden of Eden' of people who understood existentialism and phenomenology" (49–50). Kerouac's assessment is less kind. In a 1948 letter to Hal Chase, Kerouac talks of going to Paris with his friends in order to (as his friend "Burford" explains it) "show the existentialist drek the *real* meaning of anarchy" (*Selected Letters* 169). As Kerouac would later claim in *On the Road*, his is the "wild yea-saying overburst of American joy" rather than the pessimistic "negative, nightmarish position of putting down society" with "tired bookish or political or psychoanalytic reasons" (10). Overly intellectualized ennui and despair ran counter to a Beat movement that insisted on the spontaneous ecstasy of lived life. Later that year, Kerouac sums up his feelings regarding the New School to his friend Ed White: "[T]he New School with its ugly Jewesses and generally ugly intellectuals is making me sick. . . . [It] is a battleground for European ideas-of-disintegration" ("Letters" 117–18). Here, Kerouac echoes American ideas concerning existentialism in general—a depressing philosophy practiced by pseudointellectuals that is going nowhere.

Yet, numerous other references demonstrate that the Beats used existentialism as a means to better understand their own postwar generation. Discussing his coining of the term in his essay "The Origins of the Beat Generation," Kerouac describes a conversation with John Clellon Holmes when they both were "sitting around trying to think up the meaning of the Lost Generation and the subsequent Existentialism" (*Good Blonde* 57). While Kerouac's "Beat Generation" is not to be conflated with existentialism, he nevertheless makes it clear that not only was existentialism discussed among the Beats, it was used as a filter to help them better understand their own particular social situation. Kerouac makes this connection even more explicit in his "Aftermath: The Philosophy of the Beat Generation." Here he draws a parallel between the Beat Generation and existentialism: "The same thing was almost going on in the postwar France of Sartre and Genet and what's more we knew about it" (*Good Blonde* 47). Nor is Kerouac the only Beat to make such an assertion. In his *Autobiography*, Amiri Baraka claims that one of the trends he first picked up on when he arrived in New York City's Greenwich Village in the late 1950s was "the contemporary bridge into our own day, existentialism" (182). These examples suggest that the written works of existentialist authors were not simply dismissed by the Beats as scholars tend to claim. Kerouac may have been hostile to the fad of existentialism or intellectuals who wanted to practice it, but the philosophical texts themselves were read and even respected.

Despite his attacks on the New School, Kerouac retains his ultimate vitriol not for existentialist thinkers but for the intellectuals who read them. Kerouac describes his fellow students: "The only trouble is that some of those guys there are bald-faced enough to deem they are privileged to re-interpret everything from the Bible to Melville and Sartre" ("Letters"

117). The Beats did not import existentialism wholesale or accept all of its tenets. Existentialism, however, was important to the Beats as a means of defining themselves and their nascent postwar generation. In Kerouac's novel *The Town and the City*, the character of Francis is "amazed to think that a whole coherent language had sprung into being around this restless, intelligent, determined trend. . . . [T]hey had words to name the key complaints and frame the major solutions" (115–16). Some of the words Francis is amazed to hear include "Kierkegaard," "anxiety," and "Heidegger" (116). What Kerouac's quote suggests is that existentialism was a current topic among the Beats that provided them with a vocabulary for naming key complaints and framing major solutions. The Beats may have gone beyond existentialism for their answers, but existentialism was an integral component of that search for meaning.

What the Beats were seeking was a spiritual revolution but one that knew neither creed nor denomination. In his essay "The Philosophy of the Beat Generation," Holmes explains, "To be beat is to be at the bottom of your personality, looking up; to be existential in the Kierkegaard, rather than the Jean-Paul Sartre, sense" (229). Beats like Holmes and Kerouac lamented the fact that their movement was often depicted as morally delinquent and godless, when in fact it was searching for an even deeper religiousness that would bring meaning back into people's lives. Existentialism oftentimes suffered the same fate in the hands of the postwar media. But as Holmes makes clear, both were searching for spirituality free from the trappings of institutionalized church and state. Holmes's reference to Kierkegaard rather than Jean-Paul Sartre is telling. Sartre is oftentimes equated with the image of the godless, pessimistic, dystopian existentialist that thrived during the period. Kierkegaard's religious bent receives better press.[3] According to Gerald Nicosia, Kerouac passed the time on his freighter to Tangiers not just reading but "studying Kierkegaard's *Fear and Trembling*" (544). Such an insistence on spirituality led Ginsberg in search of the Jewish philosopher and theologian Martin Buber. In India, Ginsberg singled out Buber as the first "holy man" he went to see. Buber suggested to Ginsberg that he should focus on human-to-human relationships, and two years later, Ginsberg discovered, "He was right" (*Writers at Work* 314). This human-to-human relationship that Buber preaches is not codified into sectarian doctrine but instead speaks to a more essential connection that exists between human beings. Kerouac places such religiousness at the center of the Beat project in "Aftermath": "[E]ven the Existentialists with all their intellectual overlays and pretenses of indifference, represent an even deeper religiousness . . . as if the visions of the cloistral saints of Chartres and Clairvaux were back with us again bursting like weeds through the sidewalks of stiffened civilization" (*Good Blonde* 50). While the use of the qualifier "even" demonstrates Kerouac's hesitancy to fully embrace existentialism, he nevertheless includes this group as an ally in the Beat assault on a "stiffened civilization" that has forsaken any sort of "deeper religiousness." It is conformist America that is lacking spirituality, not the existentialists and certainly not the Beats.

Returning to an authentic moment is at the center of both the Beat and existentialist projects. Ginsberg relates an anecdote about William S. Burroughs, who, during a presidential campaign, quipped, "If an elephant had walked up in front of all those candidates in the middle of the speech and shat on the ground and walked away, the candidate would have ignored it. Consciousness wasn't present there on the occasion when they were talking, consciousness was an abstract, theoretical state" ("New Consciousness" 71–72). The moment is the site where life should be lived, where humans encounter one another and their environment in an immediate way. What Burroughs deplores is the covering up that existentialist philosophers examine. Instead of the reality of "elephant" and "shit," we get a covert denial, a consciousness removed from the lived reality of the situation.

The Beats formulated their new vision in an attempt to combat this trend, to step outside the inauthenticities that were being offered during the postwar years and into a real relationship with the world and its events as they occur in space and time. The Beats found themselves in a "vast American hallucination" constructed in the disembodied space of "airwaves and television and newspapers" (Ginsberg, "New Consciousness" 71–72). Their solution was to emphasize direct versus mediated experience. This insistence on the reality of the world intersects with existential attempts to recover an authenticity within the moment. As Maurice Merleau-Ponty claims in his preface to *Phenomenology of Perception*, this discipline "offers an account of space, time, and the world as we 'live' them" (vii). The Beats' desire for lived experience means that the questions of space and time are paramount for them as well. The moment is where these two vectors intersect and where the possibility of action and change takes place. Comparing the Beat approach to authenticity with the account offered by existentialist thought helps to shed light on the problem of living the moment authentically in a highly conformist postwar situation.

The Beats were not sitting in postwar libraries poring over every existentialist text they could get their hands on. Their anti-intellectualism was quite real, if a bit overstated. But that does not mean that the Beats were ignorant of the cultural and intellectual trends that were going on around them. The Beats did read the existentialists, and they found something to admire. When it came to crafting their own myths and poetics, they downplayed the role of existentialism in their projects. Yet, for all these dismissals, Beat concerns about living life authentically in the moment closely mirror the work that existentialists had conducted before them. This is not to say that the Beats copied the existentialists—on the contrary, Beat formulations of authenticity are different from these philosophers and have a specifically American hue. Yet, it is clear that existentialism played a role in Beat thinking, both as a direct influence and as a cultural backdrop that helped to develop Beat thinking along certain lines. More important than influence is that the Beats and the existentialists were bringing their thought to bear on the problem of breaking through mediation and inauthenticity to encounter the world directly. An analysis of both groups not only yields a better understanding of Beat attempts to go beyond the falseness of the world into a truer realm of experience but it also provides a better sense of how Beat texts might be employed in our current situation to live life more fully in each passing moment.

On the Road and the Authentic Beat Moment

The Penguin edition of Kerouac's *On the Road* describes it as "the novel that defined a generation." While this may be a bold claim, it is fundamentally a true one—along with Ginsberg's "Howl," the publication of *On the Road* was a watershed event in twentieth-century America. Kerouac's "spontaneous prose" heralded a new type of writing that was emerging in America, a style that was direct, open, and tied to the body. The novel introduced a new cultural movement as well, alerting society to an undercurrent of dissent and dissatisfaction with the conformity of postwar life that would eventually erupt into full-scale social revolution in the sixties. But the question that begs to be answered is what precisely "defines" this new generation that Kerouac's novel chronicled? What made *On the Road* such a challenge to the American social order at midcentury?

Kerouac's work poses a direct challenge to the ways in which the moment was conceived in postwar America. *On the Road* champions an authentic moment based on spontaneous action and desire as they respond to immediate material and social conditions. The postwar mentality, by contrast, was based on dismissal—nobody wanted to contemplate the ramification of a falling bomb or the end of a booming consumer economy. Yet, the "realities" of job, country, and home meant to replace such fears only served to distance fifties' America even further from life. The vehement criticism that *On the Road* received, then, was an indication that the vast majority of Americans did not want to be reminded of the delusions of security that they had constructed around themselves.

What makes Kerouac's *On the Road* such an excellent record of postwar American culture is that it not only provides a paradigmatic example of Beat authenticity but it also reveals the inner workings of fifties' conformity. Riding in a car with a tourist couple, Dean Moriarty explains to Sal Paradise the difference between accepted cultural notions of the moment and their Beat response:

> They have worries, they're counting the miles, they're thinking about where to sleep tonight, how much money for gas, the weather, how they'll get there—and all the time they'll get there anyway, you see. But they need to worry and betray time with urgencies false and otherwise, purely anxious and whiny, their souls really won't be at peace unless they can latch on to an established and proven worry. (208)

The tourist couple needs worries like the mill workers need the City Hall clock—it gives them a sense of security. Fretting about money, gas, and weather abstracts the couple out of the present moment, allowing them to live in an always-retreating future that never arrives since there will always be a new worry to replace it. As long as they are worrying, the couple is not truly living. Dean's authenticity resides in his knowledge that we will all get there anyway, and thus there is no need to do anything but simply experience the moment as it unfolds. Because the couple is unable to abandon themselves to the immediacy of the present, they betray time and will never achieve the direct physical and mental relationship with the world that is the hallmark of authenticity.

The work of existentialist Martin Heidegger makes this divide even clearer by drawing a philosophical distinction between authenticity and inauthenticity. The key to this difference is how one relates to his or her own death. For Heidegger, the anxiety associated with death is positive since it helps to bring the subject to an authentic understanding of its own being, one that is based on an acceptance of the finality of existence. Anxiety "throws Dasein back upon that which it is anxious about—it's authentic potentiality-for-Being-in-the-world" (232).[4] "Dasein," Heidegger's term for human existence, is caught in a world of concerns that distracts it from seizing its own life. Anxiety over death forces us to reconsider what we are doing in-the-world and thus allows us to live an authentic life that we ourselves direct. The passengers in *On the Road*, however, fail to use their anxiety to catapult themselves into an authentic relationship to the world. Instead, they lose themselves in their problems. Heidegger explains that "he who is irresolute understands himself in terms of those very closest events and be-fallings which he encounters in such a making-present and which thrust themselves upon him in varying ways. Busily losing *himself* in the object of concern, he *loses his time* in it too" (463). Inauthenticity involves a turning away from death and a losing oneself in commonplace, daily objects of concern. Such a denial is costly because Dasein loses his time as well—the chance for living a full life is constantly slipping away. Fretting about such things as money, gas, and weather, the passengers blind themselves to the one fact that could allow them to live an authentic temporal existence—death. They forget the present by constantly anticipating the future. And when the future does arrive, a new set of concerns are created to negate that present, continuing the cycle of forgetfulness. This is not to claim that the middle-class, fifties' American did not realize that he or she would die. Heidegger's point is that he or she does not embrace this knowledge but shunts it off, opting instead to deal with worldly concerns that seem to continue forever. As long as plans keep getting made, the real business of living life becomes forgotten.[5]

Earlier in *On the Road*, Dean, to lay bare their underlying assumptions, mimics the inauthenticities of the fifties. Sal travels to Denver to see his friends and asks Carlo Marx, "What's the schedule?" explaining that "there was always a schedule in Dean's life" (42). Sal then arrives at Dean's apartment, where Dean promptly treats the reader to an example of his schedule making. Dean explains to his lover, Camille, that he must go, and she replies:

> "But what time will you be back?"
> "It is now" (looking at his watch) "exactly one-fourteen. I shall be back at exactly *three*-fourteen, for our hour of reverie together. . . . So now in this exact minute I must dress, put on my pants, go back to life, that is to outside life, streets and what not. . . . [I]t is now one-*fifteen* and time's running, running—"

"Well, all right, Dean, but please be sure and be back at three."

"Just as I said, darling, and remember not three but three-four-teen." (43–44)

What immediately grabs the reader's attention in this passage is the detail to which Dean plans out his actions. Carlo's explanation of Dean's routine is fluid by comparison, rounding off to the half hour. Dean himself, however, carries his calculations to the exact minute, insisting on three-fourteen, not simply three o'clock. Such a detailed division of time is consistent with an inauthentic notion of temporality—rather than existing in the moment, Dean is instead focused on what he will be doing, and thus time is "running, running." Of course, Dean is also camping on the degree to which clock time has gained currency in America—"time is money" and should not be wasted. But what the reader soon discovers is that Dean attacks America's growing anxiety over time less through mockery than through the ways in which he employs this highly controlled temporality.

Rather than contribute to the American economy, Dean uses time to serve his own ends. Georg Lukács, in his chapter "Reification and the Consciousness of the Proletariat" in *History and Class Consciousness*, explores how inauthenticity is produced through an analysis of the notion of reification first established by Karl Marx.[6] Although Lukács is not strictly an existentialist, his critique of the ways in which inauthenticity is produced provides a counterpoint to existentialism's desire to discover the mechanisms of authenticity. Drawing on Marx's critique of the idea that "one man during an hour is worth just as much as another man during an hour," Lukács concludes that "in this environment where time is transformed into abstract, exactly measurable, physical space . . . the subjects of labour must likewise be rationally fragmented" (89–90). For Lukács, time becomes a space to be inhabited by equally interchangeable workers who form just another factor in the workings of the machine. It is this machine that then takes over, subjecting workers to its own set of laws and rules. Dean's temporal rationalization avoids such pitfalls since it is not tied to a capitalist mode of production. While the reification process has perverted time in order to constrict space and dominate the worker, Dean is able to retain control over his actions, and thus the spaces he inhabits remain his own. Time may still be subsumed by space, but it is a space that Dean is free to configure according to his own wishes. Time does not employ Dean—he employs time.

The space Dean creates is inhabited by a variety of pursuits that challenge the inauthenticities created by American capitalism. Dean's actions are indeed "rationally fragmented," but this fragmentation is figured in an economy of ecstasy, not of oppression. Running from one place to another, Dean's temporality is inextricably bound up with movement, not stasis. If David Harvey is correct in declaring that "those who command space can always control the politics of place" (234), then Dean's restless itinerary poses a threat to established notions of power. Through continual motion, Dean is able to avoid remaining in a fixed place that would render him susceptible to control. Finding a girl for Sal, making plans to go to the midget auto races, having sex with various women, and getting drunk with his friends are all activities that focus on the fulfillment of desire rather than materialist production. In fact, this frenetic activity has left Dean broke. For all of his "production," he claims, "I haven't had time to work in weeks" (45). While it would be wrong to treat Dean simply as a Marxist rebel, he is able to avoid the production of commodities that ultimately destroys the worker. Because Dean names it, the moment regains the openness to possibility that is denied it by reification, and the space filled for Lukács with "the reified, mechanically objectified performance of the worker" (90) is replaced by idiosyncratic personal experience. Thus, Dean's need to constantly "go," to perform "our one and noble function of the time, *move*," as Sal says (133), needs to be understood as a desire for both spatial and temporal movement and flux.

The Beats offer a new conception of temporality. In contrast to the inauthenticities of fifties' America, the Beats strive to live completely in the moment. *On the Road* provides ample evidence that Dean's conception of time is shifted away from past and future and towards an ever-changing present. Arriving at the doorstep of Sal's relatives in Virginia, Sal describes an altered Dean:

> "'cause now is the time and *we all know time!*" . . . [H]e roared into downtown Testament, looking in every direction and seeing everything in an arc of 180 degrees around his eyeballs without moving his head. . . . He had become absolutely mad in his movements; he seemed to be doing everything at the same time. (114)

Dean is frenetically living in the moment, trying to stay within the everunfolding horizon of the "now." To "know time" is to engage it both passively and actively. Dean accepts the belief that life must be lived in the present and practices this knowledge by filling each of these moments with as much activity as possible, attempting "to do everything at the same time." Yet, for Dean, this idea of living life to the fullest in the present is concomitant with the idea that an underlying order makes worry superfluous. Dean later explains to Sal that "we passed a little kid who was throwing stones at the cars in the road. 'Think of it,' said Dean. 'One day he'll put a stone through a man's windshield and the man will crash and die. . . . I am positive beyond doubt that everything will be taken care of for us'" (120). The present brings with it the possibility for death at every instant. But rather than recoiling from this potentiality, Dean embraces it. Here, Dean evidences Heidegger's anxiety in an authentic manner—the knowledge that life must necessarily end frees him from the excessive worry that characterizes the passengers in the car. Living the lie of inauthenticity does not negate the potential for finality and, in the meantime, serves only to keep one from experiencing the present in all its intensity. Dean opts to exist the world rather than control it. And every moment necessarily takes care of itself; it occurs.

Dean's faith in the moment is based on the knowledge that past and future are not separate frames of reference but are instead part of the present itself. There are not separate times but one time and that time is now. Merleau-Ponty has offered a similar account of temporality:

> What there is, is not a present, then another present which takes its place in being, and not even a present with its vistas of past and future followed by another present in which those vistas are disrupted, so that one and the same spectator is needed to effect the synthesis of successive perspectives: there is only one single time which is self-confirmatory, which can bring nothing into existence unless it has already laid that thing's foundations as present and eventual past, and which establishes itself at a stroke. (*Phenomenology of Perception* 421)

For Merleau-Ponty, time is a sort of continuum, and to remain fixed on a past and future is to betray the "plenitude of being in itself" (421). Thus, for Dean to fret about a rock through his windshield or any other calamity that might befall him is absurd. It may occur, but when and if it does, it is something that must occur, and as it does so, it necessarily becomes part of the present.

Such an idea sounds disturbingly close to the notion of fate. But Dean's belief in living life in the moment need not mean that life is predetermined. Dean still retains personal agency within the moment; his faith is that his actions will inevitably be the right ones for that particular present. The idea that Dean espouses, then, is to accept this moment and rather than fighting it with regrets about the past or fears for the future to revel in it as a type of momentary infinity that encompasses all of past, present, and future. In attempting to break up duration, to plan and fret about past and future, the passengers betray time because they do not allow themselves to be free in the present moment. Dean's knowledge of time is that time will take care of itself; it has to because each moment must continue. This leaves Dean free to live in the continual present that is always its own horizon. Thus, the insistence on action and movement that characterizes Dean and *On the Road* in general: one needs to continually move in order to stay in sync with time, to always live on its perpetually unfolding edge. Realizing that life will end, he seeks to make the most of it by maximizing his understanding of every moment. Focusing exclusively on the unfolding moment, Dean avoids the trap of seeing the present as anything but what it really is—the final and ultimate reality.

Of course, it would be naïve to assume that Dean was always capable of achieving the highly authentic state he obtains throughout *On the Road*. By the end of the novel, Dean's energy is spent and his once-inspirational oratory has turned to mumble: "can't talk no more—do you understand that it is—or might be—But listen!" (307). It would also be misguided to assume that every "square" American living after World War II was mired in a life of inauthenticity. One did not have to be Beat to realize that life will end and thus should be lived to the fullest. Perhaps it would be better to think of authenticity as a spectrum—one is never completely authentic or inauthentic but moving towards one or the other pole. What *On the Road* does provide, however, is an example of what the Beats considered to be authenticity within the moment. Not every American was caught up in postwar conformity every moment of his or her life, but it is clear that fifties' America presented its citizens with a baffling array of enticements and fears meant to keep them locked out of the present. As long as attention was focused beyond immediate concerns, it became easy to leave the realities of the world behind in favor of a timelessness of worry or complacency. What Beats like Kerouac recognized was that such conformity of thinking kept America from fully engaging the world in a meaningful way. True freedom was not to be found in a democratic America or in consumer choice but in giving oneself over, fully and completely, to the immediacy of the present moment.

Gendering the Moment

So far this chapter has dealt exclusively with male Beat writers and their conception of the authentic moment. Does this model change when considering women Beat writers? In *Recollections of My Life as a Woman*, Diane di Prima describes the phenomenon that she calls "Swinging." She explains that "we would sometimes go out, just go out with no particular aim ... and go where our instinct, our telepathy, our inclinations took us. We would find each other in various ways, have various adventures without preplanning, without telephones" (138). As with her male Beat counterparts, lack of planning signals a trust in spontaneous action—rather than engaging the world according to preestablished patterns, the Beats attempted to encounter each moment as though for the first time. Of course, there is a risk of failure. Di Prima explains that "on the days when nothing worked like that, you would tend to go home early and hole up" (138). Spontaneous action and openness to the event may not always work, but they at least provided the Beats, both male and female, with an opportunity to break out of existing modes of thought. "Holing up" at home, however, raises an entirely different set of issues for women Beat writers. While male Beats tended to dismiss domesticity as a stultifying experience, women Beats were more apt to attempt a renegotiation of this space. What was the dominant patriarchal notion of the domestic sphere in the 1950s, and to what extent did male Beats reinforce or attack notions of the home? More important, how did women Beat writers of this period respond to their male Beat counterparts, and how might their attempt to live domestic time and space shed light on male Beat authenticity, with its insistence on flux and mobility?

Domestic space is highly gendered. As Rita Felski notes in *Doing Time*, "modern feminism, from Betty Friedan onward, has repeatedly had recourse to a rhetoric of leaving home. Home is a prison, a trap, a straitjacket. In recent years, this critique of home has intensified" (86). Women writers such as di Prima, Hettie Jones, and Joyce Johnson agree; one must leave these confining notions and strike out on one's own if an authentic life is to be reached. Janine Pommy Vega, for instance, dates her entry into Beat life to the day she left her parent's high school graduation party for New York City. But it does not follow that domesticity is elided. Discussing the theoretical concept of everyday life, Felski cautions against easy binaries:

> Feminists have deployed a hermeneutics of suspicion vis-à-vis the
> everyday, showing how the most mundane, taken-for-granted activi-

ties—conversation, housework, body language, styles of dress—serve to reinforce patriarchal norms. . . . On the other hand, everyday life has also been hailed as a distinctively female sphere and hence a source of value. (93–94)

Felski unpacks the meanings and associations behind these viewpoints, trying to determine why it is that everyday life has become "both the most authentic and the most inauthentic of spheres" (94). The writings of women Beat writers negotiate these binaries and thus have much to tell about the inauthenticities inscribed into domestic space in the fifties as well as how authenticity might be achieved within the home.

Beat women writers certainly flee from patriarchal notions of domesticity—the memoirs of Jones and di Prima in particular clearly describe the sort of expectations that their parents had for them as women in fifties' society. Yet, these women go on to reestablish domestic spheres of their own, struggling to reconcile their Beat lifestyles with the demands of the home. What is ultimately at stake in discussions of everyday domesticity is who gets to define women's roles during the period. The temporality and spatiality of the domestic sphere are not inherently inauthentic, as some feminists may believe. This space is made inauthentic when roles and expectations are predetermined from the outside. Nor is the home a natural site of authenticity. Women must inhabit this sphere in an authentic manner, and the work of women Beat writers evidences a continual struggle to attain such authenticity.

During the 1950s, women were relegated to a highly controlled domestic sphere.[7] A telling anecdote occurred in 1959, when Vice President Richard M. Nixon and Soviet Premier Nikita Khrushchev debated the relative merits of the two countries. Nixon argued for American superiority based on "the convenience of its kitchens and the beauty of its housewives" (Belgrad 146). This "kitchen debate" epitomizes the role reserved for women during the period; they were supposed to maintain the household while remaining attractive for their husbands. Such demands limited the sort of spontaneous mobility that was a hallmark of male Beat rebellion. Relegated to the home, women were effectively immobilized. Along with this stifling of spatial mobility came a concomitant stifling of temporal freedom. The need to keep a house immaculate while maintaining the appropriate standard of beauty meant that the housewife had little time for other pursuits. As Stephanie Coontz notes in *The Way We Never Were*, "The amount of time women spent doing housework actually *increased* during the 1950s, despite the advent of convenience foods and new, labor-saving appliances; child care absorbed more than twice as much time as it had in the 1920s" (27). Coontz traces this increase to a new belief in domesticity as personal service, with the mother-wife unable to delegate work to anyone (or anything) else for fear of losing the "loving touch" that it was her job to provide. But what really underlaid this system? According to Barbara Ehrenreich in *The Hearts of Men*, "Women were, and to a large extent still are, economically dependent on men" (2). The man's sphere was outside the home in the workplace, while the woman occupied the interior domestic space. While the man earned the money for the home, the woman in turn was expected to keep it and to provide a safe and comfortable haven for her husband when he returned home from work.

The Beats' relationship to the domesticity of the 1950s is the subject of intense debate. Ehrenreich admits that the Beats' rebellion did have positive repercussions for feminism. The Beats rejected marriage and work, both fifties' institutions that established preconceived roles that kept women and men in patterns of existence that were clearly inauthentic. Yet, Ehrenreich concludes that "their adventure did not include women, except, perhaps as 'experiences' that men might have. And in their vision . . . the ideal of personal freedom shaded over into an almost vicious irresponsibility to the women" (171). Kerouac's novel *On the Road*, for example, unwittingly captures many of the stereotypes concerning women during the period. Take, for instance, Galatea's calling Dean to task for his irresponsible behavior: "You have absolutely no regard for anybody but yourself and your damned kicks. All you think about is what's hanging between your legs. . . . It never occurs to you that life is serious and there are people trying to make something serious out of it" (194). Sal, of course, goes on to defend his pal, but he does not miss the point that Dean's actions leave a wake of unhappy women behind him.

If the Beats have to fight to capture the moment, Beat women are doubly removed from authenticity—fifties' society demanded that they pick up the slack for their men's irresponsible actions. In *Dinners and Nightmares*, di Prima describes an argument with her lover over who should do the dishes. As di Prima eventually begins to do them, her lover calls out from the living room, "It says here Picasso produces fourteen hours a day" (74). Feminine production, unfortunately, does not receive such accolades. In *Going On*, Joanne Kyger has a similar experience: "No one was watching the tortillas.

/ You were. / That's my new name. No One" (41). Again the assumption, imported from general fifties' society, is that women are responsible for what is going on in the kitchen. Of course, Beat males are not entirely to blame, since this mindset was endemic to society at the time. Ann Charters, in *Beat Down to Your Soul*, admits that "it is hardly surprising that most of us who fell in love with Beat writers were conditioned to accept a traditional caretaking role, even if we chose to break away from home before marriage and rebel against our parents' ideas" (612). For women writers, this balancing act between satisfying "traditional caretaking roles" and striking out on one's own was especially difficult, since time spent in the kitchen meant time spent away from writing.

In *Recollections of My Life as a Woman*, di Prima offers an example of the difficulties inherent in the female writer's position in society. Di Prima claims that fellow poet Robert Creeley circulated a famous anecdote of her involvement in an orgy, telling it "as a man would want to have it happen" (201). Using writing as a tool to reclaim her experience, di Prima thinks that "it's time I told it like it was" (201) and proceeds to explain how she actually left the supposed orgy early in order to relieve her babysitter by 11:30 P.M. According to di Prima, "Whereupon, Jack Kerouac raised himself up one elbow on the linoleum and announced in a stentorian voice: '*DI PRIMA, UNLESS YOU FORGET ABOUT YOUR BABYSITTER, YOU'RE NEVER GOING TO BE A WRITER*'" (202). Kerouac's declaration dramatizes the difference in perspective; he believes in spontaneous freedom at all times and in all places. Yet, what he fails to understand is that he is not under the same set of conditions as di Prima. How each woman writer deals with the restrictions that gender creates varies, but such ever-present demands cannot be ignored.

The demands of the domestic sphere had repercussions for nearly all Beat women writers. Carolyn Cassady, author of *Off the Road*, was the wife of Neal Cassady, the real-life inspiration for Kerouac's *Dean Moriarty*. Unfortunately for Carolyn, the necessities of raising children and keeping house, often without the aid of Neal, meant that her hopes of painting had to be temporarily abandoned. For Hettie Jones in *How I Became Hettie Jones*, temporal demands of the home led to an unsatisfactory writing experience:

> How did I translate to words, this holding pattern of call and response, clean and dirty, sick, well, asleep, awake. Its only allure was need, and need was just a swamp behind the hothouse of desire. . . . I could only record my time, and send it on. . . . But where to go after

that? Certainly not to writing that makes any further demand on feeling, which requires strength as well as time. (182–83)

The responsibilities of her domestic situation leave Jones unable to entirely capture the events of her life. The moment is not the site for encountering the new but for taking care of the old. Jones is thus left only recording the needs of her life and not presenting the fullness of her desires. All is not lost, as some writers like Kyger are able to turn these everyday particulars into the stuff of poetry. Di Prima, too, is able to chisel out the space and time necessary to construct her work. But temporal constraints faced by these women Beat writers demonstrate that getting back to the moment is even more difficult for females than it is for males. While male writers struggle to attain the authentic moment, women Beat writers must travel twice the distance, extricating themselves not only from dominant fifties' discourse but from their male Beat counterparts, who oftentimes unwittingly refill the domestic space with just the sort of inauthenticities they are trying to escape.

Yet, women Beat writers were not content to simply suffer these gender prejudices. Writers like di Prima took an active role in constructing a new model of temporality that conformed to the needs of her gender. Consider di Prima's experience of childbirth: "I had given long and earnest thought to being conscious through the labor and the birth. Being present. . . . It seemed to my logical mind that just as pregnancy was not an illness, so too labor and childbirth were meant to be taken straight" (*Recollections* 169). Of course, di Prima's insistence on "being present" is indicative of the Beat celebration of experience in general. As a woman, however, di Prima has access to a realm of experience unavailable to her male Beat counterparts. Thus, she wants to experience all that her body has to offer, including the miracle of childbirth.

Unfortunately, di Prima will have to fight for this right and eventually loses: "But now I found myself strapped onto the delivery table, my hands and arms strapped down, and my body in the most unlikely position possible for producing a child . . . an invisible demonic being standing somewhere behind my head forced a gas mask over my mouth" (170). Medical staffing and technology, gendered masculine throughout di Prima's account, keeps her from experiencing the natural process of her own body. Not only is she physically immobilized by various straps but more important di Prima is denied access to an event that has fundamental meaning for her life. Critic Meg Fox, in "Unreliable Allies: Subjective and Objective Time in Childbirth," sees the battle between obstetrician and patient as one revolving around the perception of temporality. The doctor, as observer, sees childbirth as an expectancy to overcome and thus "does not stand by the woman, waiting for the birth to resolve itself, but hastens to intervene" (123). According to Fox, this is "phallocentrically structured time," which she sets against the time of labor itself, "the recurrent waves, the waxing and waning, of gynocentric time" (132). The woman giving birth experiences a temporality outside of the doctor's clock; contractions are not timed but felt bodily. Di Prima's battle, then, is a struggle to experience a new temporality, one that is based on rhythm, repetition, and recurrence rather than linearity. Both involve progress through a series of events, but how that progress is lived differs drastically. For the obstetrician, it involves a series of regimented steps, while for the patient, it is returning recurrence.

But before accepting this seemingly natural distinction between the time of the male doctor and the female patient, we should heed Felski's warning about easy binaries of temporality. The notion of women's time as cyclical and men's time as linear has a long history. Julia Kristeva encapsulates these positions in "Women's Time," an essay in *The Kristeva Reader*: female temporality is seen to contain "repetition and eternity" while male time is made of "time as departure, progression and arrival—in other words, the time of history" (191–92). Felski takes issue with Kristeva, as well as with the collection of essays in which Fox's article appears. For Felski, temporality is not immanent to gender. Both men and women reside in both cyclical and linear temporality, depending on the situation and personal makeup.

Di Prima, for instance, is also involved in a linear project that she defines "magickly" as her "True Will." Like a Sartrean or Heideggerian project, this "Will" is a way of being-in-the-world that subsumes everything, breaking down hierarchical barriers between life and art. And for di Prima, this being is specifically feminine: "To be available, a women's art I saw as a discipline, a spiritual path" (*Recollections* 226). This availability necessitates "the writing of modular poems, that could be dropped and picked up" (226), since one never knows when a friend, lover, or child may need one's assistance. Moments may thus be cyclical (or not), but they become combined with an overall drive to create art out of life and to make life into an art. Di Prima summarizes this sentiment in her mantra "THE RE-QUIREMENTS OF OUR LIFE IS THE FORM OF OUR ART" (227).[8] Being female means experiencing the world subject to constraints, but that does not leave women writers like di Prima helpless—they still retain an agency that allows for change, both in their lives and in the art that draws on it.

The domestic sphere undeniably posed a difficult challenge for women Beat writers in the 1950s. As both a physical and a mental limit, the ubiquitous presence of domesticity could not be ignored. Unlike male Beats, who could simply flaunt convention, women writers had to undertake a more subtle negotiation with prevailing fifties' notions if they wanted to attain a positive, authentic attitude toward their lives. Take di Prima: "Still, servitude isn't the quality or the quantity of the work, but simply in performing tasks that your heart isn't in. Where the True Will, to use a magickal term, isn't engaged" (4). Housework itself is not the problem; it is only when others *expect* her to cook and clean that she bristles. Di Prima often undertakes "mothering" (as wells as "fathering") duties in order to keep her various "pads" going. *Revolutionary Letters*, for example, demonstrates this interesting mix of the domestic coupled with the rebellious. Di Prima admonishes "store water; make a point of filling your bathtub / at the first news of trouble: they turned off the water / in the 4th ward for a whole day during the Newark riots" (7). Here, di Prima offers a new type of husbandry, one that simultaneously uses supposedly mundane "women's work" in politically subversive ways. Revolution becomes not just clandestine meetings and government coups but stockpiling "antibiotics / for extreme infections" (11). Women Beat writers are not offering a wholesale rejection of all things domestic, nor are they engaged in a project that seeks to valorize some mythic element of womanhood embedded in household chores. Rather, they are doing both. By performing what has normally been gendered female in new ways, they offer a reconception of what it means to exist inside the kitchen.

Existence outside the kitchen, however, is still another matter. In a 1996 roundtable discussion on women and the Beat generation, Joyce Johnson declared, "I'm sorry I never got to go down to Mexico with Jack. It wasn't a time when women could really go on the road, in the sense that Jack and Neal went on the road as male travelers. We women could not do that then" (Charters, *Beat Down* 629). There are numerous accounts of women traveling during this period, if not exactly in the same sense that "Jack and Neal went on the road." And not all women decided to return home after their stint at the factory during World War II. Still, Johnson's point is well taken. For the majority of women during the fifties, travel was something done in a very regimented manner on weekends or holidays and always with a male around for protection. While their male counterparts were stuck at a job in office or factory, women were expected to be stuck in front of a stove—both were rendered immobile. But Beat women were able to achieve an authenticity that reconciled larger social constrictions with their personal desire to live the moment on their own terms.

The Railroad as Challenge to Beat Mobility

In an early piece entitled "The Mystery," Jack Kerouac goes down to the railroad crossing and has one of his characteristic visions: "'Why,' . . . I asked myself, 'does not this rich cargo, these cars, that terrific locomotive belong to me? . . . and to my fellow men? . . . Are we not all men living alone together on a single earth?'" (*Atop on Underwood* 200). As Kerouac's career unfolds, such overtly marxist declarations give way to a celebration of the railroad as a means for a mobility that is championed throughout the Beat canon. Drawing on images of Western expansion, hobo America, and African American migration, Kerouac links the railroad with the freedom to move. But before we champion Kerouac's desire for movement as an unquestionable assault on the established order, it is worth paying closer attention to the dilemmas and contradictions of this return to the railroad as a site for social rebellion. Kerouac's early piece makes it clear that while the railroad may be a powerful symbol of movement and flux, its inscription in a capitalist regime means that access to its power remains mediated and unequal. The railroad itself constitutes a moving factory, a massive iron horse that chews coal and spits smoke. While Kerouac's representations of railroads in such pieces as "The Railroad Earth" may appear complimentary, closer inspection reveals that Beat mobility ran up against constraints that altered its character and effectiveness.[9]

From its very inception, the railroad has been involved in debates over spatial and temporal control. As Michael O'Malley notes in *Keeping Watch: A History of American Time*, "Railroads, canals, roads, and steamships increased the speed of travel and the flow of goods between regions," thus necessitating a means to "organize some of the temporal chaos by establishing uniform regional public times in place of local variation" (65). The railroad was instrumental in establishing time zones, punctuating temporal openness with clock precision and demarcating boundless space with distance and measurement. In the words of scholar Edward S. Casey, idiosyncratic "place" was being supplanted with an abstract "space" that was both rational and measurable. While the railroads increased uniformity and allowed the transition of capital to run more efficiently, this project met with resistance on the local level, as communities often reacted violently to the imposition of such order.

Kerouac, too, chaffed at regimentation. Interestingly, a large section of "The Railroad Earth" is devoted not to Kerouac's riding of trains but to his running after them: "2½ hours to go till the time I have to stick my railroad watch in my jean watchpocket and cut out allowing myself exactly 8 minutes to the station and the 7:15 train No. 112" (45–46). Juxtaposed with this two-and-a-half-hour interval are the personal errands and individual thoughts of Kerouac while he waits for his shift to begin. Unfortunately, Kerouac's anxiety over this interval does not prevent him from showing up late for the station, where his mad dash ends only after realizing, "It's a social embarrassment to be caught sprinting like a maniac after a train" (52). Kerouac's notion of personalized, spontaneous time conflicts with the structured time of the train, which is destined to pull out of the station regardless of whether its workers are on it. Rather than personify the locomotive, Kerouac treats it as a fixed reality that is neither positive nor negative. Thus, the train is described as running over blocks of wood, feet and legs, and bodies with equal disregard. The train is simply a juggernaut; it will roll on, with or without you.

Despite their love of travel, the Beats do not celebrate the machine. Unlike many of their modernist predecessors, the Beats are more concerned with questions of use. Gertrude Stein wrote a poem to her Ford; Kerouac just wants his to take him somewhere. In his essay "'Howl' and Other Poems: Is There Old Left in These New Beats?" Ben Lee comments that while a "lost past emerges through images of automobiles and trains, connecting industrial production and working-class employment with Beat romanticizations of American machinery," nevertheless "these machines are stationary or inaccessible as often as they move freely; they signal failure or anticipation as frequently as they signal successful movements and happy deliveries" (375). There is an ambiguity in Beat representations of the vehicles of motion. In Ginsberg's long poem Iron Horse, for example, the train is a catalyst for poetic inspiration as the poet records the impressions from his cabinette window. The train represents a microcosm of American democracy, carrying soldiers and poets, white businessmen and "negro waiters negro porters" (24). But the train is likewise implicated in the Vietnam War. America, according to Ginsberg, has been bewitched by machinery to the point where "no one knows where the flesh ends and / the robot Polaris begins—" (34). Thus, the train inspiring the poet is, at the same time, "hurrying to war" (32). This lack of investment in machinery leaves Beat writers free to contemplate its use from a distance, something Ginsberg does to a locomotive in "Sunflower Sutra," where he contrasts the "dread bleak dusty imageless locomotive" to the "beautiful golden sunflowers" (*Howl and Other Poems* 38) that we all are. The stationary locomotive becomes powerful as a vehicle of imagination, in much the same way Ginsberg builds a car of imagination to carry him to his lover Neal Cassady in the poem "The Green Automobile."

Consider, too, Gregory Corso's poem "Bomb," which both celebrates this apocalyptic device while undermining its destructive power. Corso's argument is surprisingly rational: "I cannot hate you / Do I hate the mischievous thunderbolt / the jawbone of an ass" (*Mindfield* 65). The atomic bomb is simply a tool for death, not a representation of death itself. As Corso declares, "Death's finger is free-lance / Not up to man whether you boom or not" (65). Corso's poem simultaneously deflated the importance of world leaders whose fingers were "on the button" and irked a countercultural left who felt that the atomic bomb was categorically evil. For the Beats, however, machines are simply a function of how they are conceived.

The railroad becomes, then, the battleground for two varying conceptions of space—what Gilles Deleuze and Felix Guattari call the "smooth" and the "striated." Perhaps the best way to enter into Deleuze and Guattari's spatial concept is through the sea. In *A Thousand Plateaus*, they write, "The sea is a smooth space par excellence," an open plain where trajectories run their course uninhibited (479). Here is where the "nomad" can wander without spatial constraints or limits. But "smooth" space is always being "striated." In the case of the sea, this can most readily be seen in the use of maps to navigate the undifferentiated ocean. In contrast to the "empirical nomadic system of navigation based on the wind and noise, the colors and sounds of the seas," a new system gradually came into being that employed latitudes and longitudes that fully striated the sea (479). It is easy to see Kerouac as the instigator of the smooth model of space over the striation of the railroad itself, and Deleuze and Guattari do just that, claiming that the "Beatniks . . . changed direction again, they put the space outside the cities to new use" (482). But what exactly is this new use, and how does Kerouac enact a smoothing of striated space? Just as important, how viable an alternative is this smoothing, and where might it lead in terms of fundamental social change?

If the power of the railroad involves its ability to homogenize and rationalize an otherwise idiosyncratic space, then the tool of the railroad is the mile marker. Stretched out along the track, these mile markers break the landscape into a series of measurable intervals that allow for the spatial consistency necessary for the efficient running of the train. For Kerouac, however, these abstract markers are the starting point for descriptions that invert their homogenizing functions:

> Bayshore at milepost 5.2 shows you as I say that gigantic valley wall sloping in with sometimes in extinct winter dusks the huge fogs milking furling meerolling in without a sound but as if you could hear the radar hum, the oldfashioned dullmasks mouth of Potato Patch Jack London old scrollwaves crawling in across the grey bleak North Pacific with a wild fleck. . . . [T]hat fog, that terrible and bleak Seattle-ish fog that potatopatch wise comes bringing messages from Alaska and the Aleutian Mongol. ("Railroad Earth" 60)

Personal experience, not abstract geometry, comes to measure space. Milepost 5.2 is converted from the distance between the beginning of the railyards and Bayshore at milepost 5.2 to a localized place characterized by its propensity to experience huge fogs milking furling meerolling in. The specificity of place allows the newly defined Bayshore stop to take on a richer resonance, as Kerouac's description travels both temporally back to Jack London (another Bay Arean who "mapped" the peninsula with his own yardstick of experience) as well as spatially up the coast to Seattle and Alaska beyond. Space becomes place in Kerouac's account, challenging the railroad's notion that the only difference between two sites is the distance between them.

Just as the mileposts structure the space of the railroad, Kerouac uses his inversions of these designations to structure his piece: "the following 8.6 Butler Road far from being a mystery to me by the time I became a brakeman was the great sad scene of yard clerking nights" and that "*MILE POST* 46.9 is San Jose scene of a hundred interested bums lounging in the weeds along the track" (63–64). Using the "was" and "is" of the verb "to be," Kerouac translates the abstract space of the railroad into the concrete place of his experience. "The Railroad Earth" becomes a new map of the peninsula, where users orient themselves by particular details rather than longitude and latitude. This is a lesson first learned in *On the Road*, where a naïve Kerouac decides that he will follow "one long red line called Route 6" (12) across the country. He soon discovers, however, that in reality "no traffic passes through 6" and that instead he should be trying "various roads and routes" (13). David Harvey draws on the work of French scholar Michel de Certeau to proclaim in *The Condition of Postmodernity* that "the map is, in effect, a homogenization and reification of the rich diversity of spatial itineraries and spatial stories" (253). Kerouac's prose map, by contrast, harkens to "the tactile sense of medieval representations" in its retention of the minutiae of quotidian experience (253). While Kerouac's representation literally remaps the railroad line, the ramifications of such a portrayal are not so clear-cut.

Attempts at redefining spatiality are fraught with difficulty. While the marxist Harvey envisions a space for revolutionary action, he glumly concludes that "all such social movements . . . run up against a seemingly immovable paradox. For not only does the community of money, coupled with a rationalized space and time, define them in an oppositional sense, but the movements have to confront . . . the necessary organization of space and time appropriate to their own reproduction" (238). Localized opposition can work, but it is difficult to maintain in the face of a capitalist system always ready to reclaim what it has lost. If Harvey sees little hope under such a repressive regime, Deleuze and Guattari are equally wary about the ability of fundamental change to succeed under capitalism. *A Thousand Plateaus* itself ends with an admonition and warning: "Of course, smooth spaces are not in themselves libratory. . . . Never believe that a smooth space will suffice to save us" (500). Deleuze and Guattari's concept is one of give-and-take, push and pull. There are no clear winners and no end, just an ongoing struggle. And even though a young Kerouac in "The Mystery" admits that capitalist ownership of the railroad "must not go on, that this must surely and would surely end," he can only offer a solution in the form of a dream where happy railroad men refer to each other as "Brothers" who are all invested in the ownership of the railroad (*Atop an Underwood* 202). For all of its rhetorical force, Kerouac's reconception of railroad spatiality still leaves the fundamental striation of the railroad intact.

This tension between a quest for liberation through movement and a capitulation to the necessity of striation is registered within Kerouac's text itself. Towards the end of the narrative, Kerouac describes an encounter with someone else riding the rails: "Here comes this young kid . . . obviously a bummer but on the bum from college or good family" ("Railroad Earth" 81). A conversation ensues in which the kid questions Kerouac's occupation: "Ah well I dont like going up and down the same rail, if you ask me goin to sea is the real life, now that's where I'm headed or hitch hike to New York" (81). Although Kerouac responds, "It's great and you're moving all the time and you make a lot of money," the kid retains the final word: "Neverthefuckingless you keep going up and down the same rail dont you for krissakes?" (81). The resemblances between the "young kid" and Kerouac are striking. Perhaps we are being made privy to Kerouac's own doubts about working on what amounts to a suburban train where commuters "come hysterically running for their 112 to get home on time for the 5:30 televisions Howdy Doody" (60). Kerouac may be moving all the time, but he is also moving in a closed circuit, continually doubling back over the same ground. The justification of railroad work that you make a lot of money seems equally puzzling. Kerouac is fascinated with hoarding throughout "The Railroad Earth," going as far as a "3-egg breakfast with almost dry toast and oatmeal a little saucer of, and thin sickly dishwater coffee, all to save 14 cents so in my little book proudly I could make a notation and of the day and prove that I could live comfortable in America on less than 17 a week" (42). Such pecuniary considerations appear to place Kerouac squarely within the suburban commuter frenzy that he ridicules and that his mobility is an attack against.

Kerouac may indeed be working on a commuter line, but his final destination is not a tract home in the suburbs. Like Deleuze and Guattari's nomad, Kerouac is performing a continual renegotiation with his surroundings, investing them with a topography configured in his own mental and poetical terms. Likewise with his notion of work—Kerouac accumulates not to settle into a "Howdy Doody" household but to "save all me money for Mexico" ("Railroad Earth" 72). The railroad is merely a way station where experience and resources are accumulated before another adventure begins, a delay in speed that Deleuze and Guattari claim is the basis for experimentation. What is finally at stake in Kerouac's reconception of the railroad is the level to which individual agency can effect fundamental social change. Kerouac's work is not contained by the railroad; on the contrary, it challenges the assumptions underlying the railroad's striation of space. Yet, Kerouac remains inscribed within the train's spatial, temporal, and economic systems. Kerouac must accept the railroad on its terms if he is to remain employed, and even today we are no closer to being "brothers" on a communally owned railway. Ultimately, Kerouac's work must be seen not as unconstrained flow or limited boundary but as a continual negotiation that sheds light on the possibilities and limits for spatial rebellion in America.

Race and Authenticity

In *Existentia Africana*, Lewis R. Gordon differentiates between existentialism as "a fundamentally European historical phenomenon" and "existential philosophy," which he defines as "philosophical questions premised upon concerns of freedom, anguish, responsibility, embodied agency, sociality, and liberation" (10). Gordon's point is that African Americans, by virtue of their "lived context of concern," necessarily bring different issues to "existential philosophy" (10). Residing in what amounts to a hostile environment, the ways in which African Americans achieve authenticity necessarily differ radically from options available to white Americans like Kerouac. Rebellious activity entails a stricter range of possibilities along with an increase in the severity of consequences for supposedly deviant action. The personal becomes political, and social struggle must be waged if authenticity is to be attained. In "Existence, Identity, and Liberation," Robert Birt claims that "authentic consciousness of the oppressed is an expanding consciousness which comprehends the necessity to abolish oppression. . . . There can be no liberation of consciousness separate from the total struggle for social liberation" (211). For oppressed groups such as African Americans, authenticity cannot be fully reached without a change in the underlying social order. While white authors have the option of turning their backs on society, African Americans must directly confront a prejudiced system. How is such a struggle to be waged, and how might it compare to the quest for authenticity as it is conducted by white writers such as Kerouac?

African Americans have been in flux since arriving in this country but never more so than in the 1950s. According to Coontz, "The 1950s saw a major transformation in the ethnic composition of America. . . . Prior to the war, most blacks and Mexican-Americans lived in rural areas, and three-fourths of blacks lived in the South. By 1960, a majority of blacks resided in the North, and 80 percent of both blacks and Mexican-Americans lived in cities" (30). Mobility is a destabilizing force in Kerouac's work; through his travels, he challenges dominant conceptions of spatiality. The African American exodus of the 1950s was also a threat to social order. This movement personally empowered those who undertook it, offering the chance for a better life in a new environment. As Coontz notes, the "mass mobilization of black Americans and their allies . . . produced many inroads against traditional legal and political inequalities" (243). This movement towards urban centers allowed for economic as well as social mobility—

African Americans were able to get better jobs with less discrimination. For America as a whole, the postwar experience of African Americans signaled a huge demographic shift with far-ranging cultural implications.

Unlike Kerouac's journeys, however, such movement constituted a serious danger to the traveler. For African Americans, where one is helps to define who one is. Drawing on both slave narratives and Ralph Ellison's *Invisible Man*, Nadel makes the claim that "the definition of humanity is not absolute, but rather the matrix of power organized in a given time and place" (224). Travel, for white Beats like Kerouac, was conceived of as a means of altering experience in the quest for a truer, more authentic identity. For African Americans, movement and relocation are also responses to repressive spatial constraints. The difference, however, is that while white Beats get to choose this identity, African Americans must suffer redefinition from the outside. Consider an anecdote in Jon Panish's *Color of Jazz:* "Driving into the city for a reading, Baraka crawled under the back seat of their car, surprising both Corso and Ginsberg. Baraka explained his fear to the pair—'Don't you understand, I'm in Washington D.C., I'm in a place where they don't like Blacks'" (37). Kerouac and Cassady might face cold weather, traffic stops, at worst a night in jail. But throughout their travels, their human rights were never challenged, and their journey ends with a clearer understanding of themselves. Baraka, on the other hand, is transformed from a poet to a fugitive simply by crossing a city line.

Baraka's case is not unique. Even in the most liberal of places, African Americans were still conscious of the danger of traveling in spaces not socially allotted to them. Panish explains that in the fifties, Greenwich Village was a "geographic space in which black and white members of these communities worked and socialized" (23). Despite this atypical interaction, this section of New York nevertheless remained under white control. Panish claims that Euro-Americans "owned not only the venues where black and white people interacted . . . but also the symbols of that interaction" (24). Greenwich Village was a contact zone between whites and blacks, but underlying this progressive space were white benefactors who allowed such interaction to occur.

Moreover, not every Village denizen was amenable to the idea of black integration. In his *Autobiography of Leroi Jones*, Baraka describes how the Italian population in particular was not receptive to the spatial incursions made by African Americans. Attacks on blacks by Italians, especially blacks with white girlfriends, led Baraka to defend himself: "When

I started working down around that area I used to carry a lead pipe in a manila envelope, the envelope under my arm like a good messenger, not intimidated but nevertheless ready" (197). The pliancy of the envelope represents the role that Baraka must play in a hostile society—that of the good messenger. His presence is tolerated only if it is considered to be both subservient and temporary. Within this false acquiescence, however, is housed Baraka's mettle. The lead pipe, hard and unyielding, is the real Baraka ready to strike. Here Baraka's wanderings challenge accepted notions of spatiality, smoothing the striated space of New York. However, the racism present in society means that a restriation of this space will take place even quicker and with much greater force than normal. Movement and flux decentralize, but they likewise create numerous pressures for those like Baraka who encounter resistance every time they leave their house.

The difference between white Beat rebellion and its African American counterpart is a difference in psyche. As Baraka himself explains in *Blues People*, "Young whites who associated themselves with this Negro music identified the Negro with this separation, this nonconformity, though, of course, the Negro himself had no choice" (188). It is precisely this internalization of racism that Kerouac fails to grasp that leads to his disturbing panegyrics. Perhaps his most famous occurs in *On the Road*, where he is caught "wishing I were a Negro, feeling that the best the white world had offered was not enough ecstasy for me" (180). Like Mailer, Kerouac wants to use African American experience to invigorate what he sees as a stultifying postwar society filled with "white sorrows" (180). And as with Mailer, this conception is based on a problematic assumption of African American life as inherently spontaneous and natural. But what Kerouac fails to realize is that occupying a racialized body would be tantamount to an entire change of consciousness. No more white disillusionment but a new range of material anxieties even more pressing and insidious. In *Black Skin, White Masks*, Frantz Fanon explains how the African American body is triply taxed: not only must it contend with physical repression but is likewise both racially overdetermined by whites and beholden to its own ancestry (109–16). Although writers like Kerouac and Mailer must also contend with social pressures, their right to protest does not come under direct attack.[10] For African Americans, however, seizing the authentic possibilities of the moment ultimately proves extremely difficult. Externally, one is continually subject to social constraints and the gaze of a hostile other that serves to countermand any attempts at authenticity. Worse still, such prejudice becomes internalized, making the attainment of authentic existence even more difficult. The situation of African Americans in postwar America was thus more complicated than Kerouac's or Mailer's works demonstrate.

In his 1958 piece "Suppose Sorrow Was a Time Machine," Baraka attempts to negotiate this boundary between the external and internal, the personal and social, in order to make meaning of his grandfather's death. He begins by returning to the scene of a trauma, "Dothan, Alabama, U.S.A. 1898," claiming that "this is of value" (1). Ostensibly, this value resides in the "vibration" his grandfather received, but an equally plausible reading is that value stems from the repeated injustices Tom Russ suffers. Tom's store is destroyed by arson twice, and he eventually receives an injury to the head that supposedly leaves him feeble. Complicating past and present, Baraka writes, "I too would like to know exactly what it means, here in Alabama 1898, 34 years before I am born. Fifty years before I realize you knew about the vibration, 50 years before I knew that I possessed the knowledge of your knowing. But now is what we are concerned with" (1). Baraka claims that he is concerned with "now," but where and when does this moment reside? Structurally, he seems to be speaking about the moment where the "Time Machine" has placed him—"Dothan, Alabama, U.S.A. 1898." Yet "now" could also mean the "now" of writing, the present into which this historical past is being wrenched. In any case, these traumas are going to remain with Baraka, who possesses the knowledge of his grandfather's knowing. Baraka's sorrow is that his grandfather never discloses his vibrations to his grandson, but in a curious way, he does not really need to—Baraka already knows. The burden of racial oppression bequeathed by his grandfather is carried by Baraka into every new present.

Oppression may be physical, but it quickly takes root in the mind. Baraka thus chooses to combat this inauthenticity at the mental level. Here, music is an especially important site. In his 1966 piece "The Changing Same (R&B and New Black Music)," Baraka notes:

> If you play James Brown . . . in a bank, the total environment is changed. . . . An energy is released in the bank, a summoning of images that take the bank, and everybody in it, on a trip. That is, they visit another place. A place where Black People live . . . where Black People move in almost absolute openness and strength. (*Black Music* 186–89)

Baraka's choice of the bank as the site of his example is apt. The bank connotes capitalism, authority, security, and whiteness. It is a place "Black

People" can move in but only subject to its rules and regulations. The space Baraka goes on to describe is not limited by such material conditions since it resides in the mind. The space of the imagination where "Black People live" allows them to "move in almost absolute openness and strength."

Yet, why does Baraka say "almost"? In "Some Observations on the Railroad and American Culture" in *Railroad*, James Alan McPherson states, "Although Black people were not free in the same sense that whites were free" and "owned no capital, so to them the machine could not function strictly as a symbol of economic progress," the value of the railroad to Baraka's "blues people" was that it offered "aesthetic possibilities" (9).[11] This qualification points to the uneasiness of psychic solutions to materially unequal conditions. While James Brown may catapult his listeners to a more authentic place where freedom is possible, the material world is always waiting in the background to retake any gains made in the interim. This is why one of Baraka's favorite musicians, Sun-Ra, speaks of "actual change, the actual evolution through space, not only in space ships, but of the higher principles of humanity" (*Black Music* 137). Aesthetics may open up a psychic space, but the body must still reside somewhere, and the boom-box can always be unplugged—spatial change must be made material if it is to last.

Translating the aesthetic into the material is, of course, the difficulty. The celebrated context for this attempt for both Baraka and Kerouac is the jazz club. Panish claims that while Kerouac's belief in jazz as indicative of a "universal spirituality" disconnects it from "any political, historical, or social context" (113), for Baraka jazz's social significance is clear—it captures a "secret communal expression" ("Screamers" 79) that, given the right circumstances, can lead to material change. In Baraka's short story "The Screamers," a jazz performer takes a line of dancers from the private space of the club into the public space of the street to confront "dazed white men" in cars (79). Baraka's "sweetest revolution," however, is eventually put down and spatial order is restored (79). Kerouac's description of jazz has recourse to his enigmatic "*IT*"—the moment in jazz when the musician, the audience, and individual listeners all come together as a whole (more on this in chapter 5). This intersubjective rapport elides racial difference—a positive step towards integration but also a covering-up of the fundamental social problems that created racial difference in the first place. Both Kerouac and Baraka believe in challenging the social order through the redemptive power of jazz-influenced art. By invoking the concept of shared

ancestry, however, Baraka offers what Kerouac cannot: an overtly political reconception of spatiality that is less complicit in the reigning spatial
paradigm. Ironically, Baraka's program is less effective for the very same
reason—prejudice in America means that any such rebellious activity will
be fought with an increased resistance that a white writer like Kerouac
might encounter.

Rebellion presupposes limits, and the only way to truly understand
such insurrection is to examine those limits. Kerouac and Baraka share
a desire to circumvent restrictive notions of space and time prevalent in
postwar America. The difference in their attempts to break free from these
constricting limitations is the degree of urgency in their pleas. Both want
the freedom to go where they want, when they want. For Kerouac, such
freedom is a question of personal spontaneity—to gain the widest possible
spectrum of experience his motion and time must not be restricted. Baraka,
too, is foremost an artist. But for him, freedom to travel is also essential
for revolutionary change. Baraka's visit to Cuba dramatizes the difference.
While there, he is astonished to see mobility taking place on the social level:
"The unbelievable joy and excitement. The same idea, and people made
beautiful because of it. People moving, being moved" (*Home* 147–48). Unlike Kerouac's more solitary meanderings, Baraka witnesses a communal
trip to Sierra Maestra in order to celebrate a charged political event—Fidel
Castro's first victory. Baraka comes to realize that although the Beats are
rebelling "against what is most crass and ugly in our society," it is "without
the slightest thought of, say, any kind of direction and purpose" (*Home* 131).
Kerouac is neither wrong nor misguided, but the authenticity he achieves
does not provide a complete picture of Beat resistance in the fifties. As an
African American, Baraka's quest for authenticity necessarily contains
a social valence—he is fighting for the freedom of the oppressed. What
women and African American Beats demonstrate is that conformity must
be challenged on the material as well as mental levels. Oppressive notions
of temporality must be liberated, space must be opened, and authenticity
achieved—but in a manner such that everyone has the opportunity to walk
off the clock and out the door.

2. The Visionary State
Uniting Past, Present, and Future

The visionary moment is a celebrated occurrence in the Beat canon.[1] The desire to transcend defines the Beats—their work searches for means to escape space, time, the body, and the material world. This "atemporal" moment, as Gilles Deleuze and Felix Guattari term it, creates a breakdown in the subject that exposes the Beats to new levels of experience. Despite this fleeting transcendence, however, the visionary moment necessarily ends. As champions of heightened states of awareness, the Beats are left with the difficult question of what to do with the atemporal once these moments recede. The vision must have a *use* if it is to avoid slipping into obscurity, and the ways in which Beat writers attempt to deploy their visionary experience into their daily practices reveals how they construct their early-postmodern subjectivity. The vision is an encounter with the "new"—the concept of transcendence is predicated on the assumption that one leaves the familiar behind. The question that the Beats face is what to do with the novel experience that the vision creates. To employ current knowledge as a means of understanding the new risks denuding it of its transformative power. To embrace it entirely, on the other hand, leads to the relativity of each new vision usurping the old. As early postmodernists, the Beats straddle this divide. What the Beats offer is a means of rethinking the subject. The Beats attempt to craft a subjectivity that can incorporate the changes that visions produce while retaining a stable sense of self across space and time.

Early Postmodernism and the New

The problem that both modernity and postmodernity face is how to deal with the new. In *The Politics of Time*, Peter Osborne claims that the periodizing concept of modernity registers "a break not only from one chronologically defined period to another, but in the quality of historical time itself" (16). The modern is not just another historical period. Rather, it involves a new type of temporality that "must constantly re-establish itself in relation to an ever expanding past" (20). This leaves the very notion of modernity filled with anxiety—each new present threatens all that has come before it. For commentators such as Matei Calinescu, literature is one of the sites where conceptions of the past are continually reshaped in the struggle to make sense of ever-changing conditions. In *Five Faces of Modernity*, Calinescu breaks modernity up into two sets of values, "[t]he objectified, socially measurable time of capitalist civilization" and "the personal, subjective, imaginative dúree" (5). As previously discussed, the temporality of capitalist civilization has a discomforting effect on the personal time of the subject. Modernist texts attempt to navigate this alienation, but since social activity lacks "any compelling moral or metaphysical justification," modernist texts remain mired in "unbounded relativism" (5). The problem that both Osborne and Calinescu highlight is that the modern subject lacks an uncontested vantage point from which to survey change. Modernist texts address this crisis of the ever-new that defines modernity by seeking totality in a continually changing world. Unfortunately, they cannot achieve such an end because there is no overarching perspective that can adequately include a complete range of experience.

The lack of stability that modernity creates leaves the subject in a difficult position. Living in the modern world means having the way one views that world constantly threatened. This does not mean, however, that various thinkers of the modern decide to opt out of taking sides altogether—quite the contrary. In *The Concept of Modernism*, Astradur Eysteinsson explains that modernism

> invokes the bourgeois subject, but it does so more through negation than affirmation. . . . Modernism can be seen as the negative other of capitalist-bourgeois ideology and of the ideological space of social harmony demarcated for the bourgeois subject. This appears to cohere with the historical theory of what Matei Calinescu has termed "the two modernities," according to which modernism is judged in the light of its opposition to the "progress" of social modernity. (37)

Capitalist-bourgeois ideology is not content to cede subjectivity to the relativism produced by the modern condition. It is more than happy to provide subject positions for its citizens. The problem is that these containment narratives are in the business of reinforcing a capitalist regime that desires to remain in power across modernity's changing face. The texts of modernism reject such positions but do so only in a negative sense—they do not offer a new system to replace the old. This leaves modernism still searching for a grand narrative to govern its project, even if such a conception can only be posited in the negative. According to Marshall Berman, this holds equally true for the early postmodern Beats. In *All That Is Solid Melts into Air*, Berman applauds these modernists who "sometimes called themselves 'post-modernists'" but ultimately feels that they "never developed a critical perspective which might have clarified the point where openness to the modern world has got to stop, and the point where the modern artist needs to see and to say that some of the powers of this world have got to go" (32). Berman is taking early postmodernists to task for what he sees as a simple receptivity to the world that lacks any desire to create social change through intervention. Modernism demands an agenda—better to have a grand narrative, even if flawed, than pure experimentation.

Berman is correct—the Beats directly attack modernism's insistence that the subject cohere and the world make sense. Writing in what the editors of *Boundary 2* have termed the "early postmodern" period, the Beats embrace an "openness to the modern world" that does not attempt to totalize the resulting impressions into timeless formulae. In "The Detective and the Boundary," William V. Spanos draws on the work of Martin Heidegger to criticize modernist productions that allow humankind to "perceive the immediate, uncertain, problematic, and thus dreadful psychic or historical present of Dasein as a necessary part of a linear design" (20).[2] What Spanos opts for instead is a notion of the literary that allows for a stance of openness towards the world. According to Spanos, the goal of early-postmodernist texts is to "generate anxiety or dread: to dislodge the tranquilized individual from the 'at-home of publicness,' from the domesticated, the scientifically charted and organized familiarity of the totalized world" (26). There is no grand narrative that will guide the individual through the world. On the contrary, the goal is to open up the subject, to force it to confront a world that does not contain any guarantees. The subject is not the ultimate legislator but is involved in continual process of negotiation with the objects of his or her surroundings. Early postmodernism exists on the cusp, riding the subject/object split to produce a meaning that is always contingent. The form-giving modern subject that seeks to attain ultimate understanding of the world is broken down into an early-postmodern subject that knows no one final meaning in a universe of change.

But if the Beats are postmodern, they are surely not postmodern in a way that we have come to expect in the twenty-first century. While the early-postmodern period enacted a decentering of the modernist subject, our postmodern position has gone a step further, erasing the notion of a subject capable of agential change altogether. In *The Idea of the Postmodern*, Hans Bertens traces the fall of the early postmodern to a burgeoning continental influence: "Following [Ihab] Hassan's lead in connecting postmodernism and poststructuralism, a generation of newly converted deconstructionists brought postmodernism within a deconstructionist orbit in which there was no place for a politically motivated promotion of presence or for an existentialist subject" (52). The subject became another of modernism's grand narratives—an untenable construct meant to create a false sense of security in a changing world. Of course, not all commentators see this as an unproductive turn. Critics like Elizabeth Deeds Ermarth and Linda Hutcheon laud the destruction of a subjectivity they see as producing "privileged positions based on hidden hierarchies and teleologies" (Ermarth 123). Replacing a strict Cartesian ego with a pluralized subject, postmodern critics like Ermarth call for a notion of subjectivity that is constantly changing. As Ermarth contends in *Sequel to History*, "Postmodern subjectivity is without a subject because it is without an object; the subject is dispersed in the world it observes" (123). Ermarth is not far from the existential position; she draws extensively on Heidegger to make her point. Yet, the existential subject that early-postmodern thinkers like Spanos invoke is clearly bounded. Objects affect it, but there still remains a subject that is affected. Postmodernism, by contrast, jettisons the subject altogether.[3] Postmodernism may have a political agenda, but it is one that can do without the subject as an agent of change.

Fredric Jameson is perhaps the most outspoken critic of this postmodern position. In his essay "Postmodernism and Consumer Society," Jameson equates the collapse of the subject with a schizophrenic disposition that condemns one "to live a perpetual present with which the various moments of his or her past have little connection" (119). While many postmodernists see this as an opening up of possibility and a cause for celebration, Jameson disagrees. Not only is the schizophrenic subject without an identity, they are unable to do anything "since to have a project means to be able to commit oneself to a certain continuity over time" (120). The perpetual present creates a discontinuity between subject and world that leaves the former helpless to affect the latter. The subject is literally trapped in the instant— cut off from the past in any meaningful way, he or she is rendered helpless to alter the future. Rather than generating meaning through interaction with the world, the subject must suffer continual redefinition from each new context. In contrast to modernism's conception of self as the ultimate creator of meaning, the postmodern subject lacks the ability to make sense of the world. The postmodern conception of the subject renders it passive; it is the recipient of effects, not their producer.

Jameson's contention that we are caught in a depthless present shorn of any connection to the outside helps us to understand the Beat relationship to the new. Barrett Watten draws a distinction between the new of early-postmodern poet Charles Olson, "which records either a clean or an untidy break with tradition, but one asserted nonetheless," and that of the later postmodern Leslie Scalapino, who "reinterprets the epochal break as an analytic potential to be found at all points within the habituated orders of the everyday" ("Turn to Language" 2).[4] Watten wants to use these observations to make a larger point about theory and innovation, but his binary provides a useful means of distinguishing a later postmodernism from its earlier variety. If the new is to be encountered and utilized, the modernist desire to "make sense" of the world must be jettisoned. Any attempt to extrapolate the isolated event into a law holding universal applicability is going to stifle the idiosyncrasy that gives the visionary moment its particular power. Modernism, with its recourse to grand narratives of understanding, does not leave itself free to embrace the changes that the moment brings. Postmodernism, however, errs in the opposite extreme. Embracing each instant as completely self-sufficient, postmodernism revels in the moment as each instant replaces the last. But unlike Watten's Scalapino, who wakes up "lost in the aisles of a vast postmodern supermarket" where "the claim of revolutionary newness is the oldest sales pitch in the book," the Beats are looking for a way to recoup gains made from their forays into the new, to not just shop but to bring something home from the supermarket of the world (2). The problem that the Beats face is how to stay open to the new without either settling down into one particular outlook or becoming enmeshed in the desire for continual novelty. And it is here that the concept of vision provides the best example of that Beat struggle. One must be open to the world in order to have a vision, but once one encounters this newness, how can it meaningfully inform decisions without closing down receptivity to any "newnesses" that might emerge to take its place?

The Beat Visionary Moment

The visionary moment is the perfect site for discussing the Beat's early-postmodern subjectivity because it highlights the tension between being receptive and open to the possibilities of the new while struggling to maintain a self integrated enough to avoid being consumed by the otherness that the visionary moment enacts. Examining accounts of visions by Allen Ginsberg and Jack Kerouac reveals this paradox—one must be open to the world in order to receive a vision, but one must also be careful lest this openness leads to an entire loss of self. Visions hold the possibility for a fundamental alteration of one's being, but lurking behind this opportunity is the specter of death. The stability of the modernist subject is thus challenged through a decentering of visionary experience, but the Beats are still unwilling to follow postmodernism into the extermination of the subject. Ginsberg's and Kerouac's accounts portray both aspects of the visionary experience, thus revealing an early-postmodern insistence on openness to the world that is unwilling to divest itself entirely from stable notions of self.

The first step in Beat visionary experience is to attain a stance of receptivity towards the world that will allow the atemporal to appear. In *Allen Verbatim*, Ginsberg discusses the form in which his openness to the universe took when he received his life-altering vision of William Blake's voice in a 1948 New York apartment: "I didn't understand what caused the opening of consciousness, except solitude and inattention and giving up. . . . When the soul then is passive, when it's not straining, not striving, not seeking, when it is open to the sky, then it sees" (16). Openness involves a passive state, one that eliminates the desire to place meaning on the world and instead absorbs what it finds. Too much thought, according to Ginsberg, results in a "reflecting on being rather than being" (16). This insistence on experiencing the pure presence of the moment is best accomplished in the "Beat" state. Being "Beat" implies being outside the norm—to be exhausted, lonely, and ready to give up. Ginsberg is prepared for his vision by lack—he misses his lover Neal Cassady, he has just graduated and needs to find a job, and all of his friends are currently out of the city. Deprived of such stable, recurrent elements, Ginsberg becomes more receptive to the world around him. Only after the conceptions he uses to hold the self together are destroyed does Ginsberg receive the boon of his Blake vision.

Preparation for vision inaugurates a new relationship between self and world—demarcations between inside and outside break down, leaving a precarious self that is open to new phenomenon and sensation. Ginsberg's vision of Blake produced a drastic change that would influence his life for years to come (discussed later in the chapter). But Ginsberg soon discovered that not all visions are pleasant and that policing the boundaries of subjectivity is a difficult business. After his Blake experience, Ginsberg had several more visions that week. His last one took place on the campus of Columbia University, where "some like real serpent-fear [entered] the sky. The sky was not a blue hand anymore but like a hand of death coming down on me. . . . It was not even human anymore—and was in a sense a threat, because I was going to die into that inhuman ultimately. I don't know *what* the score was there—I was too cowardly to pursue it" (*Spontaneous Mind* 44). The threat this giant octopus serpent-monster consciousness poses for Ginsberg is a threat to his sense of a stable self (Schumacher 98). Ginsberg may claim to not know the score, but it seems simple enough—pushing the boundaries of consciousness with his Blake vision, Ginsberg was nevertheless fearful of taking the ultimate step and relinquishing subjectivity altogether.

The fear of losing the self entirely marks the beginning of Ginsberg's monster vibrations that will haunt his subsequent drug experimentations. Through the use of drugs, Ginsberg attempts to approximate his Blake visions, even if their effects offer only similarities to the visionary moment. The threat to self, however, remains. Under the influence of the psychedelic drug yage, Ginsberg claims, "What I was seeing was my egoless death and it scared me" ("Interview" 274). While the drug state expanded his consciousness, it reached a limit beyond which Ginsberg refused to journey. In his essay "Mindfulness and Spirituality," Ginsberg relates that he was "scared to have my identity taken away, scared to die . . . clinging, frightened, to *stay in* this identity, this body, vomiting as it was—and seeing its doom as a living monster *outside* of me" (*Deliberate Prose* 140). The horror of the vision comes from the fear that the line between inside and outside will break down, that the outside figured as monster will overtake the inside rendered as self. Ginsberg is afraid to die before he dies. While his friend William S. Burroughs advises Ginsberg to "go right ahead, into space, outside of Logos, outside of time," it will take Ginsberg years before he is ready to heed Burroughs's advice (140).

Kerouac's accounts of his visionary experience support Ginsberg's claim that the atemporal can only be achieved through a breakdown of the self. Kerouac, too, is prepared for the visionary through his Beat lifestyle. In a 1951 letter to Cassady, Kerouac relates how he found himself with Cassady's lover LuAnne, completely broke and living in a San Francisco hotel that he could not afford. After LuAnne leaves him for an "old, bald, doddering Greek," he feels "a continent away from 'home'" (*Selected Letters* 276–77). According to Kerouac, "In this way my soul was prepared for a strange vision" (276). As with Ginsberg, openness to vision is achieved through a decentering—without home, money, or companionship, Kerouac is set adrift from his moorings and forced to confront the world without a guidepost. For these Beats, openness is not just an intellectual stance but an emotional and physical condition that leaves them ready to experience the new at any moment. Only by letting go can vision be achieved.[5]

Kerouac, however, goes further than Ginsberg in his willingness to dissolve self in service of vision. In his "fish-n'-chips" vision, Kerouac comes to a sudden realization that the woman working in the shop "had been my mother, in London, years ago, way off across the night of the world" (*Selected Letters* 278–79). Kerouac becomes "her wandering blackguard of a son, her pimp-child, her thief, returned to cheat her once more" (279). This is not simply déjà-vu but a literal reconfiguration of identity. He was standing on a street corner, when, Kerouac claims, "[s]uddenly innumerable real memories, a whole night-world of them, all of them distinct and miraculously English, whole images of old London and panged memories of streetcorners where I stood, flooded through my being" (280). No longer his 1951 self, Kerouac becomes a nineteenth-century Londoner, complete with a charged emotional history. Yet, unlike Ginsberg, Kerouac embraces this breakdown of self. Kerouac goes on to celebrate the concept of death inherent in this vision. In *On the Road*, he explains through the character of Sal, "I felt sweet, swinging bliss, like a big shot of heroin in the mainline vein; like a gulp of wine late in the afternoon and it makes you shudder; my feet tingled. I thought I was going to die the very next moment" (173). Kerouac's vision provides him with the entirely new. Giving up on a stable self, Kerouac is able to revel in his assumed identities, accepting them for the new sensations and experiences that they bring. He encounters himself as an entirely different person with an identity that he never before felt but yet is him down to the most fundamental details of memory, feeling, and emotion. During the moment of vision, Kerouac is completely other to himself.

While Ginsberg fears death, Kerouac celebrates it. However, Kerouac's death is guaranteed by his eschatological belief—the destruction of self is tolerable because an image of some afterlife stands behind it. This is Kerouac's grand narrative enacted on the level of personal history. Either heaven awaits, in which case loss of self is actually a blessing, or Buddhist rebirth prevails, and "the transitions from life to death and back to life are so ghostly easy" that there is no call for worry since self is never truly lost (*On the Road* 173). In a second letter to Cassady written the next day, Kerouac indulges in another reading of his fish-n'-chips vision:

> Of course I always felt like an orphan because my brother, who came before me, died to "save me," as it were, for my mother's arms (here I'm acquiescing to the pre-established musings of any Freudian mysterious-reader). . . . The poor Englishwoman, who is my real secret mother, and who was the wife of my sinning foul father, rejects me in the night, and I am alone like Job on the foul-heap. It's as though Jesus was my brother and I was his flesh-and-blood Judas. (*Selected Letters* 281)

Here, Kerouac is trying to secure the fundamentally divergent sense of self experienced during the vision to fixed notions of subjectivity derived from his previous self. Kerouac is not embracing the difference experienced in the vision but is attempting to ground his visionary moment in preestablished conceptions of subjectivity. Perhaps this is why Ginsberg feared his vision—he knew precisely what a loss of self would entail. Kerouac, by contrast, delves into subjectless-ness because all the while he never really loses his sense of self. He may experience a sense of otherness, but he knows that conceptions such as "heaven," "mother," and "God" will always be there to save him.

By breaking down the coherent subject bequeathed by modernism, the Beats are able to explore new realms of consciousness and experience novel ways of being-in-the-world. Kerouac and Ginsberg run up against a limit, however, when they attempt to attain a completely decentered subject. Fearful that an entire loss of ego would leave them hopelessly adrift, they cling like a drowning person to a life preserver to some stable notion of self. They are unwilling to follow postmodern thinkers like Deleuze and Guattari into a schizophrenic realm where subjectivity multiplies and nobody can be sure of returning to anything like a previous self. These early-postmodern writers occupy a tenuous position between the modern and the postmodern. Seeking to expand their range of experience, they are willing to open themselves up to the world in new ways, even if that means a loss of an absolute self. Yet, Kerouac and Ginsberg need the vestiges of the stable modern subject if they are to keep from being totally dispersed in the void. The advantage of such a venture is that the new encountered under the erasure of self can be recuperated. A purely modern self would never reach the levels of experience the Beats do, but a completely postmodern one lacks the agency necessary to utilize any gains made in the visionary moment. By retaining a link to a stable self, Beat visionaries like Kerouac and Ginsberg ensure that insights made during moments of ecstasy can return to influence their everyday lives.

Vision and the Past

Despite the newness that visions bring, they are seldom wholly original. Visions draw on the past, offering the visionary a second glance at situations normally taken for granted. If the Beat relationship to the visionary is defined as a more postmodern openness to the new that moves away from modern notions of a fixed subject, then Beat treatments of history within the visionary moment demonstrate the opposite tendency. The Beats value the past, and the postmodern insistence on a discrete, isolated instant is jettisoned in favor of a modernist sense of purpose and depth. For the Beats, the question of history's place in the atemporal moment is a question of how to usefully employ the past without becoming ruled by it in the process.

The delicate balancing act between continuity across time and periodic rupture into the atemporal can be seen in the Beat treatment of history within the visionary moment. Consider Ginsberg's Blake vision when the cornices of a building come to signify a past continually informing the present:

> I was seeing heaven in the cornice of the building. By heaven here I
> mean this imprint or concretization or living form, of an intelligent
> hand—the work of an intelligent hand, which still had the intelligence
> molded into it. The gargoyles on the Harlem cornices. What was in-
> teresting about the cornice was that there's cornices like that on every
> building, but I never noticed them before. And I never realized that
> they meant spiritual labor, to anyone—that somebody had labored to
> make a curve in a piece of tin—to make a cornucopia out of a piece
> of industrial tin. Not only that man, the workman, the artisan, but
> the architect had thought of it, the builder had paid for it, the smelter
> had smelt it, the miner had dug it up out of the earth, the earth had

gone through aeons preparing it. So the little molecules had slum-
bered for . . . Kalpas. So out of all of these Kalpas it all got together in
a great succession of impulses, to be frozen finally in that one form
of a cornucopia on the building front. (*Spontaneous Mind* 39–40)

Ginsberg's cornice is more than a simple object; it overflows instead with
a past that implicates the viewer in the long procession of history. A dense
matrix is formed between the earth itself that prepares the metal, the brute
force required to unearth and process it, and the craftsmanship required
to mold the final product. Ginsberg levels distinctions so that all of this
labor, including the act of the earth itself, is deemed spiritual. History is
not just a storehouse for stylistic possibilities but an interconnected process
whose end results constantly and intimately affect those persons living in
the present. Ginsberg claims that "about 1945 I got interested in Supreme
Reality with a capital S and a R," and in a 1948 Harlem apartment, he found
it—a vision of the world meaningfully infused with the past (35).

The early-postmodern period exemplifies a new way of *using* the past.
What is modern here is not an interest in teleological progress towards
some endpoint but the idea that there exists a human agency that can intervene to create change. Ginsberg enters history during his vision; he is
not simply carried along by the rush of events. Walter Benjamin posits a
similar notion of the atemporal in his work "Theses on the Philosophy of
History." Redefining history not as "empty time, but time filled by the presence of the now," Benjamin argues for his conception of "Jetztzeit" (261).
This now-time represents a fundamental break with history, a moment in
which possibility occurs: "Where thinking suddenly stops in a configuration pregnant with tensions, it gives that configuration a shock, by which
it crystallizes into a monad. . . . In this structure he recognizes the sign
of a Messianic cessation of happening, or, put differently, a revolutionary
chance in the fight for the oppressed past" (262–63). The visionary moment
stops time, allowing the visioner to extract the new from a configuration
pregnant with tensions. This revolutionary chance is what Ginsberg seizes
as a possibility for understanding the cornice not as a dull object carried
forward through time but a living presence that bears the aura of a past
traced back all the way to the material processes of the earth. Osborne
equates this "now-time" with the avant-garde, claiming that both disrupt
"the linear time-consciousness of progress in such a way as to enable us,
like the child, to 'discover the new anew' and, along with it, the possibility

of a better future" (150). Disrupting historical teleology, the visionary moment offers a glimpse at what might be—the possibility of seeing the past in a new light that opens up a space for change.

The difficulty in utilizing Benjamin's conception of now-time to theorize the visionary moment is that it runs the risk of making the break from history purely interruptive. Although Benjamin's use of the term "revolutionary" leads to the belief that now-time contains the potential for actual change, he fails to adequately explain how the reconsidered past is to be meaningfully employed. As Osborne claims, unless gains from the visionary moment can be reintegrated into everyday life, "we will be left with a purely interruptive conception of now-being as an exit from history into an essentially mystical space of experience" (152). Ginsberg's vision of "heaven in a cornice" undeniably represents a break with mundane reality and a step into the atemporal. However, this break is not figured as an isolated event shorn of worldly significance but rather as a peek behind the curtain that informs his subsequent thinking about reality. A theory of the visionary moment must account for both the atemporal itself as well as its impact on the present to which the seer must eventually return.

Heidegger's conception of the "moment of vision" does a better job theorizing the place of the past within the heightened present because for Heidegger, past, present, and future are already interconnected. The moment of vision occurs in an authentic present that, as seen earlier, opens Dasein to the possibilities of existence. Heidegger defines this moment as "the resolute rapture with which Dasein is carried away to whatever possibilities and circumstances are encountered in the Situation as possible objects of concern" (387). These possibilities and circumstances that Dasein encounters in the situation are not restricted to the immediate present. Dasein's "throwness," defined as the cultural condition and personal characteristics Dasein finds itself in, is a constant presence in its decisions. The future, as the possibility of death that provides the opportunity for Dasein to achieve authenticity, is a vulnerability that is always conditioning its actions. Thus, Dasein need not worry about integrating the past into future actions—the moment of vision is itself this synthesis.

Although Benjamin wants to think about now-time as a space for progress, it is Heidegger who introduces the notion of futurity that allows the past encountered in the moment of vision to do work in the future:

> Dasein temporalizes itself in the way the future and having been are united in the Present. The Present discloses the "today" authentically,

and of course as the moment of vision. But in so far as this "today" has been interpreted in terms of understanding a possibility of existence which has been seized upon—an understanding which is repetitive in a futural manner—authentic historiology becomes a way in which the "today" gets deprived of its character as present. (449)

The moment of vision unites past and future, allowing Dasein to draw upon history as a means to project itself into new "possibilities of existence." The "present," understood inauthentically as the sort of losing oneself in worldly concerns, is discarded in favor of an authentic temporality based on a vision of the past as the possibility of the future. Dasein enacts a recovery of history for its own ends, rather than being guided by the historicizing of the "they" that seeks to flatten events into a never-ending succession. For Heidegger, history is personal opportunity, a means of drawing on the past to create possibility for the future.

But if the moment of vision requires the visioner to draw on the past as a means to alter the future, why does Heidegger insist that the authentic "today" is "repetitive in a futural manner" (449)? According to Osborne, the problem is that Heidegger's past is already overdetermined: "the disruptive force of the ecstatic (death) is transformed into a moment within a national narrative of repetition through struggle" (177). The moment of vision requires Dasein to draw upon its past in order to project itself into the future, but since the past for Heidegger is already "national" in origin, the result will necessarily be prefigured in such terms.[6] Unlike existentialist appropriations of Heidegger's work that sought to portray the individual struggling to define him- or herself in an absurd world, Heidegger's insistence on the "throwness" of Dasein means that the social world will always play a defining role in its life. Heidegger himself asks, "Is perhaps the whole of existence stretched along in this historicality in a way which is primordial and not lost, and which has no need of connectedness?" (442). If this is true, then the function of the moment of vision is simply to bring the individual back to his or her heritage, to own placement in the world in such a way as to be "more free from Illusion" (443). In Osborne's view, this leads to a situation in which "authentic existence is a constantly reiterated leap into communal identification, wherein the content of action is externally determined by the authority best able to promote itself . . . as the embodiment of the destiny of the people" (170–71). Osborne is correct in questioning the assumptions that undergird Heidegger's conception. If the moment of vision is driven by repetition, where is fundamental change going to occur? Just as important, if all paths lead back to national heritage, then the notion of selfhood is predetermined, and the best we can hope for in the visionary moment is to rediscover the being we were from the outset but had lost along the pathways of history.

Of course, the result of such cultural determination need not appear so fascist as Osborne wants to claim—Ginsberg has a sense of communal heritage much less nationalistic. Consider Ginsberg's bookstore vision, where he sees each person's face in the form of a wild animal:

> Because there was a bookstore clerk there who I hadn't paid much attention to, he was just a familiar fixture in the bookstore scene and everybody went in the bookstore every day, . . . I looked in his face and I suddenly saw like a great tormented soul. . . . But all of a sudden I realized that he knew also, just like I knew. And that everybody in the bookstore knew. . . . They all had the consciousness, it was like a great unconscious that was running between all of us that everybody was completely conscious, but that the fixed expressions that people have, the habitual expressions, the manners, the mode of talk, are all masks hiding this consciousness. (*Spontaneous Mind* 41–42)

The common space of the bookstore, where everybody goes every day, becomes the site for an idiosyncratic visionary experience that fundamentally alters Ginsberg's relationship to his past. Just as ordinary cornices become extraordinary markers of human involvement and care, fixed and habitual expressions are caricatured to reveal a shared consciousness behind their masking functions. The vision makes whole the lack of connectedness inherent in everyday reality. Here is Ginsberg's "Supreme Reality"—a moment where the world is entirely complete, where the private blends into the social in such a way that both are left intact. Ginsberg will label this phenomenon "cosmic consciousness" and will return to it throughout his work. But unlike Heidegger, Ginsberg's "Real" levels distinctions in order to create a democratic visionary utopia where everybody is equally aware of everyone else and the inauthentic games they play to hide their true selves. If there is a notion of Heidegger's "nation" here, it is a nationality comprising human beings bereft of any particular shared cultural assumptions or concerns.[7]

Ginsberg's desire to attain a lost wholeness in the visionary moment is emblematic of modernism's attempt to redeem history in general. As Leo Bersani claims in *The Culture of Redemption*, "Modernism . . . included paeans to the presumably new consciousness of the times and elegiac expressions of regret for the invaluable and irrecoverable modes of consciousness presumably enjoyed in former times" (46). In either case, modernism attempts to close the gap between an unrecoverable past and a tenuous present. The work of Heidegger and Benjamin represent these two ways of recovering the past that highlight the dangers inherent in the modernist project. Osborn contrasts Benjamin with Heidegger: "Benjamin's remembrance, like the present in which it is produced, is a constructive one. History needs to be *constructed*, not made through repetition" (179). The question for the Beat visionary moment is how to use the past without being dominated by it. Benjamin's conception of constructing the past has the advantage of allowing a space for agency. The past is not simply determinate but offers a sort of raw material for the visionary. The problem with Benjamin's formalization, however, is that it runs the risk of making history superfluous. Without a future to recoup gains made from now-time, how is one ever to progress? The possibilities envisioned in one now-time are there as fodder for the next visionary moment but only nominally—there is no sense that insights are cumulative. Heidegger, on the other hand, allows for a repetition that would seem to offer a means of carrying gains forward from one "moment of vision" to the next. Unfortunately, Heidegger's appeal to an underlying national narrative means that one is never really changing, only discovering who one already was. Here, the past can become burdensome, closing off possibilities and guiding one's direction into the future. What the Beats were searching for is a midway point between these two poles—a conception of self capable of continual change but one that is simultaneously able to recover the gains made in the visionary moment.

Racialized Past, Material Present

Ginsberg's Blake vision evokes a sense of the interconnectedness of human endeavor. The cornice that inspired the vision, however, has a specifically ethnic past. While Ginsberg is living in a staunchly African American Harlem when this vision occurs, Harlem has, since its inception, been home to numerous ethnic and religious enclaves. What would Harlem's cornices signify for an African American writer like Amiri Baraka? Gilbert Osofsky notes in *Harlem: The Making of a Ghetto*, "The turning point in Harlem's history came in 1878–1881. During these years . . . rows of brownstones and exclusive apartment houses appeared overnight" (75). It is not until Harlem's real-estate bust from 1904 to 1905 that landlords "opened their houses to Negroes and collected the traditionally high rents that colored people paid" (92). For Baraka, Ginsberg's cornice is equally a symbol of economic oppression. The cornice reminds the black Harlemites that they were only welcomed when space became available and then for an exorbitant price. This point is not lost on Baraka—he infuses his conception of the atemporal with specifically racial considerations that locate the material conditions of the past squarely within the visionary present.

Baraka's concept of the "changing same" illustrates how the heightened moment can be used to negotiate the burdens of a racialized past. First, this term must be unpacked. What exactly is "changing" in Baraka's phrase, and what is staying the "same"? In *Blues People*, Baraka speaks of "consistent attitudes within changed contexts" (153). This work details the permutations that African American music has gone through in response to the continual racism prevalent in America. Here the phrase "changed contexts" seems clear enough—these are the historically contingent social realities that African Americans have had to adjust to in order to survive in America.

The "consistent attitudes" of response present more problems. On the one hand, these attitudes are continually changing since they must respond to the co-option by the dominant white society. Thus, black musicians respond to the assimilation of swing into the white vernacular with a new form of music—bop. Yet, Baraka is not content to theorize such changes as strictly a continual form of the new. Underlying these attitudes, these new stances towards white society, is a consistency drawn from the wellspring of African American tradition. As Baraka comments in a later piece, "The song and the people are the same" (*Black Music* 187). An essential blackness to experience unites disparate musical forms across space and time as they continually respond to oppressive social conditions. The difficulty inherent in understanding Baraka's "changing same" is that each side of the term contains the other. What changes is both the means by which oppression does its work as well as the form of response that African American music takes to address that oppression. What remains the same is both the continual assault on African American freedom in the form of racism as well as the consistent attitude of rebellion in the face of such an assault. Baraka's notion of the "changing same" provides a way of understanding the role of history in the present that never loses sight of the social.

Examining the "changing same" in more detail will tease out exactly how the past is coming to inform the present. Baraka's notion is firmly rooted in an African American musical tradition that is often appealed to in Beat texts as a site for transformation.[8] The first step, as with Ginsberg and Kerouac, begins with an assault on the self. In his work *Discrepant Engagement: Dissonance, Cross-culturality, and Experimental Writing*, Nathaniel Mackey explains that "since Baraka views egocentricism as the result of acculturation into whiteness, blackness represents a liberating concern for as well as openness to others. The target of the black-musician-as-saboteur thus becomes the Western cult of individualism" (36). The self is an impediment to a proper connection with blackness as a whole; the individual must open up to the social in order to gain a true sense of themselves as a subject. But unlike with Ginsberg, the resulting collectivity is not cosmic but racially specific. Tying the notion of racial collectivity to the specifically black body, Baraka writes in *Black Music*, "It is the simple tone of varying evolution by which we distinguish the races. The peoples. The body is directly figured in it. 'The life of the organs.'" (183). The black body is doubly determined—from without by white social convention, from within by a racial heredity perpetuated in every new generation. The problem for Baraka is how to carry the African American body politic into each successive moment in such a way that specifically black possibilities are formulated to address the changing conditions that limit black experience.

Baraka attempts to achieve authenticity through a judicious blending of the spiritual with the material that he finds in the African American jazz aesthetic. As chapter 1 shows, for Baraka the personal is inextricably bound up with the social. Mackey explains, "Black music, owing to a liminality that situates it somewhere between the reality away from which it recoils and the ideal toward which it aspires . . . is the appropriate unifying focus for these two forms of attention" (46). This material, this "same" that represents the undesired reality of present social conditions, continually informs Baraka's conception of the atemporal jazz moment. The past as necessity and lack is always there. In *Black Music*, Baraka writes, "We can use the past as shrines of our suffering, as a poeticizing beyond what we think the present (the 'actual') has to offer" (196). This particular social valence that the past offers Baraka means that its use in the present will always be guided in the direction of social amelioration. The present, "spiritualized" in the form of the heightened jazz moment, draws on the past to open up a space where African Americans are free to achieve an authentic stance toward the world. Ultimately, Baraka wants change. In *Black Music*, he declares that "the content of The New Music, or The New Black Music, is toward change. It is change. It wants to change forms. From physical to physical (social to social) or from physical to mental, or from physical-mental to spiritual" (199). Drawing on African American spirituality, Baraka is better able to carry the past into the present in a meaningful way. Thus, he admonishes, "The black man must seek a Black politics, an ordering of the world that is beneficial to his culture, to his interiorization and judgment of the world. This is strength" (*LeRoi Jones* 167). Ethnicity changes from a liability to an advantage: instead of seeing blackness as the site of oppression, it can become the basis for a liberating poetics that endeavors to turn a supposed weakness into a fountain of strength.

Baraka's "changing same" offers African Americans the possibility for an authentic stance towards the world. But it also shares the dangers of Heidegger's moment of vision—if authenticity involves an identification with the past, how can anyone change who they already are? This risk of "essentializing" experience has led many theorists to position blackness not as a fixed social identity but as an ongoing struggle. Houston A. Baker undertakes such a task in his work *Modernism and the Harlem Renaissance*. Adapting Baraka's changing same to "the mastery of form and the deformation of mastery," Baker draws on Baraka's conception to discuss minstrelsy and its use of the mask (15). Baker argues that the mask the minstrel show created for African Americans had to be worn in order to speak in a white-controlled society but that African Americans were able to "deform" such performances. While Baker never elides an essential blackness standing behind the social mask, his insistence on the performativity of race has been picked up on by numerous commentators. In his article "Refraining, Becoming-Black: Repetition and Difference in Amiri Baraka's *Blues People*," Jeffrey T. Nealon draws on the work of Deleuze and Guattari to make the claim that for Baraka "authenticity will need to be measured, its seems, not by prescriptive *grounds* of being, but rather by inscriptive *forces* of becoming-other" (87). For Nealon, the changing same designates a performance that must be continually repeated across time. There is no immanent blackness that must be reached but a constant "becoming-black" that even African Americans must undergo. Nealon balances essentialist views of Baraka with a Deleuzean Baraka that admonishes, "And so struggle, chance, struggle, unity, change, movement and more of, the movement, the motion" (94). This is the Baraka that Paul Gilroy wants to embrace in his work *The Black Atlantic*, where the future of black internationalism is not based on essentialism nor plurality but a constantly renegotiated hybridity. The merits of such a position are clear—blackness still exists but as a possibility available to everyone, not as an inherent characteristic of African Americans.

Baraka's conception of the changing same makes the atemporal moment dependent on the material conditions that produced it. The visionary, for Baraka, is a direct response to the racism prevalent in America. What Baraka's concept does not solve, however, is the tension between history as interruptive and history as determinate (encountered in the previous section). Defining race as an ongoing struggle with whiteness means that there must always be a limit for a "becoming-black" to work effectively. If to be black is to continually perform black, the visionary moment lacks any sort of teleology—blackness does not contain an endpoint but exists as a continually reiterated expression. This leaves us in the Benjaminian position, where the visionary moment is purely interruptive. If there is something essential about African American experience, then one runs the risk of reducing the visionary moment to pure repetition *without* a difference. As with Heidegger, the changing same comes to stand for a continual rediscovery of some essential character of the visionary subject. Despite these caveats, however, Baraka's formulation of the changing same provides an inescapable materiality to the visionary experience. Baraka grounds the atemporal in a history of ethnic conflict, making sure that the past will remain to do work as long as social equality remains unrealized.

The Future of Vision

For Beat Generation writers, the visionary state reveals the truth of the world—it is a peek behind the curtain of reality that provides an authentic glimpse of the universe. By eradicating mental structures and preconceptions, the vision provides an opportunity to see the past in a new light, thus creating potential for change. But the paradox of the transcendental is that the fullness associated with the visionary state is soon extinguished, as the seer returns to quotidian existence to make sense of his or her privileged experience. The question for the Beats, then, is how to carry insights gleaned from such ephemeral experience into the future. The revelations that the visionary moment generates must have a *use* if they are to avoid slipping back into obscurity once that moment recedes. Discussions of transcendental visionary experience in the works of Kerouac and Ginsberg grapple with this difficulty, as both authors struggle to make sense of their visions. Ultimately, both turn for an answer to the Buddhist conception of a "stillpoint" lying beyond rigid ego consciousness. While not always successful, Kerouac's and Ginsberg's deployment of the Buddhist stillpoint allows them to turn seemingly isolated visionary experience into a means of connecting past, present, and future into a meaningful whole.

The problem both writers face in their attempt to profit from the transcendental is that they make the visionary moment an end rather than a means. The allure of visions is that they seem to provide a final solution—a glance at true reality that appears to need no further elaboration. Visionary experience, however, is only the starting point for a wider wisdom that the vision makes possible. In his essay "Emerging from Nonduality," Michel Mohr explores the historical use of koans in Buddhism to induce the transcendental moment of "satori." He cautions that satori is not a "once-and-for-all goal to be reached in the future" but involves a "constantly going beyond first awareness of nonduality and aiming at integrating this insight into daily life until no trace of transient exalted states remain" (266). The vision inaugurates the beginnings of a "nonduality" that allows the seer to go beyond the arbitrary divisions created by consciousness. But the vision is a mere scaffolding, since these "transient exalted states" are not meant to leave "traces." Visionary experience is best thought of as an opening that provides an opportunity to reconceive one's relationship to the world.

This notion of the ecstatic moment of vision contrasts with the Buddhist "stillpoint." Where vision is often configured as a movement outwards that seeks to transcend the self in a search for other-worldly experience, the Buddhist stillpoint is inward focused, a result of embodied meditation that seeks to locate the center within the subject. In *Encouraging Words: Zen Buddhist Teachings for Western Students*, Robert Aitken describes the ambiguous Sino-Japanese term "sesshin" thusly: "In sesshin, you touch the mind—that is, you touch the place where there is no coming and going. . . . This breath-moment does not come from anywhere and it has no tail of association" (10). Based on the body, this breath moment creates a type of pure present where the mind can be encountered without interference. Aitken argues for a naïveté to Buddhist practice, a sort of "always starting over." Shunryu Suzuki, in *Zen Mind, Beginner's Mind*, reiterates this: "In Japan we have this phrase soshin, which means 'beginner's mind.' The goal of practice is always to keep our beginner's mind" (21). For the sake of simplicity, I am calling the type of attention that both Aitken and Suzuki describe a "stillpoint" (more on this concept later in this chapter). What is important here is that by placing the eruptive visionary state in tension with the Buddhist stillpoint, we are better able to understand the work of Kerouac and Ginsberg. These authors begin their careers through a reliance on visionary experience both as an inspiration for their writing as well as a lens to understand their place in the world. But as time unfolds, they evidence two opposite tendencies—Kerouac continually seeks new visions while Ginsberg repeatedly refers to his original visionary experience. And although both writers discover Buddhism, each man's development in this area follows separate paths as well. Kerouac typically employs Buddhism as a means of avoidance, while Ginsberg, through an increasing focus on his body, utilizes the Buddhist stillpoint to harness his visionary experience.

Prompted by Ginsberg's descriptions of Shunryu Suzuki's essays and his friend Neal Cassady's enthusiasm for the spiritualist Edgar Cayce, Kerouac began his Buddhist studies in January 1954, according to Ann Charters (*Kerouac* 191). Kerouac's "healing" vision was the result of a series of Buddhist meditations that are best described in his book *The Dharma Bums*: "I began to experience what is called 'Samapatti,' which in Sanskrit means Transcendental Visits. . . . It, the vision, was devoid of any sensation of I being myself, it was pure egolessness, just simply wild ethereal activities devoid of any wrong predicates" (147). The loss of self is a hallmark of the visionary state—destruction of the ego is required for transcendental experience to be achieved. In a 1956 letter to Carolyn Cassady, his friend's wife, Kerouac describes this feeling of samapatti:

> On March 12 my birthday my mother had a bad insistent sneeze-cough that finally got her throat all sore . . . I resolved to sit up in my bed . . . and hypnotize myself to find out what was wrong. Immediately there came a vision of a "Heet" rub bottle, and of a brandy bottle, and finally of round white flowers. I went to the parlor . . . and told her to put Heet on her throat to ease and circulate on the outside and "tomorrow we'll get brandy for the inside" and I looked and there was a bowl of round white flowers on the table and I (without saying anything) took them out and left them on my porch, and the next day her cough subsided, stopped altogether when she drank the brandy I ordered. (*Selected Letters* 572)

Kerouac's achievement of "egolessness" allows for a reconfiguration of the past placement of objects in the room and the causal connections generally established between them. The vision does not create anything new. Rather, it provides Kerouac with a new means of understanding the old. Everyday objects like a rub bottle and round white flowers gain a new significance as they are dislodged from ordinary thought patterns, and potentialities like the purchasing of brandy are called into being. Time and space get reshuffled—the flowers are moved from the table to the porch, the Heet bottle is brought to the parlor and utilized, and a new future ("tomorrow we'll get brandy for the inside") is mapped. Admittedly, Kerouac's vision is a bit mundane. But what it does demonstrate is that through a Buddhist meditative practice, he is able to leave the self and discover a visionary moment that breaks down the boundaries among past, present, and future that ordinary consciousness establishes in order to alter his life in a meaningful way.

Kerouac and Ginsberg were not the only people to discover Zen Buddhism during the postwar period. As Richard Hughes Seager notes in his *Buddhism in America*, "D. T. Suzuki and Alan Watts interpreted Zen for a broad American audience at mid-century" (91). But why Zen Buddhism, and why then? While the introduction of Buddhism to America is usually traced to the "World Parliament of Religions at the Chicago World's Fair in 1893," it did not gain widespread appeal until after the Second World War (Prebish 5). The reason for a broader public interest in the postwar period can be found in the fact that Zen in America resisted institutionalization and thus appealed to the anticonformism of the time. As Seager notes, "The shared interest of these Japanese teachers and their American students in experiential religion unconstrained by institutions was, in many respects, a perfect fit" (91). Distrust in institutions went hand-in-hand with a Zen practice which encouraged each individual student to find their own conception of self. Daniel Belgrad thus draws a connection between Zen Buddhism and the interest in spontaneity during the period: "Of all the philosophical and theoretical schools influencing the postwar avant-garde, Zen Buddhism was the least subject-centered" (167). Only through a lack of subjectivity could spontaneity be produced and authenticity achieved. But perhaps Hettie Jones explains it best in a 1996 roundtable "Women Writers of the Beat Generation," moderated by Ann Charters. In response to a question about the role of Buddhism in their lives, Jones responds, "I think in a general way the whole Beat idea and its relationship to Buddhism and its whole place in American society at that time was really an antimaterialist point of view. Buddhism was very attractive to those of us who were disaffected with the organized religion we were brought up with" (Charters, *Beat Down* 631). Anticonformist, antimaterialist, anti-institution—Zen

Buddhism offered a personalized response to the constraints of postwar culture that found appeal among the Beats.

Kerouac and Ginsberg were at the vanguard of a Beat movement that sought to replace a rigid and materialistic postwar America with a spontaneous, "Beat" lifestyle. Doubtless, then, that Zen appealed to them as a breath of fresh air in a stultifying 1950s' society. But Buddhism offered Kerouac and Ginsberg something more—a completely new relationship to their own selves. What exactly is the Buddhist stillpoint? A more detailed explanation of this concept can be found in Shunryu Suzuki's *Zen Mind, Beginner's Mind*: "When you dip your brush into the ink you already know the result of your drawing, or else you cannot paint. So before you do something, 'being' is there, the result is there. Even though you look as if you were sitting quietly, all your activities, past and present, is included" (106). According to Suzuki, to separate past and future through the wedge of the present is a mistake. The present already includes these two temporalities and thus to fret about how to remember the gains made from an old moment of vision or to worry about how to propel gains forward is irrelevant—when the next moment comes, it will already encompass these insights. Alan Watts, in his work *Zen and the Beat Way*, explains it thusly: "We live in a sort of hourglass with a big bulb at one end (the past) and a big bulb at the other end (the future); we are the neck in between, and we have no time. . . . The truth of the matter is that we have, in fact, an enormous present in which we live and the purely abstract borders of this present are the past and the future" (12). We impose "purely abstract borders" on the present, but we are actually only limiting ourselves. If we can discover this stillpoint, then the present expands to include a past and future that we normally consider beyond our grasp.

The Buddhist stillpoint, by opening up the moment to include past and future, creates a closer connection between the self and the world. In *Beat Zen, Square Zen, and Zen*, Watts remarks that "the ego finds that its own center and nature is beyond itself. . . . Here I find my own inner workings functioning of themselves, spontaneously. . . . I find that I cannot help doing and experiencing, quite freely, what is always 'right'" (6). The "self beyond self" does not need to think its actions, it simply does. The ego can be an impediment—we falsely believe that we need to think through matters on a conscious level when actually our mind already knows the appropriate course of action. Kerouac receives his healing vision not from some mystical other world but from within his very self. Kerouac's relationship to his surroundings is altered in such a way that subject and object break down to reveal the hidden connections between them. Such a revelation seems extraordinary only because what Shunryu Suzuki terms the "small mind" so often overshadows the "big mind" that exceeds it. As Kerouac explains in his Buddhist sutra *The Scripture of the Golden Eternity*, "Did I create that sky? Yes, for, if it was anything other than a conception in my mind I wouldn't have said 'Sky'—This is why I am the golden eternity. There are not two of us here, reader and writer, but one, one golden eternity, One-Which-It-Is, That-Which-Everything-Is" (23). Kerouac's "golden eternity" is the state beyond "small mind" where everything becomes One, where there is no need to think in terms of carrying gains across from one moment to another since any one moment contains all moments, past and future.

The Buddhist stillpoint thus offers Kerouac and Ginsberg a means of jettisoning their smaller, more ego-driven selves in exchange for a conception of self that expands their connection to the universe. Yet, how is this stillpoint achieved? The road to "big mind" leads through the notion of emptiness or what Buddhism terms "sunyata." According to Aitken, all too often people mistake emptiness with negativity and end up fearing what they should be embracing: "Why should you want to cling to things of the past, the present, or the future? It is because there isn't anything else. Emptiness, the void, yawns beneath the structure, so it is natural that you should hold fast to the forms of the time" (16). Rather than "clinging" to time in the hopes of avoiding "the void," Aitken counsels a letting go. The point here is to use sunyata to achieve a stillpoint within, rather than externalizing it as an "emptiness" or "void" that threatens the self from without. In terms of subjectivity, the goal becomes to bring this nothingness inward as a means of attaining the type of stillpoint that Buddhist thinkers like Aitken, Shunryu Suzuki, and Watts describe. Buddhist sunyata is not conceived of as another realm standing outside subjectivity that confronts the self with an abyss. Rather, it is an innermost possibility that lies dormant within everyone, waiting for the self to seize it.

Most commentators see Kerouac's view of sunyata as a means of breaking down oppositions in a search for wholeness.[9] But despite occasional successes like his healing vision, Kerouac either flees this emptiness or embraces it too fully—he never abides it. Those close to Kerouac have pointed out his use of Buddhism as a mechanism of avoidance, rather than as a means to self-disclosure. In Charters's roundtable, several panelists had a chance to voice their thoughts on Buddhism's role during the postwar period. Joyce Johnson, fellow Beat author and Kerouac's lover, explains that "my own feelings are that he sort of misused Buddhism as a way of rationalizing his deepest hang-ups rather than trying to overcome them" (Charters, *Beat Down* 631). Carolyn Cassady immediately agrees: "I think one of the things he liked about Buddhism was because when he got into sticky situations you could say, 'Oh, it's all an illusion.' That's how he sort of resolved things" (631). Kerouac is using the notion of emptiness as a justification for his actions, rather than as a means to attain a Buddhist conception of sunyata. This "nothing matters" attitude was likewise noted by Alan Watts, who called Kerouac to task in his work "Beat Zen, Square Zen, and Zen": "When Kerouac gives his final philosophical statement, 'I don't know. I don't care. And it doesn't make any difference'—the cat is out of the bag, for there is a hostility in these words which clangs with self-defence" (612). According to Watts, Kerouac misses the point. Any need to justify is an indication that a controlling ego is still present, that the disciple has not truly found the stillpoint beyond conceptions of self. Instead of taking the notion of emptiness within himself, Kerouac uses it as a license to flee material affairs.

Kerouac's escapism is twofold. In contradistinction to this desire to use sunyata as an excuse for his actions is Kerouac's continual abandonment to the visionary moment of "satori." Buddhism defines satori as a flash-illumination that helps the disciple reach an enlightened state. But instead of using satori to achieve a stillpoint, Kerouac often figures it as transcendence outside the self. This tendency finds its most memorable expression in *On the Road*, where Kerouac relates that "for just a moment I had reached the point of ecstasy that I always wanted to reach . . . myself hurrying to a plank where all the angels dove off and flew into the holy void of uncreated emptiness" (173). Kerouac externalizes the notion of emptiness into a "holy void" into which he can passively fall. The spatialization of nothingness that occurs here demonstrates the degree to which Kerouac has missed the concept of sunyata—rather than bringing this notion into oneself to create a stillpoint, Kerouac has instead created an external realm where the abyss is filled with action and flux. In a letter to Neal Cassady describing his fish-n'-chips vision, Kerouac ends with the pronouncement "like shortwave radio, its all in the air and is still there for me to grasp another day, and I hope to, I want to, I know I will" (*Selected Letters* 281). The benefits of the vision remain but in an externalized form that exist outside Kerouac. Despite his desire to recoup this moment, Kerouac seems ambivalent as to whether he will ever re-attain this state. Here is the root of Kerouac's problem—rather than seeking to absorb the vision as a fundamental fact of his life, he instead opts to recapture a visionary moment that, once gone, is always a step beyond him.

Ultimately, what Kerouac is after is the moment of transcendence itself, continually repeated. Take, for example, Kerouac's later novel *Satori in Paris*. In it, Kerouac explains, "Somewhere during my ten days in Paris (and Brittany) I received an illumination of some kind that seems to've changed me again, towards what I suppose'll be my pattern for another seven years or more" (7). Note the hesitancy and doubt—at this late point in his life, Kerouac is finding visions everywhere—in a conversation with an art dealer, in a look from a priest, and in the taste of creamery butter. Where satori should be a means of grasping the possibilities for an authentic existence, here it is simply a desire for transcendence that must be continually repeated. The visionary moment of satori is impossible to recuperate for Kerouac since it is not so much the insight gained that is desired as the blissful moment itself.

Ginsberg's use of the visionary errs in the opposite direction. Like Kerouac, Ginsberg saw his visions as a central aspect of his life. In an interview with Paul Portuges, Ginsberg says of his Blake vision, "But I also said at the time, now that I have seen this heaven on earth, I will never forget it, and I will never stop referring all things to it, I will never stop considering it the center of my human existence and the center of my life which is now changed" (*On the Poetry* 131). Ginsberg's Blake vision becomes the focal point for his existence and affirms his desire to be a poet. But while Kerouac continually chases after the next vision, Ginsberg staunchly refuses to leave the first. His vow to "never stop referring all things" to his Blake vision left Ginsberg locked into this single episode in his life. As he explains in *Allen Verbatim*, "I spent fifteen–twenty years trying to re-create the Blake experience in my head, and so wasted my time. . . . So I did finally conclude that the bum trip on acid as well as the bum trip on normal consciousness came from attempting to grasp, desiring a pre-conceived end" (18). Ginsberg's desire for a preconceived end is antithetical to the openness to the world that visionary experience demands. While Kerouac projects forward into a yet-to-be-conceived visionary space always on the horizon, Ginsberg repeatedly returns to a known past as a yardstick for measuring his present. Both are locked out of the immediate moment.

What does separate Ginsberg from Kerouac is the former's willingness to shift attention towards the body. The repeated overlay of past conceptions onto present experience keeps Ginsberg from engaging the present with the complete openness and possibility that is necessary for the visionary state to be adequately deployed. In his *Paris Review* interview, Ginsberg explains that if he did not renounce his Blake vision,

> I'd be hung up on a memory of an experience. Which is not the actual awareness of now, now. In order to get back to now, in order to get back to the total awareness of now and contact, sense perception contact with what was going on around me, or direct vision of the moment, now I'd have to give up this continual churning thought process of yearning back to a visionary state. (*Spontaneous Mind* 49).

Ginsberg's recourse to his Blake vision stifles his ability to utilize the insights from that past moment and keeps him from experiencing new forms of transcendence. All that remains is the conscious memory of the vision, not the immediate impact that the vision created. The problem with both Kerouac's and Ginsberg's attempts to recoup the visionary moment is that the gains achieved through the transcendental state are always figured as lying elsewhere. It is only when Ginsberg begins to think about the body that he is able to achieve a oneness with the present that, paradoxically, includes the Blake vision that he is trying so desperately to regain.

By focusing on the body, Ginsberg is able to achieve a connection with the present that allows him access to his former visionary experience. Ginsberg had encountered Buddhism as early as the 1940s while a student at Columbia University. But it was not until 1953, with the discovery of D. T. Suzuki's *Introduction to Zen Buddhism*, that his studies began in earnest (Schumacher 153). It would take a trip to India in 1962, however, before Ginsberg realized the role that the body plays in Buddhism. Ginsberg explains in an interview with Ekbert Faas that his poem "The Change" represents "a final abandonment of the pursuit of heaven ... final abandonment of the attempt to reconstruct the Blake vision I once had, and live by that. Because, finally, the memory of the Blake vision left such a strong impression of universal consciousness that it didn't seem right to abandon it" (Ginsberg, "Interview" 279). The problem is not the vision itself but Ginsberg's relationship to it. Formerly, he had read the vision as a glimpse of heaven and thus tortured himself with trying to "reconstruct" this state. His dogged attempts, however, only resulted in "monster vibrations." But once Ginsberg began to focus on his body, he was able to redirect his visionary experience and thus avoid his overreliance on the Blake vision.

The "change" Ginsberg details in his poem is the realization that his striving after the transcendental is unnecessary since it already resides within him.

> Come, sweet lonely Spirit, back
> to your bodies, come great God
> back to your only image, come
> to your many eyes & breasts, . . .
>
> (*Collected Poems* 328)

Through a return to the body, Ginsberg is able to achieve the Buddhist stillpoint that contains his earlier Blake vision. In his *Paris Review* interview, Ginsberg traces this illumination to his time spent in India, where various gurus advised, "Live in the body: this is the form that you're born for" (*Spontaneous Mind* 48). On a train in Japan, Ginsberg has another epiphany, realizing that there is "nothing more to fulfill, except be willing to die when I am dying, whenever that be. And be willing to live as a human in this form now" (48). This insistence on the body places Ginsberg squarely back into the present moment that surrounds him. Instead of continually trying to recapture his transcendent Blake vision, he can now attain the sort of insight that the Blake vision provided him through a reengagement with his Buddhist "big mind." By returning to the body, the world opens up again, disclosing the sort of interconnectedness and wonder that characterized his earlier heightened moment. Once this is achieved, there is no need to fret about losing anything—every moment exists within every other, and Ginsberg's earlier Blake vision is again made available in such a way that it does not eclipse the possibilities of the present moment.

What makes the body valuable to Ginsberg is that a receptive bodily state is more readily attainable than an idiosyncratic moment of vision. Take, for example, the meditative Zen Buddhist practice of "sitting zazen." As Shunryu Suzuki explains, "The most important point is to own your own physical body. If you slump, you will lose your self. Your mind will be wandering about somewhere else; you will not be in your body. This is not the way. We must exist right here, right now!" (27). Mind and body are inextricably linked—only by owning one's own body can one's mind focus on the moment at hand. More important, the insights gained from such a return to the present are reproducible. Buddhism is a practice, a set of techniques that allows the disciple to make steady progress towards an authentic encounter with the everyday. As Aitken comments, "You are always in a certain condition, sometimes healthy, sometimes toxic. . . . You may be in a palace with tapestries and picture windows, or you may be in a prison. But even in a prison you can practice" (18). External conditions are meaningless—as long as there is a body, then Buddhist practice is possible.

It is this notion of a Buddhist practice that separates Kerouac's stalled forays into the world of Buddhism from Ginsberg's lifelong commitment to his spiritual development. Rick Fields, in *How the Swans Came to the Lake*, comments that the Buddhism practiced in the counterculture during the postwar period "was mostly literary" (214). Lacking the physical component, many Beats were left with the purely mental aspect of Zen training. Another Zen adept, Philip Whalen, recalls that Kerouac "was incapable of sitting for more than a few minutes at a time, . . . He never learned to sit in that proper sort of meditation position. . . . Even had he been able to, his head wouldn't have stopped long enough for him to endure it" (Fields, *How the Swans Came to the Lake* 214). In "Negative Capability: Kerouac's Buddhist Ethic," Ginsberg points to this omission as the fundamental cause of Kerouac's inability to realize a true Buddhist practice: "Unfortunately, Kerouac had no teacher in the lineage of Zen or classical Buddhism. And so the one thing lacking was the tool . . . namely the sitting practice of meditation—actually to take in his body the notion of emptiness or examine it as a process of mind" (371). Ginsberg, by contrast, pays ever more attention to the role of the body as his work progresses. Themes such as the deterioration of the body, the role of death in the poet's life, keeping a "straight spine," and frank discussions of sex can be found throughout Ginsberg's later works. Ginsberg's Buddhist practice ensures that even supposedly negative bodily associations are recognized in an effort to remind himself that life is fleeting and thus attention should always be focused on the present moment.

Even with a focus on the body, the Buddhist stillpoint is difficult to maintain. Nowhere is this more in evidence than in Ginsberg's cryptic "Bad Poem." This piece, included in his last collection of verse, *Death and Fame*, encapsulates the difficulties in adhering to a Buddhist insistence on the transitory present:

> Being as Now has been re-invented
> I have devised a new now
> Entering the real Now
> At last
> Which is now.

(53)

Here the trick is to make sense of the two versions of the present being of-fered—the capitalized "Now" versus the lower-case "now" with which it gets compared. How is Now being reinvented? If this Now means the present conceived of as a space of time, then it is doomed to be remade every time it slips into the past. But why does this force Ginsberg to devise a new now and one whose lower-case spelling signals a shift from the previous Now? Perhaps because this is the subject's entry into time, placing a meaning on the undifferentiated wholeness of the abstract Now? This idea holds some merit since in the very next line this little now is going to enter the real (and why "real"?) Now and become redefined again. But the end of the poem confounds such a meaning, since it is as if the real Now somehow becomes the little now that the poet has devised. If we then loop up to the beginning of the poem, we can start anew—Now has been reinvented by the little now(s) that continually seek to replace it.

But why is this poem deemed bad? The capitalized Now is a totaliza-tion made real by the need to think of the moment in abstract terms. It is any given present moment and is therefore constantly being reinvented. Ginsberg's now, by contrast, is specific. The poem admonishes the reader not to forget that life in the moment is a personal matter, an engagement between the body and the material world. The little nows of experience make the bigger Nows of abstraction real. Yet, this still does not explain Ginsberg's title. Is the poem bad because it poorly expresses Ginsberg's sentiment or because it fails to follow the line of thought that Buddhism demands? Perhaps neither—in its inability to fully disclose meaning, it serves as a koan. Rather than searching for a meaning to a seemingly non-sensical paradox, the reader is expected to meditate on the difficulties of producing any coherent representation of something so fleeting as a now. Both literally and metaphorically, "Bad Poem" demonstrates the difficulties inherent in grasping the fleeting moment in any straightforward manner.

Despite the difficulties inherent in grounding existence on something so ephemeral as transcendental experience, the Beats view the visionary moment as the key to understanding the future. In a letter to Neal Cassady, Kerouac goes as far as to claim, "If I were ready for that vision, as I was not then, I think I would be able to understand everything and never forget it" (*Selected Letters* 278). For the Beats, the vision reveals the truth of the world, and it becomes the seer's job to prepare for, experience, and interpret this event. The heightened moment is what provides the possibility for a new trajectory into the void, a chance to change the direction of one's life. Visions do not create entirely novel possibilities. Rather, they reconfigure the visionary's understanding of the world. Consider Ginsberg's pronouncement regarding the predictatory powers of the visionary moment in *Allen Verbatim*: "I think the experiences made sense by hindsight and have come true since. In a sense they were glimpses of what I feel now, all the time. . . . In other words I was imagining my own potential awareness from a limited virginal shy tender blossom of feeling" (21–22). The vision does not fate one to a particular future, nor does it produce a pathway that was never there before. It allows the visionary to seize opportunities that were always there but never consciously realized. Such an understanding remains dormant, always available to those who allow themselves to find it. The Buddhist stillpoint has already "predicted" the past and will always already make use of the future. The visionary's job is to reach that stillpoint in the present that, once attained, dissolves the self into a "momentless" moment that subsumes past, present, and future into a meaningful and immediate whole.

3. Immanence and Transcendence
Reich, Orgasm, and the Body

The moment of orgasm catapults the human body into two spheres simultaneously. It is a crucial element in the continuation of the species, an "essential" act that calls us back to the importance the body plays in our lives. Yet, orgasm is also figured as ecstasy, a moment when the body is euphorically left behind. This twofold nature of orgasm makes it the perfect vehicle for discussing the sexual politics that the Beats were embracing. As Daniel Belgrad notes in *The Culture of Spontaneity*, "The recovery of an awareness of human experience as embodied experience became one of the most insistent themes of postwar culture" (156). But what exactly does this embodied experience look like, and how were the Beats using it to theorize a new "human experience"? The discourse surrounding the moment of orgasm provides an answer.[1] While the Beats draw on modern notions of the body as a marker of authenticity, they also use the body as a site for experimentation that prefigures a move to the postmodern. Beat representations of orgasmic experience rely on a modernist preoccupation with the body as a "natural" ground for experience and communication. As with Ginsberg's Buddhist return to corporeality, the body situates the subject in an authentic way within the material world. But the Beats also seek to transcend the body in their search for new experience. Here orgasm opens the body to a rhetoric of diffusion. The body undergoes a multiplicity of forces, sensations, and desires that reorganize subjectivity. Examining Beat representations of orgasm helps us to understand their desire to use the body as a site for both wholeness and experimentation.

The Beats' perpetual novelty as archrebels and timeless hipsters emanates from the desire to isolate the postwar decade as an anachronistic island, an example of when times were simpler. Nowhere is this more apparent than in discussions of sex. Hollywood is especially fond of appropriating the 1950s as a nostalgic site where time travelers in films such as *Back to the Future* and *Pleasantville* return with the wisdom of the late twentieth century to inspire and invigorate a sexually repressed (if refreshingly naïve) postwar culture. Foisting such representations onto the past, however, does a disservice to our understanding of the fifties as a transitional decade in American culture. Witness the tumultuous reception of Alfred Kinsey's publications *Sexual Behavior in the Human Male* (1948) and *Sexual Behavior in the Human Female* (1953). Observers compared the publication of these works to the explosion of an atomic bomb. From 1938 until 1956, Kinsey and three of his associates conducted approximately eighteen thousand interviews designed to assess sexual behavior in America (Robinson, *Modernization of Sex* 44). What he found debunks the myth of the 1950s as a prudish decade. According to Miriam G. Reumann in *American Sexual Character*, Kinsey discovered that "much of Americans' sexual activity took place outside marriage, and that the majority of the nation's citizens had violated accepted moral standards" (1). Kinsey delighted in using his findings to "shock the squares" with the true licentiousness of American sexual behavior. Rather than viewing the Beats as the sole voice of dissent in a sea of morality, Beat representations of sexuality must be situated within a decade struggling to determine what sex "means" for them.

Americans were shocked over the Kinsey report not because it revealed the kind of sex they were having but because the discourse surrounding sexuality was intimately connected with nation building and the question of American "character" as a whole. Reumann comments,

> Narratives of sexual danger could and did attach to specific kinds of acts or bodies: homosexuality was often rhetorically linked to political subversion and the betrayal of male institutions, women's extramarital sexuality associated with the decline of female nurturance and motherhood, and male heterosexuality viewed as potentially becoming either passive or excessive, either of which would threaten family life and gender roles. (35–36)

The Kinsey report did not "out" individuals; it "outed" a nation. Individuals whose sexual activities generated the report found their actions addressed on the national, rather than the personal, level. In fact, a more open sexuality was oftentimes the prescription for a country viewed by many to be on the verge of moral collapse. Discussing this inherent contradiction in American sexual discourse, Reumann explains that "authorities simultaneously maintained that sexuality had the potential to ruin families and community standards and sought to harness its appeal for the maintenance of traditional lifestyles" (4–5). Sex was both the cause and the cure—the rampant sexuality found in the Kinsey report showed how demobilization and a culturally changing America were intertwined with promiscuity and homosexuality. But rather than returning to a Victorianism that relegated sex to procreation, America turned towards a more open view of sexuality as a means to promote satisfying marriages that would form the backbone of a stronger nation.[2] Male orgasmic satisfaction meant an end to promiscuity and homosexual relations, while female sexual fulfillment, first demanded by women earlier in the century as part of first-wave feminism, meant less infidelity and a happier domestic sphere.

This chapter takes as its premise that sexual intercourse is the most essential act one can perform and, simultaneously, the most transcendent—orgasm both creates and negates bodies. Kinsey and his reports demonstrate the tension in the early-postmodern period between a desire for wholeness and totality characteristic of the modern, and a belief in openness and multiplicity that is a hallmark of the postmodern. The representation of orgasm is at the center of this divide. In *The Modernization of Sex*, Paul Robinson notes, "The most striking example of Kinsey's materialism . . . was his decision to evaluate sexual experience strictly in terms of orgasms, and orgasms themselves strictly in terms of numbers" (57). Kinsey's method was deceptively simple—measure sex in terms of orgasms. For Kinsey, sex is a biological function, divorced from the Victorian moral prescription that it always be in the service of procreation, but nevertheless a measurable, calculable event that defines sex in relationship to its connection with the body. I am arguing that the body is the site of modernist wholeness and totality par excellence—a singular, essential, and authentically natural site that implicates the subject in a tradition of biological necessity. Kinsey's recourse to orgasm as a defining human characteristic seeks to normalize sexual relations, arguing that anything adult humans do with their bodies in the privacy of their bedroom must automatically be acceptable and proper. Harnessing orgasm to conjugal success fits the logic of modernism perfectly—the natural act of orgasm legitimizes and sustains an institutional practice designed to ensure the continual reproduction of healthy citizens.

Kinsey's proclivity towards postmodernity resides in his implicit belief in the inherently positive and liberatory nature of sexual exploration. Robinson points out that while Kinsey's methodology of compiling orgasms appears to produce a straightforward portrait of American sexual practice, in actuality he relies on a "systematic structure of assumption that underlies his examination of human sexuality" (*Modernization of Sex* 43). Kinsey anticipates the more postmodern argument that sunders the bond between sex and gender by arguing for sexual desire measured on a spectrum instead of through binaries like heterosexual/homosexual. One of Kinsey's major contributions, according to Robinson, is his "dissolution of the very category of homosexuality. . . . It is suggested not merely that homosexual acts are extremely common, but that homosexuality, since it is not a state of being, exists as a potentiality in all persons" (116–17). For Kinsey, the discovery that 37 percent of adult American males had engaged in homosexual activities to orgasm meant that homosexuality, far from being an anomaly, was an integral part of natural sexual practice (51).

This challenge to accepted notions of American masculinity was debated on the national level. According to Reumann, "Boundaries between hetero- and homosexuality were policed so rigorously precisely because of the nagging fear that they were breaking down altogether" (198). While many saw an increase in homosexual behavior as a threat to the nation, Kinsey thought otherwise, embracing almost all sexual practice as inherently liberating. In the film *Kinsey*, the scientist and statistician, eminently "square" in a bow-tie and gray suit, is also shown to be a flaunter of moral custom, engaging in wife-swapping and homosexuality while condoning any sexual activity short of forced pedophilia. This desire to explore is chronicled later in the film in a scene where his wife discovers him piercing his foreskin with a needle in order to "see how it feels." The film renders this scene pathetically as the desperate act of an aging man, but from a wider historical vantage point, this is clearly the beginning of such bodily experimentation and alteration, not the end.

To achieve a better understanding of how the Beats theorize the body in the early postmodern moment, we need to position Beat depictions of orgasm within a range of modern and postmodern sexual representations. The cover to William Carlos Williams's prose work *Kora in Hell: Improvisations* (1920) provides a paradigmatic example of modernist thinking on sexuality (see fig. 3.1). This picture, produced by modern artist Stuart Davis, depicts the moment of conception as a struggle amongst various sperm to impregnate the female egg. This battle to conceive life mirrors the titular Kora's (also known as Persephone) yearly sojourn "in Hell" as she awaits her return to the earth as a reviver of crops. Critics have tended to read Kora as a surrogate for writerly creativity in general and as a valorization of the feminine within Williams's work in particular. Williams is the sperm, extending its individuality into the next generation through a reconnection with the feminine. Certainly, the modernity of Williams's project resides in the privileging of the hero-author, the seminal genius who struggles to free himself of the hell of chaos to craft his brainchild that will live generations beyond him, carrying his name forward into time. Though the feminine is invoked, it is involved only passively, as a container and nurturer of male

Fig. 3.1. William Carlos Williams uses modernist painter Stuart Davis's image of sperm attempting to fertilize an egg as cover art for his *Kora in Hell: Improvisations*. Photo courtesy of Harry Ransom Humanities Research Center, The University of Texas at Austin.

genius. There is a singularity here (one sperm enters) that is saved from the ravages of history through an appeal to the trope of rejuvenation. Williams is modern not only in his invocation of the Greek myth of Kora but likewise in the way he deploys this myth—spring, as a natural occurrence, provides the sort of rebirth that does battle with modern civilization's decline. As with T. S. Eliot's "Tradition and the Individual Talent," the modern writer is allowed unfettered creative license for his talent, all the while knowing that mythical grand narratives of tradition will ensure that his work will not end up as just another modern novelty destined to be replaced by the next generation. Williams is not linking orgasm to reproduction in order to stifle a nonprocreative sexuality as does his Victorian predecessors. His use of Davis's picture has a more modernist agenda—to make artistic production into a singular act of will that is nevertheless reproduced across moments of history.

Andres Serrano's postmodern depiction of the orgasmic moment stands in stark contrast to Williams's modernism. Serrano, a New York–born artist, became the focus of intense criticism for his 1987 piece "Piss Christ," a photograph of a crucifix immersed in the artist's own urine. Serrano went on to photograph other bodily fluids, including male ejaculate (see fig. 3.2). The relationship between the title of his piece, "Untitled VII (Ejaculate in Trajectory)," and Serrano's representation of male orgasmic experience lends insight into the way in which postmodernism tends to depict the body. The image of semen here is decontextualized—without the title, we would have difficulty identifying the image as ejaculate at all. Yet, the title adds little to our understanding, besides clinically naming the subject within the frame. Unlike Williams, Serrano offers no myth, no grand narrative, to recoup his image. Not only is there no connection here between ejaculate and reproduction, there does not appear to be any subject either. The "Ejaculate" simply exists "in Trajectory," without a past point of emanation or a future to provide meaning for the act. Of course, Serrano's work cannot escape the larger historical moment that necessarily frames it. But here, too, we see Serrano's postmodern distance from Williams. While Davis's picture draws on images of fertility and rebirth, standing behind Serrano's work is the specter of death—the late 1980s was a time when the threat of AIDS was gaining national attention. Bodily fluids such as semen became markers of disease and bodily disintegration, a fact Serrano draws on in his 1990 work "Blood and Semen II," which makes a microscopically alien world out of these two essential bodily fluids.

Fig. 3.2. Andres Serrano's 1989 work "Untitled VII (Ejaculate in Trajectory)" presents a more postmodern depiction of orgasm. Courtesy of Andres Serrano and Yvon Lambert Paris, New York.

I am not arguing that Serrano's work, as a marker of the postmodern, elides the body. On the contrary, Serrano and the postmodernism he represents are extremely concerned with the body and how it is depicted. The argument here is that thinking about the body undergoes a transformation from the modern to the postmodern. Rather than seeing the body as a natural site for wholeness, postmodern artists like Serrano are more concerned with the moments when the body breaks down. This allows representations of an altered body to enter the social with new force, as markers of difference rather than as shared essential experience. Serrano's "Untitled" series does not represent male orgasmic experience in a timeless myth of reproduction; it strips the sexual bare, challenging the viewer to place new meaning on what should be one of the most essential acts of humanity.

Beat representations of orgasm ground the body in the natural world and simultaneously utilize it for transcendence. This wedding of both the modernist and postmodernist relationships to the corporeal is evident in Gregory Corso's volume of poetry entitled *Long Live Man* (1959). The cover of Corso's volume looks very much like a photograph of the night sky, a collection of stars, gases, and planets that resembles the solar system (see fig. 3.3). Although the back cover credits the photo to "Mount Wilson

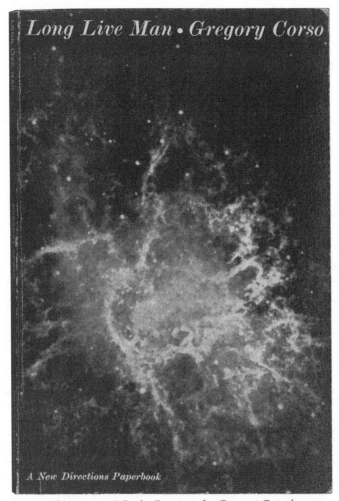

Fig. 3.3. Sky or semen? Both. Cover art for Gregory Corso's 1959 book *Long Live Man*. By Gregory Corso, from *Long Live Man*, copyright © 1962 by Gregory Corso. Reprinted by permission of New Directions Publishing Corp.

and Palomar Observatories," the critic Gregory Stephenson relates in his study *Exiled Angel* that, according to Corso, the cover "while seeming to depict a nebula or a galaxy, is, in fact, a magnification of the poet's own semen" (44). Regardless of the facts, the conflation of sperm and firmament is characteristic of Corso's desire to elevate the moment of orgasm to cosmic significance. The first poem of the collection, "Man," celebrates both an essentialism of body as well as the infinite capacity for growth and adaptation: "Air his fuel, will his engine, legs his wheels, / Eyes the steer, ears the alert; / He could not fly, but now he does—" (9). The body is what grounds "Man" in the universe. Through legs, eyes, and ears humankind navigates the world. Yet, humankind is also able to transcend the body, to will a world in which he is able to achieve what nature would not allow—flight. The body is a legacy, centuries in the making, that connects humankind to the larger cosmos that the cover photograph represents. Thus, Corso claims that "The penis is a magic wand, / The womb greater than Spring—"(9). The penis is magic and the womb great in two interrelated senses. A hereditary gift from eons of ancestors, they come to signify an unknowable past that must be accepted and celebrated. But these reproductive organs are also what allow humankind to propel itself forward spiritually, attaining ever-higher levels of achievement. Corso sees "death simply [as] a hygiene" for an escaping "soul" that is continually "Building, unbuilding, rebuilding" (9). The moment of orgasm stands on this cusp between body and soul, microcosm and macrocosm, past and future. As an essential act in the making of humanity, it implicates every individual body in that history. At the same time, orgasm is implicitly related to the magic wand that drives the species forward in a never-ending process of building, unbuilding, rebuilding that knows no teleological end. Orgasm, for a Beat like Corso, becomes the most essential act a human male can perform and the most transcendent.

The sexualized body serves an even more polemic function in the work of Allen Ginsberg. His poem "Kral Majales," for example, is framed by two images of a naked Ginsberg ensconced in an erect penis drawn by his friend Robert La Vigne (see fig. 3.4). The poem was written upon the occasion of Ginsberg's expulsion from the former Czechoslovakia for what Communist officials considered to be his negative (read homosexual) influence on the country's youth (Schumacher 443). Ginsberg locates the poem graphically between the two penises and metaphorically between the two major systems of postwar government, "when Communist and Capitalist assholes tangle the Just man is arrested or robbed or had his head cut off" (*Collected Poems* 355). Ginsberg offers an alternative. In Prague, he is crowned "Kral Majales," or "King of May," by Czech students. His doctrine is one of sexual liberation—Ginsberg announces, "And I am the King of May, which is the power of sexual youth" (355). Though his coronation occurs in the spring, the power of sexual youth is not located so much in

Fig. 3.4. Robert La Vigne's drawing of two naked Ginsbergs for the poet's "Kral Majales" welds the modern and the postmodern. Illustration courtesy of Robert La Vigne. All lines from "Kral Majales" from *Collected Poems, 1947–1980* by Allen Ginsberg. Copyright © 1965 by Allen Ginsberg. Copyright renewed 1993 by Allen Ginsberg. Reprinted by permission of HarperCollins Publishers. "Kral Majales" taken from *Collected Poems 1947-1997* by Allen Ginsberg. Copyright © 2006, the Allen Ginsberg Trust. All rights reserved.

the trope of reproduction (as in Williams) but in the revelation of sexual desire. Keeping with the modernist tendency to view the orgasmic body as naturalizing, Ginsberg's reliance on the nakedness of his pictures offers the viewers a sexualized body as a means to liberation. The power of sexual youth is its willingness to get naked and have sex—be it heterosexual or homosexual. Ginsberg considered the naked body as a means to authenticity and was fond of removing his clothes for both photographs and public events. One of his favorite mantras was "Candor ends Paranoia," and nakedness was instrumental in breaking down the social distance that caused interpersonal conflict and strife. The naked body is rebellious because of its naturalness—it is an immediate marker of a sexuality that implicates every human being that witnesses it.

But while Ginsberg draws on the sexualized body as a marker for an inherent humanism that can topple the grand narratives of capitalism and communism alike, at the same time La Vigne's drawing is not quite "natural" either. The figure of Ginsberg has three misshapen hands, each playing finger cymbals. This gives the figure, according to one critic, the appearance of a "Hindu temple relief sculpture" (Sullivan 148). Further complicating matters is that Ginsberg is wearing both glasses and tennis shoes. The point here is that Ginsberg celebrates more than just the sexual power of the natural body. In postmodern fashion, he goes on to craft an updated body that draws on an array of historical precedents. As the poem itself explains, Ginsberg is a new type of king, one

> who worships the Sacred Heart of Christ   the blue body of Krishna
>   the straight back of Ram
> The Beads of Chango the Nigerian   singing Shiva Shiva Shiva in a
>   Manner which I have invented
> and the King of May is a middle   european honor, mine in the XX
>   century.

> (355)

The sexualized pictures of Ginsberg are built of such bricolage, as ancient Hindu rites denoted by finger cymbals playing on three hands are wedded to the fashionably comfortable sneakers of a burgeoning consumer culture. Of course, all of these bodily adaptations and additions are framed by the phallic. Certainly, the homoeroticism of Ginsberg's piece, years before the Stonewall riots of New York in 1969 (in the poem, Ginsberg is called a "BOUZERANT," Czech for "faggot"), prefigures a later postmodernism of sexual-identity politics. But where Serrano's work recalls the AIDS epidemic as merely a backdrop to the work, here Ginsberg's phallic imagery enters directly into the political—the abrupt sexuality that "Kral Majales" displays is meant to galvanize support for the counterculture. Still, one would be correct in challenging the politics of such an image. Ginsberg invites everyone to take refuge under the sign of the phallus, but is that the only (or the most desirable) place to think a politics of the body?

An investigation of Beat representations of orgasm has the advantage of raising the vexed question of sexual difference within the Beat canon. The role of women underwent a change in the 1950s. Women were indeed relegated to a constraining domestic sphere, but intertwined with the rhetoric of woman as homemaker was the desire to see American women as exceptional: "It was important to national legitimacy for them to be seen as unhampered by political oppression, domestic responsibility, and male domination and as free to enjoy leisure, consumer resources, and egalitarian family lives, as well as free to play public roles as civic housekeepers" (Reumann 92). Women had "public roles" as well as private ones, and American interests required their freedom even as it discouraged it in practice.

This schizophrenic split in American consciousness provided Beat women with the space both to explore the essential qualities of their bodies in a struggle for a newly defined sense of self and to critique the constructed nature of gender hierarchies that kept them civic housekeepers. This quest for feminine identity relied on modern notions of autonomous wholeness to posit a natural womanness that could form the basis of both a politics and a poetics. This has already been seen in a writer like Diane di Prima, who explores gendered experience such as childbirth in an attempt to craft an understanding of herself as a woman in a patriarchal world. Thus, Beat women are squarely imbedded in a second-wave feminism that sought to ground definitions of femininity in the particularity of women's bodily experience. Yet, the obvious misogyny of the male Beat desire to subsume sexuality within a male-dominated register evident in Corso's link to men's sperm as constitutive of the cosmos or Ginsberg's cock rendered as emancipation pushed female Beat writers to explore the more postmodern argument that gender relations are a construct. Reumann explains that the discourse surrounding marriage in the postwar period called for new forms of gender relations, but "[t]he version crafted by marriage reformers was, however, largely divested of its feminism and progressive political implications" (144–45). Beat women challenged the more Victorian assumptions that undergirded the rhetoric of domesticity that prevailed during the 1950s. By sundering the traditional bonds uniting sexuality, the home, and marriage, women Beat writers were able to craft representations of sexual and orgasmic experience that prefigured the second-wave feminism of the late 1960s. As with their male counterparts, female conceptions of orgasm reside in a liminal space between the modern and the postmodern. While women Beat writers are all too aware of how the social impinges on the body, they nevertheless celebrate a feminine sexuality that is far more diffuse, diverse, and polymorphic than their male Beat counterparts. At their best, in their representations of orgasm, women Beat writers achieve what the men oftentimes cannot—a body that is both holistic and open to change.

Reich and the Beats

Any examination of Beat orgasmic experience must begin with the infamous figure of Wilhelm Reich. A "second generation" Freudian psychoanalyst who fell out with Sigmund Freud in the early 1930s, Reich's theories of genital sexuality are important for understanding the role ascribed to the body in the modernist period as well as Beat appropriations of his work. In *The Freudian Left*, Paul A. Robinson explains what distinguishes Freud from his disciple: "Freud had stated earlier that no neurosis arose without sexual conflict, but he had meant 'sexual' in the widest possible sense. For 'sexual' Reich now substituted 'genital,' thus undermining that broadening of sensibilities which had been one of Freud's hardest-won accomplishments" (14). The shift from the broadly sexual to the specifically genital signals a profound shift in Reich's procedure. Whereas Freud devoted his studies to the psychic problems that created neuroses, Reich opted instead for a conception of actual neuroses that catapulted the body to the forefront of his technique. Cure the body, and the mind will follow. Thus, in his 1942 work *The Function of the Orgasm*, Reich claims that "every individual who has managed to preserve a bit of naturalness knows that there is only one thing wrong with neurotic patients: the *lack of full and repeated sexual satisfaction*" (73). In a modern period of grand narratives, the concept of a normative sexuality designed to cure ills both material and psychological is perhaps the grandest narrative of all. Here Reich's naturalness is easily translatable into authenticity, while neurosis bespeaks the fall into inauthenticity described in previous chapters. For Reich, authenticity clearly resides in the body—the trick is to know how to achieve the sort of orgasm that will break through neurosis and restore a healthy, functioning, natural state in the individual.[3]

Reich's insistence on the body as a natural site of authenticity is made even more explicitly in his 1933 work *Character Analysis*. In this influential volume, Reich presents his notion of "character armor." Discussing the content of psychoanalytic sessions, Reich complains of the "underestimation, if not total neglect, of the patient's bearing, the manner in which the patient makes his communication, recounts his dreams, etc." (31). The character of the patient forms an armoring that tells the analyst as much as Freudian clues like dreams, associations, and slips. The truth of the psychic interior is written on the exterior like a text to be deciphered. Moreover, character armor can be read like a history as well. In *The Function of the Orgasm*, Reich explains that "every muscular rigidity contains the history and the meaning of its origin. . . . The armor itself is the form in which the infantile experience continues to exist as a harmful agent" (267). The body functions both as a site for authenticity and as a script upon which inauthenticities are written. In either case, truth comes to reside in corporeality, and only through the body can a natural state be restored. As Robinson observes, "Character was in fact the economic antithesis of the orgasm. . . . It 'consumed' the psychic energy not discharged in sexual intercourse" (*Freudian Left* 25). Standing behind Reich's discourse of orgasm was the fundamental belief in the desirability of the natural state—only through healthy orgasmic release could authenticity and wholeness ever be attained.

Reich's theory of the inherent authenticity of the orgasmic state found ready adherents among artists, psychologists, and intellectuals in the postwar period. However, just as Reich had amended Freud before him, these new followers only borrowed what they needed from Reichian psychoanalysis. Take, for example, the case of Paul Goodman. Barbara Ehrenreich locates Goodman's work within a new psychology, started in the 1950s, that came to be known alternately as the "human potential movement," "third force," or "humanistic psychology." Its insistence on change is what distinguishes this wave of thinking from the psychological outlook that came before: "Psychology discarded maturity as the universal developmental goal and introduced the doctrine of *growth*" (88). While Reich offered a means to attain a normative state, third-force psychologists were more concerned with fostering continual change in their patients. As Belgrad notes, Goodman combined elements of "gestalt, existential, and Reichian psychologies" but went on to "redefine 'body armor,' substituting a cognitive argument for

Reich's exclusively sexual emphasis" (143, 151). The physical attitude of the body was still important in disclosing mental problems, but the solution for Goodman was not simply "orgastic potency" but an increased spontaneity to the world. In *Gestalt Therapy*, Goodman, Frederick Perls, and Ralph E. Hefferline compare their method to those of Freud and his followers:

> We must contrast this conception of the self with the otiose "consciousness" of orthodox psychoanalysis which has as its function merely to look on and report to the analyst and cooperate by not interfering. And accordingly the revisionist para-Freudian schools, for instance, the Reichians or the Washington School tend to reduce the self altogether into the system of the organism or the interpersonal society. . . . But the self is precisely the integrator; it is the *synthetic* unity, as Kant said. It is the artist of life. (235)

Freud is too much consciousness, Reich is too much organism. Goodman is striving for a mind-body holism that sees the patient as an *act* taking place at a specific place and time. Authenticity thus involves not a return to a more primal state of being but a constant negotiation with the surrounding environment that must be continually performed. Stasis is precisely the problem, not the solution.

The debt humanistic psychology owed to Reich and the importance on change and adaptation to the surrounding environment that this movement added to his theories aligned third-force psychologists with Beat thinking on the body. The Beats, too, owe Reich. References to Reich abound in Beat texts, but the credit goes to Burroughs for first introducing his colleagues to Reich. According to Lardas, "Burroughs introduced Kerouac and Ginsberg to Reich's unorthodox theories in 1947 after hearing about the Food and Drug Administration's investigation into Reich's Orgone Institute in Rangeley, Maine" (101). Burroughs was no doubt attracted to Reich because of the censorship Reich suffered at the hands of governmental bureaucracy. But the Beats' use of Reich demonstrates that he was more than a political martyr. According to Ginsberg in *Composed on the Tongue*, Burroughs was "exploring the Reichian orgone therapy. I went to a Reichian around that time myself. . . . And he psychoanalyzed us. I spent one year talking, free-associating on the couch everyday while Burroughs sat and listened" ("Improvised Poetics" 82). This belief in Reichian analysis is especially striking given the Beats' general skepticism of psychoanalysis. Even Kerouac, quick to dismiss Freud, endorses Reich wholeheartedly. In *The Subterraneans*,

Kerouac cites *The Function of the Orgasm* specifically, then summarizes the text: "Orgasm—the reflexes of the orgasm—you can't be healthy without normal sex love and orgasm" (47). Further examples could be adumbrated, but the previous quotes are sufficient—Wilhelm Reich stands behind Beat thinking on the orgasm.

But if third-force psychologists deviated from Reich by positing a middle ground where the body and mind's interaction with the world leads to growth, it was left to the Beats to experiment with such a formula. The Beats certainly invoke Reich, but the uses they put him to oftentimes deviate immensely from his own theories. Take the colorful example of Burroughs's experimentations with his "orgone accumulator." This bit of machinery was supposed to be able to cure cancer, a claim that would eventually cost Reich his freedom. In *The Cancer Biopathy*, Reich states that "healthy, vigorous orgone systems capable of absorbing a strong orgonotic charge must be present for the elimination of protozoal or bacterial foreign bodies" (309). Although Reich's "orgone accumulator" was meant as a prophylactic against disease, Burroughs puts it to quite a different use—he would sit in his accumulator and experience blue flashes of light. For all the discussion about Reich, the Beats often seem to be more concerned with the transcendent possibilities of orgasm than with a Reichian return to an authentic body. Drawing on both Count Alfred Korbyzki's theory of general semantics and Church of Scientology's use of biofeedback, Burroughs argues for a new body unencumbered by the taint of the "word virus." For Burroughs, the body is literally besieged by language at the neurological level, thus requiring a complete overhaul of the nervous system if the disease is to be cured. The body, far from being authentic, must first be altered in order to function correctly.

This desire for a new body is even more evident in Norman Mailer's essay "The White Negro." Although not specifically a Beat writer, Mailer considered himself a "near-beat adventurer" (and was also a competitor), and his essay partakes of a similar rhetoric concerning Beat sexuality (355). As with the Beats, Mailer names Reich specifically as one of the "intellectual antecedents of this generation" (340). Yet, the hipster's desire for what Mailer terms the "apocalyptic orgasm" does not lead to the natural state that Reich is hoping to achieve (347). Rather, Mailer's hipsters are seeking to create a "new nervous system for themselves" since the "antiquated nervous circuits of the past ... strangle our potentiality for responding to new possibilities which might be exciting for our individual growth" (345). While humanistic psychology sees the body as a ground for encountering growth experiences in the environment, Mailer goes a step further, arguing for a new body altogether. As already seen, Mailer's article is problematic—by equating the "apocalyptic orgasm" with African American experience, he perpetuates the stereotype of the black male as sexual aggressor. His formulation has unsettling implications for women as well (discussed later in this chapter). But both Mailer and the Beats make the Reichian orgasm serve two divergent functions—they see orgasm as a central fact of existence and simultaneously use this knowledge to experiment with building a better body.

The Beat desire to build a new body in place of the old positions their orgasmic project more in line with postmodern theories of the body. Postmodern thinkers like Gilles Deleuze and Felix Guattari go beyond notions of the body as normative and even beyond third-force therapeutic conceptions like growth. In *Anti-Oedipus*, Deleuze and Guattari take Freud to task: "A classical theater was substituted for the unconscious as a factory . . . an unconscious that was capable of nothing but expressing itself—in myth, tragedy, dreams—was substituted for the productive unconscious" (24). The problem with Freud's schema is that it renders the unconscious passive. Instead of "producing" something new, it can only consume the preformed oedipal grid. Deleuze and Guattari thus champion Reich's attack on his mentor: "the fact remains that Reich, in the name of desire, caused a song of life to pass into psychoanalysis. He denounced, in the final resignation of Freudianism, a fear of life, a resurgence of the ascetic ideal, a cultural broth of bad consciousness" (119). Freudian bad consciousness serves to inhibit change and to maintain the psychic status quo.[4] Oedipus is erected as the norm, and any configuration that deviates from this is an aberration that must be brought back into line. For Deleuze and Guattari, this functions as enslavement. Rather than giving the unconscious full reign, the Freudian dynamic stifles the creative production of the unconscious necessary for a revolutionary challenge to the existing social order.

Production, however, is not relegated strictly to the mental register. For Deleuze and Guattari, a fundamental mechanism for alteration is the body. This can easily be seen in one of their most celebrated formulations, the "Body without Organs." At issue here is nothing less than the construction of a new body. Thus Deleuze and Guattari query, "Why not walk on your head, sing with your sinuses, see through your skin, breath with your belly" (*Thousand Plateaus* 151). As amazing as this sounds, these authors emphasize that the BwO is *not* a metaphor but a "practice, a set of practices" capable of fundamentally altering the way a user perceives the world (150). The BwO is a means to bypass the tyranny of the oedipal mind. Through a focus on the body, the ego is elided, and the user is able to come closer to the real world that is truncated by mental and physical structures. Rather than relying on a rigid, fixed conception of the body as a means of experience, these philosophers are calling for a reorganized body in which "experimentation has replaced all interpretation" (162). By producing a BwO, the user becomes active, creating a bodily condition receptive to stimuli occluded by the dominant systems of thought.

The difference between an authentic Reichian body built through orgasmic potency and a postmodern Body without Organs can be seen most clearly in Deleuze and Guattari's conception of masochism. Consider their discussion of the misconceptions surrounding the concepts of orgasm, pleasure, and masochism:

> It is claimed that the masochist, like everybody else, is after pleasure but can only get it through pain. . . . This is inaccurate; the masochist's suffering is the price he must pay, not to achieve pleasure, but to untie the pseudo bond between desire and pleasure as an extrinsic measure. Pleasure . . . is something that must be delayed as long as possible because it interrupts the continuous process of positive desire. (*Thousand Plateaus* 155)

The masochist is building a new body, one that experiences pleasure not simply through orgasmic release but on the way to orgasm. For Reich, the masochist would be an example of orgasmic impotency for several reasons. Reich does not recognize the master-servant relationship as authentic but as a sign of a deviant sexuality. More important, the moment of orgasm is what provides for the reinstitution of the natural state. Prolonging orgasmic release (or denying it altogether) makes for a decidedly "unnatural" sexual act that cannot result in a productive orgasm.

But what is being produced? For Reich, it is a terminal state of authenticity, while for Deleuze and Guattari's masochist, it is a zone of intensity that is pleasurable in itself. These two authors will go on to demonstrate this point again with regards to both courtly love, where "the slightest caress may be as strong as an orgasm," and in Taoist treatises, where "it is not a question of experiencing desire as an internal lack" but of "constituting an intensive body without organs" (156–57). Deleuze and Guattari, like the

Gestaltists, leave Reich's notion of an authentic return to the body behind in favor of a concept based on growth and change. Yet, the postmodern BwO goes a step further. Where Goodman and others still need some notion of an organized body in order to ground such change, Deleuze and Guattari see any norms as an invitation to control. Better to build an entirely new body, one unencumbered by the organs of the past, than to fall prey to a totality.

Deleuze and Guattari make repeated use of Beat texts to illustrate the body without organs. In *Anti-Oedipus*, they invoke Allen Ginsberg and Jack Kerouac as "men who know how to leave, to scramble the codes, to cause flows to circulate, to traverse the desert of the body without organs" (132–33). Later in that same text, Deleuze and Guattari quote from Ginsberg's "Kaddish" at length. And in *A Thousand Plateaus*, excerpts from Burroughs's *Naked Lunch* form the prime examples of the "drugged" BwO. While there are numerous examples of the BwO in Beat writing, a slightly different picture emerges from Beat manifestoes. Truth is in the body. But it is a truth that must be produced and, for the Beats at least, communicated. While the Beat body is undergoing constant change as means of attaining newer levels of experience, the Beats rely on the modern notion of an authentic body to ground their poetic practice. They may build a new body for experimentation, but expression depends on a body that everybody can understand.

The Beat return to the body as authentic site is more pronounced in their discussion of poetics. Here, Reich continues to play a pivotal role in the equation between the act of writing and orgasmic release. The work of Maurice Merleau-Ponty, however, explains what Reich cannot—how writing allows bodily gestures to be transferred from one person to another. In *Phenomenology of Perception*, Merleau-Ponty differentiates between two types of language: original and secondary: "I may say that 'I have been waiting a long time,' or that someone 'is dead,' and I think I know what I am saying. Yet if I question myself on time or the experience of death . . . there is nothing clear in my mind. This is because I have tried to speak about speech, to re-enact the act of expression" (391). Original, authentic expression is already full, since in the act of saying something, one attains an "immediately apprehended clarity" (391). Problems arise only when one attempts to speak about speech. The sentence turns into a reified object that loses its immediacy and thus its immanent meaning. This is important for the Beats because only writing that is original and authentic can be fully understood by the reader. Merleau-Ponty claims that "as the parts of my body together comprise a system, so my body and the other person's are one whole, two sides of one and the same phenomenon" (354). It is only through encountering the other's body that communication can be established, that this "system" can be constituted. Writing done through the body allows for intersubjectivity to be established between bodies via the medium of the text.

At its best, Beat writing partakes of a bodily gesture that the reader cannot help but receive. In discussing a threatening gesture, Merleau-Ponty explains, "[T]he gesture does not make me think of anger, it is anger itself" (184). The meaning of a raised fist contains the concept of anger within it—it is not a representation of anger but the presence of anger itself. For Merleau-Ponty, the spoken word is also a gesture, and thus "the meaning of words must be finally induced by the words themselves. . . . Their conceptual meaning must be formed by a kind of deduction from a gestural meaning, which is immanent in speech" (179). Original speech is not concerned with simply communicating a set of facts to the listener but aims at conveying a "style of being" from one body to another. Thus, Kerouac has recourse to the simile of gesture in explaining his technique. In "Essentials of Spontaneous Prose," Kerouac compares the line to "a fist coming down on a table with complete utterance, bang!" (*Good Blonde* 69). This "bang!" denotes the "telepathic shock and meaning-excitement" that the reader receives from such an expression (69). Language is not first a matter of communication but of alteration. Merleau-Ponty claims, "I begin to understand a philosophy by feeling my way into its existential manner, by reproducing the tone and accent of the philosopher" (179). Before content comes form, and "a certain style of being" gets communicated from the speaker to the listener, causing not a "process of thinking on my part, but a synchronizing change of my own existence" (183–84). Original speech can bridge the gap between self and Other since, as Kerouac maintains, the listener has the "same laws operating in his own human mind" (69). Beat poetic theory employs a conception of the body that makes it a centerpiece of communication. It is only because Beat writing is embodied from the outset that the reading process can attain such a heightened level of intersubjectivity and rapport.

For the Beats, a proven means of attaining such authentic writing is through crafting their work orgasmically. In his "Essentials," Kerouac proceeds to offer advice on how to achieve such ego-less writing: "Write excitedly, swiftly, with writing-or-typing-cramps, in accordance (as from center to periphery) with laws of orgasm, Reich's 'beclouding of consciousness.' *Come* from within, out—to relaxed and said" (*Good Blonde* 71). The body becomes intimately connected with artistic production, from cramps affecting the fingers to the moment when words spill out onto the page. Such embodied writing allows the author to bypass the ego in order to create work free from the taint of consciousness. Of course, Beat claims regarding their poetic practices must be approached with caution. I am not arguing that orgasm is always taken literally by the Beats—oftentimes it is simply a metaphor, as is obviously the case in orgasmic writing. And as archival materials clearly demonstrate, spontaneously crafted work was sometimes edited, cut, or re-presented in other forms. Ginsberg would typically cull the initial drafts of his poems from journal notes, and even Kerouac's celebrated *On the Road*, whose single-sheet manuscript is continually on display in museums and libraries across America, is actually the fourth version of the book (Hunt 77). Nevertheless, spontaneous composition formed the basis of Beat aesthetics. The work might be revised or rewritten, but the Beats strove to write "through the body," believing that only through such writing could they achieve a rapport with their readers.

For Ginsberg as well, writing intentionally as orgasm attains an authenticity that is the hallmark of literary production. Discussing the use of mantra in his poetry, Ginsberg observes "the . . . rhythmic . . . units . . . that I'd written down . . . were basically . . . breathing exercise forms . . . which if anybody else repeated . . . would catalyze in them the same pranic breathing . . . physiological spasm . . . that I was going through . . . and so would presumably catalyze in them the same *affects* or emotions" ("Improvised Poetics" 36). Writing that takes its cue from the body imbues language with a physical presence that can impact the reader corporeally. When the text is infused with such a bodily presence, the reader is able to connect with the work on a visceral level. Although Ginsberg's conception of poetic intersubjectivity seems to privilege the breath over other bodily functions, he does not exclude orgasm. Discussing his poem "Television Was a Baby Crawling toward That Deathchamber," Ginsberg describes "a series of staccato comes, spurts, within the line" that lead "up toward the end where its like a come, that begins the orgasm, the climax" ("Improvised Poetics" 22). Ginsberg makes the connection between a Reichian body and poetic expression more explicit: "because that's the key to suddenly wakening up like a whole Reichian chain of muscular reactions . . . its touching jujitsu pressure points on the body, by pronouncing them—so its doing like a physical exercise or yoga involved with the breathing" ("Improvised Poetics" 33–34). The Beats may not always agree with the return to naturalness of the Reichian orgasm, but for purposes of intersubjectivity, the notion that everyone has a body capable of sending and receiving communication makes Reich's work highly amendable to Beat poetical theory.

Beat thinking on the subject of orgasm is complicated. The Beats pay lip service to Reich's theories; allusions to his texts can be seen throughout the Beat canon. But it would be incorrect to conclude from this that the Beats were Reichian. They incorporated Reich's thinking into their works and lives but just as often deviated from his central tenet that saw orgasm as a means to recover a natural state. Orgasm is routinely in the service of transcendence. The Beats are least modern, then, when they seek to exceed the body, to place experimentation ahead of the authentic state. Going beyond their counterparts in humanistic psychology, the Beats are more in accordance with the postmodernism of Deleuze and Guattari. Here, the body becomes more than a means to ground the subject in the world. Rather, the subject finds itself in experimentation. Even the Gestaltists need a modern body to return to in order to understand the changes taking place in the field. The Beats typically do without such assurances and are willing to take bodily experimentation to the brink of death. This is why Deleuze and Guattari are so fond of Kerouac, Ginsberg, and Burroughs—one has to go to the limit in order to attain the BwO. If the Beats look forward toward the postmodern, however, they equally look backwards toward the modern. Notions of the body as authentic are essential in understanding Beat poetics. Relying on the idea that there is a truth spoken through the body, the Beats need the modern to ground their written practice lest it be reduced to an incomprehensible howl. The Beats' early postmodernism thus resides between these two poles. Believing in the natural and authentic so as to retain a link with expression, the Beats nevertheless push the body as far as it will go in order to constantly uncover new domains of experience.

Death, Orgasm, and the Body without Organs

But is there a "too far" in the Beat quest for experience? Death stands as a limit to the Beat desire for bodily experimentation through an "apocalyptic" orgasmic moment. As Georges Bataille comments in *Erotism: Death and Sensuality*, "In the hushed silence of that one moment, that moment of death, the unity of being is revealed through the intensity of those experiences in which truth stands clear of life and of its objects" (275). Truth lies beyond reality, beyond discourse, and beyond the body. The Beats are in a difficult position—to truly experience the male Beat body, one must first leave it. But this desire to transcend the material limitations of the body has disturbing consequences for Beat sexuality. By linking death with orgasm, the Beats opt for a Body without Organs that is oftentimes problematic. If bodily experimentation is not pursued far enough, nothing happens. But if it goes too far, the altered body cannot be utilized or maintained. Beat orgasmic experience thus shares the same sort of problems that characterizes their quest for the visionary moment—how does one explore consciousness and simultaneously remaining capable of recuperating gains back into everyday, embodied existence?

The Beats are not the first to link orgasm with death. There is a long tradition of equating the reproductive act with the cessation of life. In *The Use of Pleasure*, Michel Foucault finds just such a parallel in Greek thought: "medical and philosophical reflection describes it [orgasm] as . . . prefiguring the death of the individual while assuring the survival of the species" (125). This doubling of the orgasmic act as both an end and a beginning is the inevitable result of viewing sperm as a type of "life force." Thus, there is an economy to the production and expulsion of semen in the individual—lose too much life force, and risk losing the "essence" of life itself. Foucault relates that, according to authors such as Aristotle, Plato, and Hippocrates, "[b]y expelling their semen, living creatures did not just ejaculate a surplus fluid, they deprived themselves of elements that were valuable for their own existence" (130). Such a belief then led to a discourse of regulation and regimentation that sought to control this expenditure in order to ensure the healthy functioning of the individual and the society. Perhaps the most celebrated example of this type of thinking occurs in the work of Freud. Contrasting the "pleasure principle" to his recently discovered "death drive," Freud argues in "The Ego and the Id" that "after Eros has been eliminated through the process of satisfaction, the death instinct has a free hand for accomplishing its purposes" (*Freud Reader* 650). The pleasure principle is a sort of holding out against death. Once satisfaction is achieved, the lack of tension propels one even closer to the death instinct that one is constantly fighting. At the same time that orgasmic experience is seen as a hallmark of embodied existence, it has the potential to bring male Beat writers to a near-death state that is antithetical to the very life it makes possible.

Most Beat writings are willing to ride this cusp, to court death in an effort to get as close as possible to the unattainable. Take, for example, Burroughs's treatment of hangings. In *The Job*, Burroughs offers a standard connection between orgasm and death: "Freud referred to the orgasm as '*la petite mort*'—the little death. It is a moment of unconsciousness, in some cases, that approximates some of the manifestations of death" (114). But Burroughs goes on to offer a more novel possibility, speculating that "it might represent possibly the transfer of the ego into another body at the moment of ejaculation" (115). This formulation shares similarities with received notions of orgasm—it contains an aspect of death while retaining the ability to foster new life. In Burroughs's formulation, however, death is not transcended through successive generations but in the lateral movement from one body to another. Burroughs goes on to explore this possibility in *The Soft Machine*, where a medicine man explains to the narrator that "only one body is left in the switch they were going to hang me and when I shot my load and died I would pass into his body" (16). The hanging is enacted, with the result that "the jissom just siphoned me right into Xolotl's cock and next thing I was in his ass and balls flopping around spurting all over" (17). Transcendence is enacted but at a cost. Because "only one body is left in the switch," somebody must pay the ultimate price for the barrier of death to be crossed. Burroughs's work is certainly parodic, and I am not arguing that such representations should be taken at face value. However, Burroughs's repeated recourse to the trope of ejaculatory transcendence demonstrates that these formulations are not idle speculation. What they do reveal is a desire to jettison the body as an unworthy vessel. The insistence Burroughs places on orgasm as an exiting from the body signals an uneasiness with corporeality that permeates the male Beat canon.

The negation of corporeality is a theme that runs throughout Beat works, despite their insistence on embodied writing. Ginsberg's later work is replete with such images of the body as an obstacle. In "Scatalogical Observations," the epigraph reads, "The Ass knows more than the mind knows" (*Death & Fame* 85). However, the ass's knowledge is less than reassuring, as Ginsberg observes, "Shit machine shit machine / I'm an incredible shit machine" (85). The body becomes reduced solely to its excretory functions. A survey of the poet's work shows that Ginsberg grappled with the question of the body his entire life. The body is oftentimes conceived of as a limitation, a check on what consciousness would rather accomplish. Ginsberg attempts to negotiate his bodily disdain through a Tantricism that advocates acknowledging the embodied condition. Yet even here, the emphasis comes to reside on denial. Ginsberg acknowledges his physical pain but only in order to realize that it is illusory. Thus, in *Gay Sunshine Interview*, Ginsberg says, "We are so free of our bodies that we are able to stay in them; and it's all right to be in them and use them. That's the Buddhist position. You're so free of the body you don't have to be afraid of it" (38). And while David Savran declares, apropos of Burroughs, "No writer of the period is as obsessed with bodies, fluids, organs, consumption and excretion, and the mechanics of sex and reproduction," the Burroughsian body is never satisfactory (90). Burroughs's writing is a litany of transubstantiation, disfigurement, hybridization, and mutation. Rather than residing in their bodies, Burroughs's characters desire to escape them. All these examples demonstrate an uneasiness with corporeality. In contradistinction to the modernist impulse to see the body as inherently authentic, these Beat writers oftentimes evidence an intense mistrust of embodied existence. The goal thus becomes to either amend the body or flee it—at present, the body is nothing more than an unworthy vessel.

Even at their most immanent, the Beats seem unable to escape the excessive desire for transcendence that sends their sexual program beyond the realm of recoverability. During Kerouac's early Buddhist phase, for instance, he tries to build a different BwO that relies on abstinence rather than fecundity. In *Some of the Dharma*, Kerouac dismisses a Reichian discourse on orgasm that he will pick up again in *The Subterraneans*, asking rhetorically, "Buddha didn't have sexual frottings of his part from age 29 to age 83—did he die of Reich's cancer?—did lack of 'proper orgasm' pile up Neurosis & Cancer in his repressed backlog of 'sexual emotion'? No" (113). Kerouac will use such observations as a starting point for conducting a bodily program that eschews materiality through a denial of the senses. Thus, he makes a commitment:

> *—resolved—*
> One meal a day
> No drinking of intoxicants
> No maintaining of friendships.
>
> (127)

And no sex. What Kerouac is hoping for, in addition to curbing his alcoholism, is to construct a pared-down BwO that leaves his mind open to exploring the illusory nature of the universe. Kerouac, of course, is not the first to conduct such an experiment.[5] As Foucault observes in *The Use of Pleasure*, the equation between abstinence and wisdom is long-standing. Truth resides in denial, and understanding demands a relinquishing of desire.

Abstinence becomes transcendence—through negation, a higher truth is revealed. Kerouac hopes that through a denial of his present body, he will be able to reconnect with an earlier body untainted by his subsequent lasciviousness: "Drink is the curse of the Holy Life . . . coupled with No Publishing and No Loosing of Sexual Vitality, would return me to the original pristine state of the child . . . 6 year old Ti Jean seeing the red sun in the snow windows of Lowell" (*Some of the Dharma* 240). Mind and body are inextricably connected, and building the body of a six-year-old Ti Jean would allow Kerouac to return to a mental state of childhood. Thus, his injunctions—no drugs, no sex, no liquor, no adult literary complications, and no troublesome friends. In his novel *Tristessa*, Kerouac will not have sex with his junkie "Madonna" since he had "sworn off sexuality and the inhibiting impulse—I want to enter the Holy Stream and be safe on my way to the other shore" (22). This explains why Tristessa's statement that she does not care whether or not her friends pay her back because "'my Lord pay me—and he pay me more—M-o-r-e'" becomes a refrain in Kerouac's novel. Denial and abstinence are in the service of transcendence—sacrifice now, and receive the payment due upon reaching the other shore.

If the goal of Beat body politics is to fashion an authentic body grounded in the natural that is nevertheless capable of adaptation, then the Beat denial of the body raises serious doubts as to the efficacy of such an approach. In *Taking It like a Man*, Savran links this preoccupation with death to a masochistic tendency running throughout the Beat canon. Drawing on Freud's conception of "feminine masochism" (33) as well as on "what Kaja Silverman calls the Christian masochist" (82), Savran argues that Beat works "enact an obsessive oscillation between feminized and masculinized positionalities, between victim and street tough, martyr and tyrant, aesthete and proletarian" (67). Savran's persuasive account has the added appeal of being able to explain how the Beats could envision themselves as both the "beaten" victims of a repressive 1950s society as well as its most potent critics. Savran points out that while Ginsberg's "Howl" documents a "generation of victims," it, ultimately, retains a "deep ambivalence toward this process" (80–81). For Savran, this is the inevitable result of a process whereby the masochist courts his demise with the clear expectation that it will inevitably be redeemed. Thus, in Burroughs's account, orgasm within death is embraced so that the ego can transplant itself into another body. Savran notes that in many Beat texts, the authors undergo a masochist feminization that ultimately allows phallic masculinization to return even more triumphantly. Mailer's "White Negro," for instance, "allows the white male subject to take up the position of victim, to feminize and/or blacken himself fantasmatically . . . all the while asserting his unimpeachable virility" (33). These oscillations between pain and pleasure, between subservience and power, threaten to leave the Beats in a dualistic trap that renders any attempt at subversion meaningless.

A sadomasochistic body, however, need not be theorized in the negative terms Savran employs. Savran is offering an account of masochism that links pain to pleasure; Deleuze offers another account that sunders this bond. In an early book entitled *Masochism: Coldness and Cruelty*, Deleuze explains, "Freud gave two successive accounts of sadomasochism, the first in relation to the duality of the sexual and ego-instincts, the second in relation to the duality of the life and death instincts. Both accounts tend to treat sadomasochism as a particular entity within which transitions occur from one component to the other" (103). Deleuze argues that this formulation is misguided. Through a detailed reading of masochist texts by Leopold von Sacher-Masoch, Deleuze demonstrates that the sadism evidenced by its namesake the Marquis de Sade differs radically from the masochism encountered in Sacher-Masoch's texts. Thus, sadism is not a component of masochism, or vice versa—they are two separate formulations, each with its own set of demands and goals. Savran cites Deleuze's text in a footnote: "Deleuze argues that sadism and masochism are not complementary. . . . This distinction between the two kinds of sadist seems to me to be particularly useful for analyzing what usually is called S/M" (351n49). Nevertheless, the formulation Savran uses throughout his work looks very much like the sort of concept that Deleuze is attacking in *Coldness and Cruelty*. Savran even uses the term "sadomasochism" in *Taking It like a Man* as a means of describing how the pain of masochism is often intertwined with the desire for mastery associated with sadism. Thus, Savran reads Ginsberg's "Kaddish" as the "ambivalent taking up of a feminine position, of the role of victim" that ultimately desires to be "penetrated both physically and metaphysically, and so, as if by magic, to be transubstantiated or, in effect, remasculinized" (81–82). For Deleuze, "Kaddish" is a schizophrenic BwO, a "family gasping for breath and stretched out over the dimensions of a social field that does not reclose or withdraw" (Deleuze and Guattari,

Anti-Oedipus 278). Is the Beat link between orgasm and death evidence of a sadomasochism running through their work, or is it a body without organs seeking a maximization of intensity? Is orgasm death doomed to vacillate between pain and pleasure, or can it break free to create a new type of body?

The key to answering these questions is to see Beat thinking on the orgasm as an open-ended project that constantly risks failure. Savran is correct in locating a problem in male Beat sexuality. There is a tendency to move back-and-forth between positions, to continually replace one extreme with another. Kerouac is an excellent example of this tendency. Dissipation gives way to abstention, as Kerouac attempts one means of transcendence after the other. But just because Beat writers explore alternate routes to enlightenment does not mean that they are doomed to remain within a binary. Meaningful change does occur within the Beats' sexual framework. Savran's reconsideration of the Beats prompts one to take male Beat sexuality with a grain of salt—passivization can quickly become phallocentricism (and vice versa) in Beat texts. But what Savran terms "remasculinizations" and "feminizations" considered from another perspective are what Deleuze is calling "intensities." What is important for the Beats is that change and growth result from their sexual explorations—the process itself is thus more important than the results obtained.

The problem is not that the Beats are stuck in a binary but that they constantly overshoot the mark. Deleuze considers the BwO as a desirable instrument of change, but he is also aware of the dangers it involves. In *A Thousand Plateaus*, Deleuze and Guattari argue for prudence in creating a BwO:

> And how necessary caution is, the art of dosages, since overdose is a danger. You don't do it with a sledgehammer, you use a very fine file. You invent self-destructions which have nothing to do with the death drive. Dismantling the organism has never meant killing yourself. . . . You have to keep enough of the organism for it to reform each dawn . . . and you have to keep small rations of subjectivity in sufficient quantity to enable you to respond to the dominant reality. (160)

The Beats are not drawn towards death purely through sadomasochistic desire—their negation of corporeality is an attempt to experiment with subjectivity and embodiment. But as Deleuze and Guattari warn, such a program runs the risk of overdose. Attaining the limit that is the BwO requires finesse not strength, a "fine file" rather than a "sledgehammer."

That the Beats oftentimes court danger through excess is obvious—Burroughs's work exudes all of the warnings that Deleuze and Guattari make about the drugged BwO. But the Beat equation of death and orgasm should be seen as a sign of experimentation pushed to the brink and not simply as a binary constantly reproduced.

The male Beat orgasmic program founders on the shoals of death. How does one bring back gains made at the expense of the body if a body no longer remains to transport them? One answer is to be found in Beat poetics. Beat writing attempts to capture the state achieved at the abyss and bring it back for the reader to witness. Yet, this seems a tragic solution; it sets up a situation in which the writer must sacrifice his body so that art may live. The artist thus becomes the proverbial addict, and the romantic notion of suffering for art becomes needlessly invoked. A better solution is to be found in modern notions of the body as a ground for experience. The Beats certainly rely on this notion to bolster their artistic practice, but perhaps the lesson to be learned from their oeuvre is that an insistence on corporeality should inform their embodied experimentation as well. In the words of Deleuze and Guattari, a little less sledgehammer and a little more fine file might be in order. Because the Beat body is so easily discarded, these writers run the risk of not being able to return from the transcendent state. Every Beat foray into the beyond risks an overshooting of the mark that leaves them incapable of returning with knowledge gained. A little less transcendence and a little more bodily immanence are in order if the Beat sexual program is to be realized.

Beat Women's Response

Women Beat writers were just as concerned with the orgasmic body as were their male counterparts. But their conception of this moment, along with the uses they put it to, make Beat women's representations of orgasm vastly different. One reason for reading Beat women is that they provide a necessary corrective to the rampant misogyny found throughout the Beat canon. As Barbara Ehrenreich notes in *The Hearts of Men*, women, for male Beats, were often little more than "'experiences' that men might have" (171).[6] A comprehensive account of the Beat sexual project can only be attained by expanding the Beat canon to include marginalized female authors. But female Beat conceptions of orgasm provide more than just a check on the phallic excesses of their male partners—these women offer novel conceptions of sexuality that demand attention in their own right.

Beat women writers are a crucial link between the first-wave feminism of the 1920s and a second-wave feminism that began in the late 1960s. In *Desiring Revolution*, Jane Gerhard examines how second-wave feminism provided the impetus for the current third-wave feminism's investigations of the cultural, political, and social meanings of the term "woman." If Gerhard is correct in arguing for a return to second-wave feminism to tell "the story of how 'woman' became a political category" (5), then it makes sense to take another look at the women Ronna C. Johnson and Nancy M. Grace, in their collection of critical essays *Girls Who Wore Black*, claim where "forerunners of women's movements of the postmodern, post-1968 era" (9). Like male Beats, female Beat writers exist on a cusp—they return to the body as a way of understanding their distinctly feminine experience, but they also understand gender as a construct and thus anticipate a more postmodern argument. An essentialism of body grounds their experience as women, but theirs is a much more polyvalent body—Beat women writers emphasize multiplicity in their representations of the sexualized body. Beat women writers are postmodern in a different way as well. The postmodernity of female Beats lies not so much in their willingness to adapt and mutate (though they also do this) but in their recognition of the constructedness of gender. For male Beats, the body is a given; for women Beat writers, it is a text scripted and controlled from the outside. This attempt to understand their multivalent female sexuality and deploy it as a politics amidst recognition of the socially constructed nature of femininity affords them a reflexivity rarely found in the male Beat canon. Women Beat writers are thus extremely relevant for a third-wave feminism trying to bridge the gap between the universality of feminine experience and the specificity of individual bodies, each with its own racial, social, and political history.

The work of Beat women can only be understood by locating it in a postwar decade that sought to "liberate" women only in order to recontain them in a larger national narrative. As described earlier in this chapter, the 1950s woman was in a contradictory position—exhorted to explore and express her sexuality, she was nevertheless forced to do so for the benefit of family and nation. Sexuality was ultimately in the service of larger interests. Through an analysis of the popular discourse surrounding sexology in the postwar years, Gerhard, too, discusses the implicit demands made on the 1950s woman:

> She was told to use feelings of romantic love to overcome any deficiencies in sexual technique that left her unsatisfied. She heard, once

again, that the highest expression of her sexual self lay in vaginal intercourse that resulted in simultaneous orgasms. Such a portrait of "liberated" womanhood, while certainly more sexually expressive, continued to embody the tortured and convoluted ways in which ideas about sexuality worked in tandem with views of gender. (80)

The disjuncture between pleasing oneself and pleasing a partner, between sex as enlightenment and sex as a means to a more stable marriage, placed Beat women in an awkward position. Rebellion against sexual mores was not just deviant but culturally and socially subversive. Yet, this schizo-phrenic discourse held revelatory potential for Beat women. Although many postwar women explored sexuality, Beat women's iconoclasm revealed the constructed nature of gender that would become a mainstay of second-wave feminist critiques a decade later. By leaving their parents' homes to forge alternative partnerships outside the strictures of marriage, Beat women gained special insight into the workings of patriarchy. The novelty of Beat women's representation of orgasm is that it pushes bodily exploration in an attempt to discover a distinct femininity of experience while rejecting the "femininities" prescribed by a world of predominantly male experts.

The tension between feminine sexuality as an immanent body experi-ence and gender as a construct is important because it locates Beat women squarely within the early-postmodern register of this study. In her intro-duction to *The Irigaray Reader*, Margaret Whitford discusses the problem of the modern-postmodern split for feminists: "Feminist politics, up to now, appears to be grounded in a modernist category, 'woman,' with essentialist implications, while the possibility of founding a political programme on a postmodernist base is, to say the least, still a matter for debate" (12–13). For postmodernists, a return to the body is linked with an essentialism that has all the trappings of a modern grand narrative. Ironically, in an attempt to redefine the feminine on its own terms, feminism ended up installing an understanding of woman that was equally suspect. As Rita Felski notes in *Doing Time*, the attempt by second-wave feminists to "reclaim the femi-nine" was attacked by poststructuralism for its "blindness to material and cultural differences among women" (117). This blindness is precisely what led to the division between second- and third-wave feminists, as divergent race and class concerns in the 1970s led to a dismantling of the narrative category "woman" that became even more pronounced in the 1980s.

Unfortunately, postmodernism has not fared any better. For although postmodernism avoids the reductiveness of modernist essentialism, its denial of any type of normative criterion leaves it unable to galvanize political support. Postmodern feminism's insistence on "social construction" means that any conception of the female body, even ones that allot to it a privileged site for knowledge, is actually the result of cultural and political forces that exceed personal agency. Feminism is indeed in a difficult position. On the one hand, it needs essentialism in order for the term "feminism" to have any meaning at all. But on the other hand, once it starts to define what constitutes "womanhood," it risks creating a structure that is likewise exclusionary and normalizing.

The representation of female orgasmic experience is at the center of this debate. Freud believed that vaginal orgasm was the natural state for women and that a focus on the clitoris indicated a regressive sexuality. Reich, following Freud, focused on the vaginal orgasm as well, claiming that during intercourse, "the muscle contractions in the woman follow the same course as they follow in the man" (*Selected Writings* 33). As Juliet Mitchell explains in *Psychoanalysis and Feminism*, "Freud thought the later importance of the clitoris infinitely variable but that clitoridal sex alone indicated an arrestation of the development of femininity; to feminists it indicates an independence of men" (107). Bolstered by Masters and Johnson's 1966 study *Human Sexual Response*, which demonstrated both the dominance of the clitoridal orgasm in the majority of woman as well as women's ability to attain multiple orgasms, feminists rallied around the clitoridal orgasm as a distinctly feminine experience denied them by a male discourse that sought to tie sexual satisfaction with procreation. The celebration of the clitoris allowed women to claim a sexual independence from male models, a "third space" of desire to call their own. Gerhard relates, "This new view of the clitoris enabled feminists to reclaim the sexual ambiguity first introduced by Freud in the 1920s and later pathologized by Freudians in the thirties and forties. Feminists used the health of the clitoris, established in sexology, to breath new life into Freud's account of the instability of female heterosexuality" (104). Second-wave feminists reclaimed this space of "sexual ambiguity" that was so troubling to Freud and that had been corrupted by Freudian psychologists to appropriate female sexuality into accepted channels of marriage and procreation. The switch from the vaginal to the clitoridal, then, signals a rejection of phallic-centered constructions of the feminine by substituting a sexuality that was conceived of as both multiple and outside standard norms.

Of course, Beat women were not strictly second-wave feminists, and their writings reveal both a struggle with and an acceptance of the dominant codes prescribed them. Much has been made of the duplication of negative gender stereotypes within Beat culture itself. As Johnson and Grace comment, "they were or became cognizant of, on one hand, resisting and, on the other hand, participating in their own marginalization by forces of social construction in both Beat and establishment cultures" (*Girls Who Wore Black* 8). Many Beat women did ultimately succumb to the social insistence that they remain the silent, invisible objects of men's attention. But many Beat women questioned these stereotypes while being forced to live them. Looking back on this period in *Recollections of My Life as a Women*, di Prima adds "the imprisonment and death of Wilhelm Reich" to her list of "madnesses" during the late 1950s (203). Yet, di Prima's memoir is replete with references to Reich that cast doubt on his contributions. In another section, di Prima relates that she was less sexual than her lover Bonnie, oftentimes reaching the point of satiation early. Di Prima remarks, "Was it, I wondered, simply that I was not sexual enough? This was the big fear of women in my time, exacerbated by Wilhelm Reich, and I often stayed with the lovemaking past any point of interest, just to see if there was something I had missed" (195). Reich's insistence on orgasm as a means of attaining authenticity actually becomes a hindrance to sexual satisfaction. Feeding into 1950s' assumptions that expected women to be the guardians of domestic space and then chided them for being sexually complacent, Reich "exacerbates" the problem of women as responsible for sexual excitement. Such realizations of the constructed nature of sexuality places Beat women writers at the postmodern vanguard. Realizing that the sexual codes bequeathed them were not essential at all, they fought to at least become aware of the facades by which the dominant culture operated.

Many women Beat writers went a step further and fought against gender constructions. Questioning the assumptions that undergird sexual politics by demonstrating their reversibility, these writers performed a deconstruction of the prevailing sexual mores of the 1950s. Joyce Johnson's *Come and Join the Dance* is exemplary in this regard. Johnson's novel, published under the name Joyce Glassman, chronicles the growing disillusionment of a young college senior as her graduation approaches. Feeling as though life has not offered her enough experience, Susan searches for sexual fulfillment in Beat circles. Rather than becoming the passive object for masculine affection, however, Susan instead opts to seek out sexual experience herself. As Ronna C. Johnson argues, Susan is "rendered a Beat subject by her capacity for masculine privilege, the ultimate expression of this being her (re)positioning as the privileged consumer of sex" ("And Then She Went," 87). At the end of the novel, her lover Peter apologizes, "'I didn't even make you come.'" Susan responds, "'It was good anyway,' she said. But his face had gone blank and she knew he didn't believe her. 'It was what it meant,' she said. 'I knew what it *meant*'" (Glassman 175, italics in original). Rejecting the male Beat insistence on orgasm leaves Susan empowered—her main interest was in experience, not sexual satiation. Had Susan followed prescribed male Beat assumptions, she would have remained frustrated. Although both of Susan's lovers fail to bring her to orgasm, it is they who are disappointed by this lack, not Susan. Her decision to challenge sexual assumptions demonstrates that gender differences are supported not by a natural essentialism but by an interested construction that seeks to maintain the domination of one gender over another.

Beat women recognized the constructedness of gender that is the hallmark of postmodern feminism's critique of patriarchy. Yet, these writers did not eschew the notion of essentialism altogether. On the contrary, they ceaselessly explored sexual conceptions specific to femininity that empowered both their lives and their writings. In her *Reader*, Irigaray insists that for women, "it is important that we discover the singularity of our *jouissance*. Of course, it is possible for a woman to come [*jouir*] in accordance with the phallic model. . . . But if we are to discover our female identity . . . there is a relationship with *jouissance* other than that which functions in accordance with the phallic model" (45). For Irigaray, the female body has a "singularity" that must first be discovered if women are to recapture their "female identity." Males are all too happy to provide models for female pleasure, but these only entangle women in a dominant masculine network where women are unable to find their true selves. Di Prima configures this female knowledge as a reversal of the prevalent conceptions embedded in the phallocentric order. In *Recollections*, the inward thrust of the penis so celebrated by male Beats is replaced with the outward movement of the child: "Childbirth, of being opened *from the inside out*, I thought, was how you truly lost your virginity. Torn open so the world could come through. Come through you. Not that semipleasant invasion from a man, excursus from *the outside in*" (190). Through the act of childbirth, Di Prima comes to realize "what flesh really is. A woman's secret knowledge" (190). This secret knowledge that di Prima discovers through childbirth is an engagement with the strictly feminine body that critics like Irigaray invoke as a privileged site for feminism. Thus, in *An Ethics of Sexual Difference*, Irigaray likens the female body to a "place": "The maternal-feminine remains the *place separated from 'its' own place*, deprived of 'its' place. She is or ceaselessly becomes the place of the other who cannot separate himself from it" (10). Woman is a container—for man, for his children, and for his conceptions. For women to recapture themselves, they must first reinhabit their own bodies.

Female embodiment is essential in more ways than one. Not only does it provide a means for attaining an authenticity specific and necessary for Beat women striving to attain a sense of self in a male-dominated society but it is also a crucial component if the reciprocity Beat women demand is ever going to be reached. A coming together on equal terms will only occur if each partner has an appropriate relationship to his or her own private subjectivity. In *Tracking the Serpent*, Janine Pommy Vega describes her desire for a sexual liaison in just such terms: "I didn't need to be shorter or younger or less experienced than the man I picked, but I did need to need him. I needed to own up to my own need squarely, face to face. I needed to enjoy myself at play. I was not David's woman, or anyone else's—not even my own. My passion exceeded ownership" (66). The bid for equality here is obvious; Vega bridles at the concept of ownership. But what is more interesting is Vega's attitude toward herself. The sexual act requires that an openness exist in the interchange that is predicated on Vega's own need. Thus, she writes that the "play was in how it pertained to no one in particular, but where I felt a response, a stirring. To what my eyes, lips, breasts, and vagina wanted" (66). Vega's entire body becomes a dowser's wand, dipping toward desire and need. This intense engagement with the body, this movement inward, ultimately allows for a transcendence all the more revelatory for its immanence. In *Ethics*, Irigaray gives the reader a hint of what a sexual union based on equality might look like: "What would man and woman have in common? Both conception and perception. Both. And without any hierarchy between the two. . . . To receive the self and to envelope the self" (93). Irigaray will go on to label the third component created from such an interchange "God," but a notion of mutual becoming will likewise serve. The point is that both partners can transcend, instead of one simply utilizing the other. Only by journeying within the body first can a fruitful sexual union be consummated.

The female Beat desire to use an altered body to achieve sexual union culminates in the work of Lenore Kandel. While *The Love Book* (1966) was admittedly written later than most Beat works, it shares a Beat desire to craft a specifically feminized body that has the capacity for a higher level of lovemaking (see fig. 3.5). Kandel was no stranger to the constructed nature of gender—her work was seized as pornography in San Francisco as late as 1966, and one wonders if *The Love Book*'s highly sexual vocabulary and blasphemous style might have been overlooked had it been written by a man. But what is truly iconoclastic in Kandel's work is her depiction of female sexuality. As the cover illustrates, *The Love Book* is a celebration of heterosexual union. She writes,

> the barrier of noumenon-phenomenon
>   transcended
> the circle   momentarily complete
>   the balance of forces
>   perfect
> lying together, our bodies slipping into love
> that never have slipped out.
>
>   (5)

Here, transcendence is not figured as movement away from the body but rather as a balance of forces. Where male Beats want to flee the corporeal, Kandel uses it to attain the heightened state—it is this lying together that allows the dualities of gender to be (at least temporarily) succeeded by a union of opposites. What allows such a connection to occur is an emphasis on the sexuality not just of the genitals, but of the entire body. Just as Vega includes eyes, lips, and breasts in her depiction of sexuality, Kandel claims that "my whole body is turning into a cuntmouth / my toes my hands my belly my breasts my shoulders my eyes" (6). Male Beats have a tendency to focus on the phallus in their bid for the "apocalyptic orgasm." Kandel, however, provides a rhetoric of diffusion—the orgasm is not linked to a single ejaculatory instant but to a spreading of pleasure across the body. Kandel thus turns the sole site of feminine pleasure according to male experts, the "cuntmouth," into a polymorphous sexuality of the "whole body." Of course, Kandel is not alone in this regard. In the 1960s, radical psychoanalysts like

Herbert Marcuse and Norman Brown, along with third-force psychologists, likewise championed a full-body sexuality. But Kandel, along with other Beat women writers, placed such formulations into a poetic register, challenging male Beat representations of orgasm's phallic singularity and opening the door to a new version of the feminine both equal to and different from male sexuality.

Fig. 3.5. Cover art for Lenore Kandel's 1966 *The Love Book* presents a union of opposites. Photo courtesy of Harry Ransom Humanities Research Center, the University of Texas at Austin. Reproduced by permission of the Estate of Lenore Kandel.

4. Recording the Moment
The Role of the Photograph in Beat Representation

In *The Electric Kool-Aid Acid Test,* Tom Wolfe provides a description of Neal Cassady that epitomizes the Beat quest for the moment: "Cassady in his movie, called *Speed Limit,* he is both a head whose thing is speed, meaning amphetamines, and a unique being whose quest is Speed, faster, godamn it, spiraling, jerking, kicking, fibrillating tight up against the 1/30 of a second movie-screen barrier of our senses, trying to get into . . . *Now*" (131). Cassady's desire to go faster, to get into the now of experience, is what drew Jack Kerouac and Allen Ginsberg to his side. But while these latter two have myriad works to their credit, Cassady only produced a short novel and various letters. There are undoubtedly multiple reasons for the fact that Cassady exists mainly in the tributes of others, but one central consideration is the disjunction between experiencing and recording. A consummate participator, Cassady had literally less time to produce—actions spoke louder than words. Cassady is given the moniker "Speed Limit" because his one-thirtieth of a second comes closer to the real movie of life than anybody around him. But his attempt to move beyond the movie-screen barrier of the senses points to another limit, that of representation. Cassady apprehends experience at a mere one-thirtieth of a second behind time's flow, but Wolfe doesn't indicate whether he ever revisits these instants once they have passed. Kerouac and Ginsberg, on the other hand, have the difficult problem of not only living as fully in (and closely to) the fleeting present as Cassady does but of also recording and reflecting on their experiences.[1]

While Beat writing often presents itself as an authentic testimony to lived experience, the Beat relationship to photography provides a parallel site for exploring the role representation plays in "capturing" the events of the moment. Beat writing often directly imitates the "flow" of spontaneous experience, but in photography, freezing a moment of time into an image creates a series of gaps in temporal continuity. Photography lets the past become present again but with a difference. The photo is evidently not the event itself, and captions, commentary, and textual addition meant to bridge this distance only serve to highlight the gap between the primary moment and its subsequent representation. But Beat writers do not passively suffer such gaps; on the contrary, they theorize, inhabit, and produce them. Exploring this gap and its place in Beat thinking gives a better understanding of the Beat project of returning to the moment. This gap is not simply a lack but a space of fullness. Photography is well suited to such an inquiry. The photographic image's status as a representation calls into question the relationship between spontaneous life lived in the moment and mediations that seek to re-present the present as it fades away. As an index of the real that exists in two dimensions, as an arbitrary boundary marker among past-present-future and as a cultural emblem of ever-contested truth, the photograph is inextricably implicated in the question of the gap between living and recording.

Image, Caption, Gap

Upon first glance, however, it does seem as though the Beats often accept the photograph as a simple reproduction of the real. In his introduction to Robert Frank's *Americans*, Kerouac writes: "As American a picture—the faces don't editorialize or criticize or say anything but 'This is the way we are in real life,'" and then continues on to describe the photos as "the gray film that caught the actual pink juice of human kind" (6). For Kerouac, the picture corresponds directly with its subject matter, and thus the photo is capable of capturing the "actual pink juice" of the real world. William S. Burroughs, too, is not immune to such declarations. In his film script *The Last Words of Dutch Schultz*, Burroughs describes a street crap game and then advises in a parenthetical, "Actual street game must be photographed and recorded for this scene" (12). Later, when discussing a scene in Harlem, Burroughs again advises, "The following shots of Harlem in the 1930s can use any available documentary material of the period and place. This not only saves expensive reconstruction but gives the background shots more authenticity" (60). Although Burroughs is more concerned with how such seemingly "natural" images are used to manipulate viewers, the photograph occupies a privileged place in Burroughs's work as an index of "reality."

Ginsberg goes further still in this direction. In the commentary to his book *Photographs*, Ginsberg explains, "My motive for taking these snapshots was to make celestial snapshots in a sacred world, recording moments in eternity with a sense of sacramental presence" (1). Again, there is a faith that the photograph will retain the sacramental presence of actuality, that these fleeting moments can be recorded. The photograph is not just a simple representation but an actual trace. Thus, in a 1991 interview, Ginsberg claims that "in portraiture, you have the fleeting moment to capture the image as it passes and before it dissolves. And in a way, that's special for photography. It captures the shadow of a moment" (*Spontaneous Mind* 523–24). In other words, photography has a claim upon the real that sets it apart from other forms of mediation. Capturing the moment in meticulous detail, it provides a window on a past forever gone.

The Beats are certainly not alone in viewing the photograph as a privileged site for capturing the world as it unfolds; as Martin Jay explains in *Downcast Eyes*, "Without a doubt the commonplace view of photography ever since its inception during the heyday of the Realist reaction to Romanticism is that it records a moment of reality as it actually happened" (126). There is a verisimilitude to photography that sets it apart from other forms of representation. The photograph seems to "be" the subject in a manner that exceeds painting, sculpture, or drawing. In *On Photography*, Susan Sontag declares, "But a photograph is not only like its subject, a homage to the subject. It is part of, an extension of that subject" (155). The exterior physical world comes to reside within the confines of the photograph, and it is such a formulation that allows photographers like Henri Cartier-Bresson to speak of "trapping" items from the real world: "I prowled the streets all day, feeling very strung-up and ready to pounce, determined to 'trap' life—to preserve life in the act of living. Above all, I craved to seize, in the confines of a single photograph, the whole essence of some situation" (22).[2] One of photography's most famous commentators, Roland Barthes, writes,

> In the Photograph, the event is never transcended for the sake of something else. . . . It is the absolute Particular, the sovereign Contingency, matte and somehow stupid, the *This* (this photograph, and not Photography), in short, what Lacan calls the *Tuche*, the Occasion, the Encounter, the Real, in its indefatigable expression. (4)

In the realm of photography, as Barthes claims, "a pipe, here, is always and intractably a pipe" (5). At first glance, Kerouac and Ginsberg would appear to agree.

But despite rhetoric that equates the photographic image with veracity, a closer inspection reveals uneasiness with the photograph's ability to directly present reality. This is most clearly seen when the Beats attempt to supplement the image. Take, for example, Robert Frank's film *Pull My Daisy*. Long seen as an example of cinema verité, this movie nevertheless relies heavily on the audio soundtrack provided by Kerouac. Jack Sargeant remarks that with his narration, Kerouac "is not just recounting events and telling a story, but also observing and commenting on events transpiring within the film, and simultaneously speaking for all the protagonists" (22). *Pull My Daisy* is full of holes—the characters are silent, and the location is nondescript and undisclosed. Kerouac's commentary fills in these gaps, speaking where the film must remain mute.

This same sort of supplementary impulse is also at work in Ginsberg's photos. In both *Photographs* and *Snapshot Poetics*, which contain selected photos from throughout his career, Ginsberg provides each shot with a handwritten caption. In the event the reader is unable to read his handwriting or is unfamiliar with the people in the photos, Ginsberg reprints the text of these captions, along with biographies of his subjects, at the end of each work. A photo of Burroughs is thus captioned "William Burroughs on roof of apartment house Lower East Side Fall 1953 New York where I lived, we worked on editing his Yage Letters, and mss. of Queer, not published till 1985" (*Snapshot Poetics* 82). Ginsberg's captions explain what the photo often cannot—date, place, person, circumstance, and relevance. But like Kerouac's voice-over for *Pull My Daisy*, Ginsberg also indulges in improvisational flights of verbal fancy, as in the caption to a photograph of Burroughs and Kerouac engaged in a mock battle: "Bill and Jack in mortal combat with Moroccan dagger & broomstick club on the couch. 206 East 7th Street, Fall 1953" (see fig. 4.1). Ginsberg's captions reveal hesitancy about the photograph's ability to adequately capture a moment in time. If Ginsberg were truly "recording moments in eternity with a sense of sacramental presence" with his photos, there should be no compulsion to supplement each image with language. Like Kerouac's voiceover, Ginsberg's captions suggest that the photographic image is always falling short and must be added to if the viewer is to properly comprehend the recorded moment.

Historically, the practice of captioning photographs serves to curb a proliferation of meaning while guiding the imaginative use of the photograph. Ginsberg's captions often replicate this pattern; to appropriate Barthes's words, the text becomes a "parasite" on the image. Yet, Ginsberg also places text and image into a tension to produce affects that exceed the sum of their parts. Ginsberg's analysis of a dream he had of Joan Burroughs

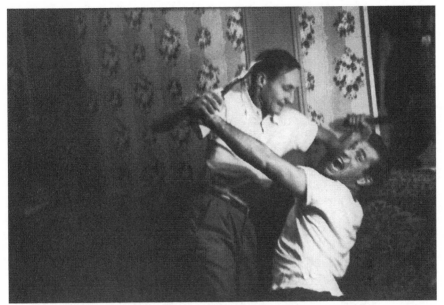

Fig. 4.1. Jack Kerouac and William S. Burroughs (with dagger in hand) are in mock battle; Ginsberg's handwritten caption tells what the photo cannot: "Bill and Jack in mortal combat with Moroccan dagger & broomstick club on the couch. 206 East 7th Street, Fall 1953." Photo courtesy of Allen Ginsberg Estate.

in 1955 offers a keen insight into the aesthetic potential of his method of juxtaposition. The deceased Joan appears to him in her former beauty, and as Ginsberg speaks to her, she fades into a tombstone. Ginsberg uses this contrast between these two images of Joan to fashion what might be called a theory of the gap: "What is needed in a poem is a structure (magical, miracles in the head) of clear rational actualities put next to one another to suggest (in the eclipse of Time between the images) Eternity. The 'intervals.' The *gap* of time. Joan's live body—Joan's tombstone" (*Journals Mid-Fifties* 138). For Ginsberg, the gap comes to stand not for lack but for fullness. The intervals create a magical feeling of the eclipse of Time, leaving the reader not with a simple understanding of time's passing or the nature of Joan's death but the physical sensation of time itself. I argue that from this perspective, the caption is not necessarily supplementary. Rather than control the photograph, the caption can work with the photo to create a useful gap. When that happens, what is privileged is not one moment over another but the movement from one moment to another that eclipses time itself. Rather than making one representation delimit another, at his best

Ginsberg opts for a practice that places representations in service of each other—only through working together can the juxtapositional interval between clear rational actualities be effected.

Ginsberg's insight into this interval's potential has many literary antecedents, and the influences he lists are unsurprising: John Keats, Hart Crane, Ezra Pound, and William Carlos Williams, among others. Also unsurprising is his recognition of the limits of their precedent:

> The Cantos are too literary and [much of] the experience is aesthetic experience of aesthetic experience. . . . Williams has refined the reproduction of images to a science—that is stripped bare for utility. We have not yet had a crystallization of real grief in a poem since imagism, or any gamut of human experiences. To say nothing of experiences of the superhuman. . . . Do away with symbols and present the facts of experience. (*Journals Mid-Fifties* 141–42)

Pound is overly concerned with an aesthetics that is distanced from the real world of experience. Williams, with his emphasis on the reproduction of images, comes closer to the sort of feeling that Ginsberg is attempting. But it appears that even Williams does not go far enough in capturing what Ginsberg calls "subjective emotion" (142). The interval is not merely technique but a means of arriving at an affect that exceeds literary experience. Ginsberg is searching for a method that will allow him to convey the emotional impact of an event to the reader, even into "experiences of the superhuman." Not content with formal invention or imagistic representation, he seeks a method that will convey the physical and mental import of a moment to the reader.

Ginsberg's quest to present subjective emotion and the facts of experience (which he theorizes in literary terms—though imagism plays a conspicuous role in his analysis) finds a parallel in the photographers of this period. One of the major figures in this turn towards interiority was Minor White. Through his periodical *Aperture*, White sought to push an aesthetic that favored the subjective over what had come to be known as the "documentary" photography of the 1930s and 1940s. Like the Beats, White was deeply influenced by Eastern mystical experience and sought to capture it in his work. As Jonathan Green and James Friedman observe, photographs for White were readable, which meant that "they had to push beyond the concerns of documentation, the pictorial, and the informational. The most fitting photograph for 'reading' was a visual *koan*" (73).

As with Ginsberg's juxtapositional method, the photograph as Zen koan serves to jolt the viewer out of commonplace experience. The photo sheds its indexical quality and comes to stand for another level of experience. Joel Eisinger explains, "White used Aperture as a forum in which to revive Alfred Stieglitz's idea of the equivalent, a photograph that is meant to subordinate or obscure its literal subject matter so as to work metaphorically" (146). Just as Joan's live body and Joan's tombstone are less important individually than they are as units of meaning that open up a gap, White's emphasis on inner truth instead of objective reality meant that the image itself was subordinated to the feeling it produced.

Ginsberg clearly believes in the power of the gap to reproduce subjective experience in the reader. But the question remains: what kind of interval is going to best produce the experience of subjectivity that the Beats are seeking? Ginsberg speaks of two or more "image points" and "clear rational actualities" that bound the given interval (*Journals Mid-Fifties* 138–39). In his primary example, Joan's live body and Joan's tombstone represent two such points; I'm arguing that at their best, his photographs and their captions succeed on exactly these terms, as "clear rational actualities put next to one another to suggest . . . Eternity." That said, Ginsberg's use of the caption often sets up a parasitic relationship between text and image that actually collapses the gap rather than expands it. Consider his *Indian Journals*, in which his captions convey factual details that only supplement the photographs. Thus, a picture of a Calcutta street is captioned, "A woman rolling spices into red spice on the sidewalk." This straightforward description draws attention to the center of the photograph, where a woman is hunched over the sidewalk. The end of his caption directs the reader to a page number, where the text itself yields merely another description: "a woman rolling spices into red paste on the sidewalk, the bare sidewalk itself her rolling board, grinding stone on stone in the red patch by the curb" (113). Text and caption are descriptive, seeking to relay a set of objective facts about the woman in order to guide interpretation. Ginsberg's reliance on a textual supplement to his photographs does not demonstrate the "jump or interval or ellipsis of consciousness" but rather reiterates the image that came before it in a slightly different register (*Journals Mid-Fifties* 139). Such a use of captions and text does not widen the gap but closes it.

More disruptive in *Indian Journals* are the images themselves, which articulate extremes of embodiment. Take, for example, the photograph of a disembodied foot (see fig. 4.2). According to the caption, the foot has been "severed from body along railroad tracks." Ginsberg's caption is redundant: it tells what is self-evident in the photograph and fails to create an interval. But what is interesting here is the excessiveness of the image. *Indian Journals* contains other such images, including a photograph of a severed arm. Ginsberg is attempting to represent death with these photographs. Barrett Watten views *Indian Journals* as an exploration into the limits of representation as a whole: "Beginning with the limit case of language as unable to represent consciousness, both of visionary experience and death,

Fig. 4.2. Ginsberg's photograph of a severed limb from his work *Indian Journals* demonstrates the limits of representation.
Photo courtesy of Allen Ginsberg Estate.

Ginsberg realizes an arbitrariness of representation that returns writing to an embodied state after experiencing the nonexistence of the other" (165). The moment of death as the state of pure otherness is impossible to represent in a subjective register. The best Ginsberg can hope for here is to write as closely as possible to the experience of death. Watten believes that Ginsberg's photographs are "fascinating precisely in the gap in comprehension they provoke" (164). But in this case, the gap in comprehension is more of a lack than a productive interval. Existing solely within the frame of the picture itself, Ginsberg's ghastly photographic depictions work more as a Benjaminian "shock" than an interval that promotes a jump in consciousness. Ginsberg himself seems aware of this, complaining earlier in *Indian Journals* that he is "hanging on to habitual humanistic series of autobiographical photographs," unable to move beyond "a few cool imagistic photo descriptions" (39). Although he reveres the photograph, Ginsberg fears that his writing is incapable of moving beyond what he imagines is its flatly objective technique of pure visual description.

A more successful combination of photographs and text can be found in *Bixby Canyon Ocean Path Word Breeze*. Collaborating with photographer William Webb, Ginsberg is able to create a richer nexus of writing and image that produces the sort of interval that he failed to achieve in *Indian Journals*. Quotes from Kerouac's novel *Big Sur* form epigraphs and postscripts that bookend the work, creating *Bixby Canyon*'s first set of gaps that Ginsberg will use. Ginsberg goes on to describe the intimidating automobile bridge that spans the canyon and will come to drive the central image of the poem:

> Brooktrickle deep
>   below Airplane
>   Bridge
>   Concrete
> arches balconey'd
> Pendant over
> Oceancrash
>   waves

(6)

On the next page is a photograph of the bridge set against the sky. Unlike his captions to most of his own photographs, Ginsberg's text comments on Webb's photograph only obliquely. Rather than attempting to control the meaning of the photo, it provides another vantage point from which to view it.

Later in the poem, Ginsberg describes a

> Car's rusty
>   under carriage
>   kelp pipes
>   & brown chassis,
>   one rubber wheel
>   black poked from
>   Sand mattresses
>   rock wash

(12)

Two pages later is a photograph of an engine block sitting in water beside an assortment of kelp and organic debris (see fig. 4.3). The text supplements

Fig. 4.3. Ginsberg creates a more successful gap in his poem "Bixby Canyon Ocean Path Word Breeze" by incorporating photographs of Big Sur by William Webb, such as this image of an engine block. Photo courtesy of Harry Ransom Humanities Research Center, The University of Texas at Austin.

the image but comments on it from an entirely different register. Gaps begin to emerge. There is a movement here that is undeniable, if invisible: at some point in the past, a car fell off the bridge and landed in the water. The intervals of time continue to proliferate, from shiny to rusty under carriage, from full car to a simple chassis, and from a clean crash site to one encumbered by kelp pipes and sand mattresses. Ginsberg then ends with a quotation from Kerouac: "Underneath the bridge, in the sand right beside the sea cliff, hump, your heart sinks to see it: the automobile that crashed through the bridge rail a decade ago and fell 1000 feet straight down" (15). Kerouac attributes the sadness he feels at the sight of the car to the fact that there are "no more people," a statement doubly significant when one considers that *Big Sur* is a novel of alcoholic disintegration and breakdown. There is death here, but Ginsberg also makes Bixby Canyon a site of rejuvenation—grasses and flowers grow, spiders and ants crawl, the sea absorbs.

In contrast to the photographs and captions in *Indian Journals*, the photograph of a rusted engine block is surprisingly efficacious, setting in motion a series of intervals that binds it with the bridge above it and the ocean across from it and simultaneously looking back to Kerouac's novel and forward to the moment when the sea will ultimately dissolve the engine's metal. Unlike the abrupt shock of a severed hand, Ginsberg's image of a rusted engine block creates intervals that the reader can actually inhabit productively.

Severed hands, smashed automobiles, Joan's tombstone—all of these examples are traumatic. How does one create an appropriate ellipsis of consciousness? According to Ginsberg, a key component is trauma. In his *Journals Mid-Fifties*, Ginsberg explains that he is looking for a technique that will reproduce the "awe & terror & knowledge" of his Joan dream (137). It is not unimportant that Ginsberg is searching for an "Aesthetic experience of the sublime," since it is precisely appeals to this philosophical concept that best elucidates his method (137). This mixture of awe and terror is inextricably bound to notions of the sublime as they appear in the works of Edmund Burke and Immanuel Kant. In his *Philosophical Inquiry*, Burke explains, "The passions which belong to self-preservation, turn on pain and danger; they are simply painful when their causes immediately affect us; they are delightful when we have an idea of pain and danger, without being actually in such circumstances" (51). For Burke, whatever creates this "delight" is termed the sublime. Fear of death is an integral part of Burke's project. It is only distance, the physical gap between what induces this terror and our bodily condition of safety, that turns the potentially traumatic into a source for sublimity. Kant's sublime occurs on the mental level but is likewise implicated in a mixture of pain and pleasure that characterizes Burke's thinking. According to Jean-François Lyotard in *The Inhuman*, when confronting something beyond our capacity to represent, "This failure of expression gives rise to a pain, a kind of cleavage within the subject between what can be conceived and what can be imagined or presented" (98). Yet, for Kant, this pain induced by the inability to imagine or present actually creates a two-fold pleasure, as Lyotard explains: "The impotence of the imagination attests *a contrario* to an imagination striving to figure even that which cannot be figured" and that the "inadequacy of the images is a negative sign of the immense power of ideas" (*Inhuman* 98). A gap is produced between an "impotence of the imagination" and the joy in discovering that this imagination is capable of striving—awe and terror work hand-in-hand to produce a gap where the sublime can do its work.

Lyotard draws on these theories of the sublime to make a distinction between the modern and postmodern that places Ginsberg's theory into an early-postmodern register. According to Lyotard in *The Postmodern Condition*, the modern is characterized by a desire to "present the fact that the unpresentable exists" (78). In *The Inhuman*, Lyotard expands on his definition: "the unpresentable is what is the object of an Idea, and for which one cannot show (present) an example, a case, even a symbol. The universe is unpresentable, so is humanity, the end of history, the instant, space, the good" (126). Modernism works, then, by demonstrating the unpresentable as pure absence. This technique follows the logic of the sublime—there is a pain at the inability to present but likewise a pleasure in the attempt. Thus, Lyotard concludes that modernism focuses on forms and techniques that provide a means of comprehending (or attempting to) that which is ungraspable. Postmodernism, on the other hand, attempts to do the opposite. In *The Postmodern Condition*, Lyotard writes:

> The postmodern would be that which, in the modern, puts forward the unpresentable in presentation itself; that which denies itself the solace of good forms, the consensus of a taste which would make it possible to share collectively the nostalgia for the unattainable; that which searches for new presentations, not in order to enjoy them but in order to impart a stronger sense of the unpresentable. (81)

Rather than demonstrating the unpresentable through negativity, post-modernism opts instead for a direct presentation of the ineffable itself. For Lyotard, the consequences of this shift are that postmodern practice jettisons modernism's reliance on the solace of good forms and a nostalgia based on a consensus of taste. In its place, postmodernism installs a regime in which the unpresentable is continually reiterated as affect. The idea is not to contain or enjoy but to perform.

Ginsberg's theory of the gap marks a turning away from much of modernism's desire for wholeness and totality in order to free up possibilities for subjectivity. In *Journals Mid-Fifties*, Ginsberg, after discussing his Joan dream, immediately follows with a telling addition to Williams's poem "The Red Wheelbarrow":

> So much depends
> Upon
>
>   Gap
>
> A red wheelbarrow.
>
>   (140)

What Ginsberg is interested in here is the gap that occurs between Williams's images. The images themselves are there merely to facilitate the jump in consciousness that Ginsberg is striving to achieve. The unpresentable is not contained in order to provide solace or nostalgia but to create an affect in the reader that can transport him or her into another realm of feeling. Again, this feeling is not meant to be enjoyed as a recuperation of an absence into new forms but to be experienced as "the grief-realization of time, or the cold shiver of eternity" (142). Contrast this to Williams. In Ginsberg's journals, he added parts of Williams's *Selected Essays*, including the "Prologue to Kora in Hell": "The true value is that particularity which gives an object a character by itself. The associational or sentimental value is the false. . . . Much more keen is that power which discovers in things those inimitable particles of dissimilarity" (*Journals Mid-Fifties* 131). Here is Williams's "Objectivism," where the poem becomes a material object, presented for its own sake rather than as an "equivalent" of something else. A red wheelbarrow, white chickens, and rainwater are, in a sense, unpresentable in their unique objectness. Yet, Williams's poem organizes them into a coherent whole. Williams is less interested in the gap between them as he is in using each of their dissimilarities to bring out each item's own particularity. He focuses on the plenitude of the objects themselves and not on their lack. This reliance on the concrete thingness of the objects and the formal arrangement within the poem ("so much depends") provides a modernist totality. Thus, while Ginsberg draws on Williams for inspiration, he shifts focus towards the gap itself. As Michael Schumacher claims in *Dharma Lion*, Ginsberg "worked with what he considered to be the best aspect of existing forms" (139). Ginsberg adapted "no ideas but in things" as a means to bound an interval with concrete images that would nevertheless yield the ineffable sentiment *between*.

If the gap has a content, then, it is one of movement and action. Throughout *The Inhuman*, Lyotard is obsessed with the simple question, "Is it happening?" (99). For Lyotard, this query is at the heart of the postmodern sublime. Following Burke, Lyotard explains, "What is terrifying is that the *It happens that* does not happen, that it stops happening" (99). Burke's sublime is based on a fear of privation, with the ultimate fear being that soul and body will cease altogether. Thus, Lyotard explains that "thanks to art, the soul is returned to the agitated zone between life and death, and this agitation is its health and its life" (100). Such agitation is clearly a goal of Ginsberg's aesthetic of the gap. While the modern renders experience safe through its recourse to forms, the postmodern seeks to jar the reader into an encounter with the unrepresentable. Ginsberg, too, is concerned that "it happens." If it does not happen, then the interval collapses into two simple imagistic points. The gap is not a representation but an event.

William V. Spanos conceives of the early postmodern in much the same manner. Describing the contemporary writer's task in "The Detective and the Boundary," Spanos speaks of "undermining the detective-like expectations of the positivistic mind, of unhoming Western man, by evoking rather than purging pity and terror—anxiety" (39). Movement, flux, and happening—only through a constantly reiterated challenge to fixed expectations can the subject change instantiated notions of self. Yet, what is one to make of the fact that Lyotard labels this project "postmodern" when it sounds very much like the early postmodernism that Spanos champions? The answer lies in Lyotard's own definition of the term in *The Inhuman*: "What I've here called rewriting clearly has nothing to do with what is called postmodernity or postmodernism on the market of contemporary ideologies. . . . Postmodernity is not a new age, but the rewriting of some of the features claimed by modernity" (34). For Lyotard, the postmodern is a constantly nascent form of modernism, one that predates historical location and is subject to emerge at any future time. It is this belief that allows

Fredric Jameson, in his foreword to *The Postmodern Condition*, to claim that "although he has polemically endorsed the slogan of a 'postmodernism' and has been involved in the defense of some of its more controversial productions, Lyotard is in reality quite unwilling to posit a postmodernist stage radically different from the period of high modernism" (xvi). Lyotard's postmodernism actually resembles the Beats' early-postmodern position. Opening up representation into the realm of the dislocating event, both utilize the sublime sentiment in service of a poetics that seeks to present the unpresentable to the reader.

Although Ginsberg's aesthetic practice sought to distance itself from modernism, he was nevertheless unwilling to venture into the realm of the postmodern, where subjectivity is lost and indeterminacy reigns. His desire to retain some center can clearly be seen in the ways in which he constructs the gap. The last picture in *Photographs* depicts a triple image of Ginsberg that leaves the viewer wondering which Ginsberg is actually taking the picture (see fig. 4.4). Upon closer inspection, however, it becomes clear that the hand and head on the left side of the frame is the "true" Ginsberg, while the other two are reflections. Ginsberg opens up a multiplicity of selves in this photograph, yet the stable center of photographer is still discernable. In *Snapshot Poetics*, he includes two similar photos. In the first, a seated Ginsberg appears naked holding a camera, while a double image appears to his right. The "real" Ginsberg is on the left again, but just in case there is any doubt, the caption relates "mirrored bathroom wall on my right meeting mirror in front of me" (11). The doubling that occurs here does not open out into indeterminacy. There may be two images of Ginsberg, but the photo and caption reveal which one is "true." The picture represents the possibility of imagining multiple selves while still retaining a central self that creates the reproduction. Another example occurs using a mirror in a sushi bar restroom, where Ginsberg sees himself "several dozen times multiplied" (15). These photos all create a gap between the mirrored image of the photographer and the multiple representations created from that mirror image. Of course, no image is "truer" than another within the frame; they are all reproductions of the actual Ginsberg, who stands outside taking the picture. Yet, the photograph is not simply a dispersion of Ginsberg images, but a field that can be organized through appeals to the reality outside it (where is Ginsberg standing, which mirrors face which doors, and so forth). These images are a perfect example of Ginsberg's mantra "Notice what you notice." Ginsberg undoubtedly noticed the play of

Fig. 4.4. Triple image of Ginsberg from *Photographs*. Although Ginsberg multiplies subjectivity, the origin of the image is still discernable. Courtesy of Allen Ginsberg Estate.

images that mirror and lens can create, but at the same time it is important to remember that it was Ginsberg who "noticed."[3] Subjectivity remains to guide images that would otherwise move towards the indeterminate.

The perfect counterpart to Ginsberg's reflexive photographs is the work of postmodernist Andy Warhol. Consider, for example, Warhol's "Double Elvis," composed in 1964 (see fig. 4.5). As with many of his works, Warhol drew on photographs (both taken, found, and stolen) as the basis for creation in other media. "Double Elvis" is a silkscreen taken from a movie still of Elvis in *Flaming Star*. The two Elvises, while not exactly alike, are close enough allied to confound any notion of originality. The original photograph is actually absent here, tucked away in some Warhol archive. Multiple Ginsbergs, by contrast, provide a sense of center. There is a Ginsberg in the photo that is responsible for the image, even if the photograph overall is still a reproduction. Ginsberg speaks to this difference directly in a tribute to Warhol published in 1989. Although Ginsberg praises Warhol for his "almost Zen-like nonattachment," he continues on to discuss the major break between the two: "In the long run, effort to evade egocentric subjectivity by making cool anonymous art is unnecessary. Friendly relationship to a tamed transparent ego encourages more passionate intensity without disillusioning backfires" (*Deliberate Prose* 457). Warhol's problem, according to Ginsberg, is that he is unwilling to enter subjectivity into his art. Creating art through "cool anonymity" rather than "passionate intensity" keeps Warhol from the emotional affect that the Beats are so clearly seeking. This difference is likewise seen in Warhol's 1962 work "Baseball," in which an idiosyncratic moment of a batter swinging at a pitch is reproduced

Fig. 4.5. A reproduction of a reproduction. Andy Warhol's "Double Elvis," a silkscreen produced from a movie still, challenges the viewer to name which Elvis is the original.
© Andy Warhol Foundation/CORBIS.

over and over. Where writers like Williams and Kerouac celebrate baseball for its temporal specificity and Americaness, Warhol is more interested in the image as image and the results of multiplication. The difference here is between an instant of time as "sacramental reality" and representation as infinitely repeatable. Thus, Ginsberg's "Notice what you notice" can be contrasted to Warhol's quip "I don't know where the artificial stops and reality begins" (*Photography* 9). Ginsberg's mantra is firmly grounded in subjectivity; the "you" speaks to an actual person capable of discernment and action. Warhol's statement, by contrast, demonstrates confusion. There is no possibility for discernment since the "artificial" bleeds into "reality," leaving any notion of a subject in doubt as to what constitutes fiction and what constitutes fact.

Of course, for many postmodernists the distinction between "fiction" and "fact" is spurious. They are not absolutes at all but positions that define each other by contrast. For Jacques Derrida, it is the movement between such poles that constitutes the focus of his theory of difference. In his *Of Grammatology*, Derrida writes about the flaw of Rousseau's critique of representation:

> It supposes at once that representation follows a first presence and restores a final presence. One does not ask how much of presence and how much of representation are found within presence. In criticizing representation as the loss of presence, in expecting a reappropriation of presence from it, in making it an accident or a means, one situates oneself within the self-evidence of the distinction between presentation and representation, within the *effect* of this fission. (296)

Warhol does recognize that representation is already within presence. This is precisely why he focuses on celebrities—while they are indeed actual people, we think them through representation. An encounter with the presence of the silver screen or a Hollywood tabloid is already mediated by a vast system of image that we cannot escape. The indeterminacy of Warhol, the constant slippage between the "fact" and the "fiction," makes his program of Pop Art align with Derrida's insistence on movement. Ultimately, Derrida is interested not in the "effect of this fission" but instead on "the productive movement of the effect of difference: the strange graphic of difference" (296). The Beats also seek the sort of movement that Derrida champions. Yet, their difference lies in teleology.[4] For Ginsberg, the goal is to attain the sublime sentiment, not to merely slide between positions endlessly. Representation does "restore a final presence," even if that final presence might be ineffable, difficult to attain, and in the end, fleeting.

Even amidst tenuous uncertainties, the Beats are repeatedly called back to a subjectivity that grounds them in the world. In "Howl," Ginsberg comments explicitly on the technique used in his poem: "Who dreamt and made incarnate gaps in Time & Space through images juxtaposed" (*Collected Poems* 130). Representation is not simply an abstraction that functions like a "dream" but a concrete process that can have a profound impact on individual consciousness. Figurative gaps can literally be made incarnate, actualizing and embodying a new order of "Time & Space." In a note to this line (in Barry Miles's facsimile edition), Ginsberg points to the phrase "hydrogen jukebox" that occurs earlier in his poem as emblematic of the "flash of recognition" that he is seeking in his work (130). "Hydrogen jukebox" is a heavily-laden juxtaposition. "Hydrogen" suggests the atomic bomb, a weapon capable of annihilating vast territories in an apocalyptic instant. And "jukebox" speaks to temporality in an entirely different register, where the moment relates to the exuberance of music, to the beat of time filtered through trumpet valves and across guitar strings. This phrase is likewise embroiled in a social field that Ginsberg was at the forefront of critiquing. "Howl" was written against the backdrop of the cold war, a mere eleven years after the bombing of Hiroshima and Nagasaki. Like Kaufman's parking meter, the word "jukebox" implicates the consumerism of American culture, implying a *metered* encounter with music in a public space. The collision of these disparate connotations creates the realization that Ginsberg is striving to achieve—an understanding of time, unalloyed and pure. Not every juxtaposition is successful, and Ginsberg's method relies on the assumption that language has the ability to radically alter subjectivity. At its best, however, Ginsberg's method has the ability to open up a space that allows for a fundamental alteration of existence. The photograph may not record reality directly, but when the contents of the frame are juxtaposed with caption, text, and referent, the result is a gap not in the service of a representation but rather an event in its own right.

The gaps created by the photographic image are essential to understanding Beat poetic practice. How does one actually "capture" the moment? Representation does not provide a nostalgic solace for a lost moment by creating a new object meant to replace the immediacy of the past event. Nor does it level invidious distinctions between the original moment and the flatness of subsequent representations that erases this question altogether.

It is not the moment itself that is "caught" in Beat representation but the quality of affect inherent in any experience. Rather than attempting to hold the past steady, the Beats instead opt to record the intensity of the event that transcends its specific temporal bounds. As Ginsberg's best work with photography reveals, the Beats use the space between to effect a subjective experience in the viewer (who is also a reader) in order to represent not the content of an event but rather a feeling of the movement of time itself.

Memorializing Childhood

The photograph can serve a myriad of purposes—artistic object, evidential record, commemorative decoration. But it finds its true calling, especially in the hands of an amateur, as a mnemonic device. But what type of remembering does the photograph make possible? The memories that it evokes differ radically from the reminiscences that occur spontaneously to the mind. Although the photograph certainly offers a type of proof of an event's occurrence, the memories that it prompts are subject to the flat, two-dimensional surface that provoked them. Are recorded memories doomed to suffer a sort of reduction in intensity, or is there a better means to capture the import of an experience? This is precisely the question that Jack Kerouac asks throughout his corpus. Focusing on Kerouac's works that attempt to re-present his childhood experiences to the reader, this section sets out to explore the terrain among memory, the photograph, and the use of writing to capture the fullness of events that are continually slipping farther and farther into the past.

Kerouac is obsessed with recalling the past events of his life, crafting them into his "Duluoz legend," as he calls it, in an attempt to protect his memories from the ravages of time. But if capturing the kernel of the present is a tricky affair, then relating past events takes on added difficulties posed by the intervention of temporal distance. It is not enough for Kerouac simply to save his memories; he wants them to retain a force and intensity that makes them *useful* in the present. Here we see Kerouac's writerly disdain for the photograph. As a static representation of the past event, the photo fails to capture the import of experience that Kerouac is desperately seeking in the recollection of memory. The photograph defines Kerouac's project by contrast, highlighting the shortcomings of the filmic image when compared to the depth and range of his prose method of recording. Ginsberg uses the photograph to create a gap that produces an affect in the reader. It is not the photo itself that generates a sensation of time but the interval between the photo and a caption, text, or referent. Kerouac's work evidences the same tendency. The photo is too "rigid" to produce the affect he is seeking. But where Ginsberg employs the gap to jolt the reader into sublimity, Kerouac takes the opposite tack—using the photograph as a starting point, he attempts to write the gap between the present and the past.

Kerouac prided himself on his memory. According to Ann Charters's biography, Kerouac's childhood friends called him "Memory Babe" in tribute to his "possession of a very accurate, very detailed memory" (*Kerouac* 63). Despite Kerouac's ability to recall the past, his memory is still subject to the ravages of time. Thus, in his novel *Dr. Sax*, Kerouac muses on the stability of representation. Kerouac relates an incident involving two of his boyhood friends, then comments,

> That gray's forgotten too, as I say Cy and Bert were dreadfully young in a long-ago of moving Time that is so remote it for the first time assumes that rigid post or posture death-like denoting the cessation of its operation in my memory and therefore the world's—a time about to become extinct—except that it can never be, because it happened, it—. (75)

Kerouac's dilemma is to reconcile personal memory with a representative form that will allow it to exist beyond himself. If memory's cessation means the end of the event, then once Kerouac becomes extinct, the memory will be lost forever. Kerouac wants to see the event as ultimately "unerasable" (75), but it is clear from his hesitant prose that positing some extratemporal zone where an event of the past is necessarily collected simply because it happened is an uneasy solution at best. For memory to remain it needs a vessel, a form that can carry it through time with as much richness and depth as possible.

An easy question emerges—why not a photograph? The function of a photo has long been seen as a means to capture the passing of an event in minute detail so that it can live on beyond its allotted position in time. Kerouac references photographs throughout his work, but his rejection of their efficacy as a mnemonic device is telling. For Kerouac, scenes from his memory are always "unphotographable." This adjective appears throughout *Dr. Sax*, Kerouac's novel of the loss of boyhood innocence: "It is Sunday afternoon in Lowell, absolutely unphotographable it is that I am sitting in my room in good Sunday clothes just home from a drive to Nashua" (101).

Later, Kerouac will deploy this term again to describe a memory of "when I was a little kid of five on Hildreth I used to make the Great Bird pursue the Little Man . . . my eyes rounden in the silence of this old thought—unphotographable moment" (102). Why does Kerouac deem these moments unphotographable? As memories, they are already past and thus cannot be recalled through the camera's lens. Yet, this is not Kerouac's point—after all, someone could have conceivably taken a snapshot of Kerouac in his Sunday clothes or while playing his bird-and-man game. The scenes themselves are photographable, but their affect is not. Even if the shutter had closed on Kerouac's memories, the resulting picture would still not contain the event. "Sunday afternoon" is inseparable from a host of sensations, feelings, and perceptions that the memory creates but would not be captured by a photograph of Kerouac sitting on his bed in his Sunday best. The term "unphotographable" thus points to a litany of responses that such memories evoke and that the camera is helpless to capture.

Kerouac's antiphotographic bent places him in a French tradition of photographic skepticism that dates back to Charles Baudelaire and Marcel Proust and culminates in the work of the philosopher Henri Bergson.[5] In *Downcast Eyes*, Jay describes how Baudelaire was mainly concerned with photography's "artistic pretensions" and its "incursions into the realm of 'the intangible and the imaginary'" (138). But for Proust and Bergson, more troubling was the photograph's corruption of memory. In *Remembrance of Things Past*, Proust attacks the filmic image: "What we call reality is a certain relationship between these sensations and the memories which surround us at the same time (a relationship that is destroyed by a bare cinematographic presentation, which gets further away from the truth the more closely it claims to adhere to it)" (2:1008). For Proust, the photographic image is ironically too precise. Its mimetic efficacy destroys the delicate interplay between sensation and memory that creates reality itself. As with Kerouac, the photograph is incapable of capturing the multitude of nuances that lend memory power and force in the mind.

Bergson views the photograph as yet another attempt to delimit a temporality that is in perpetual flux. In *The Creative Mind*, Bergson discusses the use of film to break up duration into equal and successive increments: "Succession thus understood, therefore, adds nothing; on the contrary, it takes something away. . . . In short, time thus considered is no more than a space in idea where one imagines to be set out in line all past, present, and future events" (18). The photographic image removes movement and duration, making temporality appear to be nothing more than a succession of dislocated instants. Bergson thus concludes that it is "not the 'states,' simple snapshots we have taken once again along the course of change, that are real; on the contrary, it is flux, the continuity of transition, it is change itself that is real" (16). The continuity of transition reaches back into the past and forward into the future—for Bergson, memory is contemporaneous with the present. The spatialization of time that the photograph enacts makes it feel as though the past is distant and unattainable. For all of these writers, the photograph serves as an artificial and undesirable limit. By presenting a reality enclosed strictly within its frame, the photograph keeps its viewer from feeling the widest possible range of experience.

How exactly does Kerouac write himself into this gap between memory and the present? The type of quality that Kerouac seeks in his relation of memory is best explained through Gilles Deleuze and Felix Guattari's concept of "hecceity" in A Thousand Plateaus: "Climate, wind, season, hour are not of another nature than the things, animals, or people that populate them, sleep and awaken within them. This should be read without a pause: the animal-stalks-at-five-o'clock" (263). Here the animal is inseparable from the external qualities that effect it. Conditions like five-o'clock and the stalking of prey are not simply factors that the animal confronts but are instead enfolded into the organism in such a way that a new manner of existing, a new being, is created in the process. As Deleuze explains in The Fold, "However abruptly I may flog my dog who eats his meal, the animal will have experienced the minute perceptions of my stealthy arrival on tiptoes, my hostile odor, and my lifting of the rod that subtend the conversion of pleasure into pain" (87). The event that turns pleasure into pain is not a discrete moment. Rather, it reflects an entire assemblage of affects, from a stealthy arrival to the physical sensation that will accompany the application of the lash. Affect is not punctual but depends on a series of infinitesimal perceptions that cross the barrier between internal subject and outside world.[6]

Deleuze and Guattari's conception of hecceity helps to elucidate the shortcomings that Kerouac experiences with regard to photographic representation. If the affect of the lash on the dog's body is composed of a series of perceptions that form a hecceity of the type "dog-being-whipped-by-man," then a static photograph of such an event can never fully capture the import of the experience. Movement is inextricably linked to affect. Flux creates a constant push and pull, bringing elements together and driving them apart. Movement is necessarily denied the photograph, leaving the viewer with a chance arrangement caught at an indiscriminate point in time. A photograph of a dog being lashed or an animal stalking would necessary highlight only one small temporal fraction of an otherwise continuous event. Cinema is privileged for Deleuze because it has the capacity to offer a sampling of fluid movement. Photography, however, must remain static, and thus movement and affect remain beyond the threshold of perception. The frozen frame might offer a visual representation of a dog-lash hecceity, but from this one is unable to derive affect. One may insinuate and argue by visual analogy, but a perception of the interaction that movement through time makes possible necessarily resides elsewhere.

Neal Cassady, the real-life inspiration for many of Kerouac's works, voices the same concern when discussing the function of memory. In *Visions of Cody*, Kerouac includes a tape-recorded session of his late-night, marijuana-fueled discussions with Cassady. In these dialogues, Cassady explains the danger of "skeletonization" when attempting to convey a past event to a present audience:

> And so you say it three or four times, so pretty soon, especially if it's a thought, not a happening, but a thought, so if you have to go through a thought again and again pretty soon it becomes an abstraction of the thought and you still follow the form and structure of it but you just say "Well this happened and that happened," and it becomes just a dry, drab nothing, see? It's not like it was at first. (215–16)

Cassady's fear is that emotional spontaneity achieved in the present becomes lost as a tale receives a "skeletal" undergirding. The "form and structure" that become erected to support the memory bear much resemblance to the photograph's reliance on a frozen depiction of temporality that forces the viewer always to consider the caught moment within the parameters that the picture constructs. The event happens "at first," and then subsequent returns to that past are forced to proceed along demarcated lines. Cassady's solution is to simply remain in the present, to "complete whatever thought comes, see, instead of making myself hurry back" (145). Yet, Kerouac, as a writer, is in a more tenuous position. He needs to record events, but in order to do so, he must first find a form that will allow his memory to be re-presented with as much spontaneous force as possible.

Taking his cue from Cassady, Kerouac's solution to the problem of adequately representing memory is to focus on the act of remembering as it occurs in the present. Thus, in his manifesto "Essentials of Spontaneous Prose," Kerouac admonishes, "Begin not from preconceived idea of what to say about image but from jewel center of interest in subject of image at *moment* of writing, and write outwards swimming in sea of language to peripheral release and exhaustion" (*Good Blonde* 70). As its title suggests, Kerouac's poetic theory stresses the spontaneous nature of composition. Rather than building a skeletal structure around a preconceived idea of what to say, the writer is advised to focus on the moment of writing instead. What becomes essential is not how to recapture a moment fading into the past but instead how that past moment is impinging on present-tense consciousness. The intersection of memory and perception of that memory is the starting point for a writing that will then carry itself outwards towards the release and exhaustion that marks the memory's effective limit. Memory is not rendered static as in the case of the photograph but set in motion in order to recover the import of a remembered experience as it plays itself out in the present context.

This dichotomy between fixed photographic representation and the continual flux of Kerouac's spontaneous prose is nicely demonstrated in a memorable scene from *Visions of Cody*. In the section entitled "Joan Rawshanks in the Fog," Kerouac provides a description of a film crew taping a movie in San Francisco's Russian Hill district. Although the scene revolves around what Kerouac terms "the actual moment, the central kill, the riddled middle idea, the thing, the Take, the actual juice suction of the camera catching a vastly planned action," Kerouac spends numerous pages describing the scene around "the Take" (281). The moment of the camera's click becomes almost anticlimactic, a mere excuse for hundreds of people to mill about a house in San Francisco. This section of Kerouac's novel highlights the difference between the hecceity of an entire street (night, fog, people, lights, and the like) and the delimiting nature of the moment of the camera's shutter. Ultimately, Kerouac is more concerned with what happens around the cameras and between the takes. Recording everything from the movement of the crowd to the director's "red lollipop" (282), Kerouac draws attention to the fact that a moment caught on film is but a small fraction of the event in which it occurs.

Spontaneous prose replaces the fixed with the mobile and stasis with flux. Although Kerouac admonishes to stay in the present when writing memory, the present itself never stays the same. Thus, Kerouac's writing must always move with the present in order to truly register the impact of a memory, scene, or occurrence. As he proclaims in "Essentials," "Time being of the essence in the purity of speech, sketching language is undisturbed flow from the mind of personal secret idea-words, *blowing* (as per jazz musician) on subject of image" (*Good Blonde* 69). To "blow" is to continually move, catching the essence of the performance as it unfolds in time. Kerouac is not immune to the effects of photographs, but by themselves, they remain insufficient to enact the sort of affects that Kerouac desires. Thus, in all his descriptions of photos, he makes them *happen*. Take, for instance, a memory of looking at a friend's baseball cards in his 1953 novel of high school love, *Maggie Cassady*:

> He took me to his house and showed me his scrapbook full of pasted pictures of baseball stars of 1920's and 1930's with incredibly old stars whose bones are long interred in crumbling files in the archives of red sun sinking in the Ninth Inning with Nobody On. . . . Lost forever the still figure in right center with a tanned taut expression on solid legs waiting for the crack of the bat as a little shrill creamy whistle splits the atmosphere stadium hush. (90)

The photo is insufficient. Kerouac moves from the card itself, to the physical players whose bones are long interred, to a reanimated present tense where the crack of the bat sends a little shrill creamy whistle into the stadium. The photos escape their function as a mere record of the physical appearance of a player along with his statistical performance and instead become an actual event, an actual occurrence in the mind of Kerouac. And even more important, Kerouac is not recounting how as a boy he made these baseball cards come alive but is doing so in the present tense of writing. Through his spontaneous prose, Kerouac is able to breathe new life into a photograph of a baseball star long since gone.

Kerouac's attempt to fill the gap between the present and the past with his spontaneous prose is best theorized by Deleuze and Guattari's conception of becoming. In *What is Philosophy?* these thinkers explain becoming as "a zone of indetermination, of indiscernibility, as if things, beasts, and persons (Ahab and Moby Dick, Penthesilea and the bitch) endlessly reach that point that immediately precedes their natural differentiation" (173). Becoming involves a tandem movement, each element towards the other in a zone of indetermination. While partners such as Ahab and Moby Dick do not entirely transform into one another, they each draw out affects and sensations from the other that create a change in their very beings. In *A Thousand Plateaus*, Deleuze and Guattari speak of a "becoming-dog":

> If I wear shoes on my hands, then their elements will enter a new relation, resulting in the affect or becoming I seek. But how will I be able to tie the shoe on my second hand, once the first is already occupied? With my mouth, which in turn receives an investment in the assemblage, becoming a dog muzzle. . . . At each stage of the problem, what needs to be done is not to compare organs but to place elements or materials in a relation that uproots the organ from its specificity, making it become "with" the other organ. (258–59)

One does not literally turn into a dog. Rather, one places oneself in various positions that allow one to experience, as closely as possible, the conditions of dog-ness. The assemblage created with the dog-body pushes into a zone of indeterminacy that is neither person nor dog but a movement between the two. What is experienced, then, is the affectual qualities not of dog but of a becoming-dog that open up into new sensations and perceptions unavailable to the merely human. Becoming is experimentation, and according to Deleuze and Guattari, literature provides one of the most fecund sites to conduct such an exploration.

The idea of becoming has vast implications for thinking about memory. Becoming is movement and thus escapes the sort of memory that seeks to pin down a past event in time. In *A Thousand Plateaus*, Deleuze and Guattari expand upon this distinction:

> One may contrast a childhood block, or a becoming-child, with the childhood memory: "a" molecular child is produced . . . "a" child coexists with us, in a zone of proximity or a block of becoming, on a line of deterritorialization that carries us both off—as opposed to the child we once were, whom we remember or phantasize, the molar child whose future is the adult. (294)

The use of the indeterminate here is important because the goal of becoming is not to produce a static form but to create an in-between where novel perceptions can occur. By producing "a" child rather than "the" child, becoming creates a "zone" or "block" where change happens. Contrast this with the "molar child." This conception implies that the adult is already encompassed in the child, and, thus, the possibility for adaptation and flux is negated. Here, "molar" designates a way of thinking about the event as an already-happened that is incapable of promoting change. Everything hinges on how memory is deployed. If by memory is meant an ossified form of the past that must remain consistent through time, then the molar child is invoked, and nothing can become other than it is or already was in the past. On the other hand, if one conceives of memory as intensity, then childhood changes from what one once was into what one is continually becoming in the present.

Deleuze and Guattari's conception of becoming provides an insightful means of understanding the use of memory in Kerouac's corpus. In *Dr. Sax*, Kerouac relates one of his earliest childhood memories of his mother's brown bathrobe. He describes this "Great Bathrobe Vision":

> I'm in my mother's arms but somehow the chair is not on the floor, it's up in the air suspended in the voids of sawdust smelling mist blowing from Lajoie's wood yard, suspended over grass at corner of West Sixth and Boisvert—that daguerreotype gray is all over, but my mother's robe sends auras of warm brown (the brown of my family)—so now when I bundle my chin in a warm scarf in a wet gale—I think on that comfort in the brown bathrobe—or as when a kitchen door is opened to winter allowing fresh ices of air to interfere with the warm billowy curtain of fragrant heat of cooking stove . . . say a vanilla pudding. . . . I am the pudding, winter is the gray mist. (18–19)

The strict relation of the facts of the memory tends toward the molar. Locations like Lajoie's wood yard and West Sixth and Boisvert anchor the memory in space, while a suspended chair and a mother's arms provide the scaffolding on which the reminiscence is built. Yet, Kerouac quickly sends these discrete facts into motion, heightening the intensity of the image in an effort to make it become. This becoming takes place on two levels. Daguerreotype gray is contrasted to warm brown in order to create affect in the reader—the sadness of an old photo is replaced with the familial conviviality of a mother's robe. Here, childhood comes alive in the present, and the young Kerouac is less an expired entity than a present force in the reader's mind. But Kerouac goes even further, building an assemblage that allows him to turn a childhood memory into an act of becoming. Kerouac takes the comfort that the memory of the brown bathrobe creates to foster a sense of security in the present. The comfort in the brown bathrobe that Kerouac uses to ward off a wet gale is not simply an association lock that he has developed. Rather, it is a becoming-child that sends Kerouac racing towards a new state of being. Thus, the declaration "I am the pudding, winter is the gray mist" is not an analogy but the expression of a becoming. The goal of memory for Kerouac here is not to recall but to enact—memory makes something happen in the present by causing a shift in the consciousness of the rememberer.

The difference between memory's static, "photographic" depiction and writing as becoming can clearly be seen in Kerouac's later works. *Dr. Sax* was composed in 1952; Kerouac's *Vanity of Duluoz* was written in 1968, a year before his death. By drawing attention to the difference between the occurrence of the memory and the time of writing, Kerouac gives *Vanity of Duluoz* a feeling of nostalgic looking back that is absent in *Dr. Sax*. Consider the beginning of *Vanity of Duluoz*, where Kerouac opines that "my anguish as I call it arises from the fact that people have changed so much, not only in the past five years . . . or past ten years . . . but in the past thirty years to such an extent that I don't recognize myself as a real member of something called the human race" (9). Many of *Vanity*'s passages are prefaced with such statements, alerting the reader to a value judgment implicit in the text—things were better back then. This reminiscent style displays a longing for the past that serves to extract the reader out of the narrative's present. Memories do not become, as in *Dr. Sax*, but are rather presented as rigid past events. Kerouac calls these moments "cameos" and presents them in list form throughout his work: "Weekends at Ray Olmsted's apartment with his parents and kid brother, in Yonkers, the affair with Betty there, skating on the Yonkers pond and a few kisses here and there. Sharpy Gimbel yelling 'Hi' from his convertible at the dance" (51). Here the affair with Betty fails to provide the occasion for a becoming. Kerouac does not create any sort of intensity that might influence the reader's perception of the event, nor does his affair develop an assemblage that might launch him into a becoming. Instead, what is given is flat description that is filmic in quality. Events are rendered as mere visual occurrences devoid of affect. Memory in *Vanity of Duluoz* does not reenter the space of present time, and thus it is forced to remain as an already-taken-place that is an expired force rather than a current intensity.

The difference between *Vanity of Duluoz* and *Dr. Sax* is the difference between a history and a becoming. Later in *Vanity*, Kerouac goes on to explain his conception of the Duluoz Legend, a chronicling of "what I'd seen with my own eyes, according to the style I decided on at whether twenty-one years old or thirty or forty or whatever later age, and put it all together as a contemporary history record for future times to see what really happened and what people really thought" (190). Here, Kerouac is concerned with fixing historical events in time, so that future times can see the supposed truth of the moment as it occurred in the past—the event as it really happened and what people really thought. This conception of "Legend" assumes that history is indeed recoverable and presentable as objective fact and runs directly counter to the becomings achieved in Kerouac's other works. Drawing on the work of French essayist and poet Charles Péguy, Deleuze and Guattari explain in *What Is Philosophy?* the two ways of considering the event: "One consists in going over the course of the event, in recording its effectuation in history. . . . But the other consists in reassembling the event, installing oneself in it as in a becoming" (111). History thwarts change. Instead of creating a textual moment in which writer and reader can become something else, historical recording such as occurs in *Vanity* seeks to pin down the nature of an event once and for all. In *The Spontaneous Poetics of Jack Kerouac*, Regina Weinreich correctly observes that Kerouac composed his works "not in the terms of the linear chronology we might expect from mere Legend. Kerouac abandons the linear narration of saga for a literary strategy based on the juxtaposition of the images that produce experience, each expressed differently at different points in time" (12). Each of these repetitive turns back to childhood, how- ever, are not created equal. Many of Kerouac's later works rely on a wistful nostalgia that lacks the intensity of earlier works like *Dr. Sax*. Kerouac is always turning towards the past, but the way in which he reencounters the past in the present marks the difference between recording a past event and re-creating the intensity of that event again in the present.[7]

Ultimately, what is at stake in recording memory is control over the past. Given the battle with the media that Kerouac conducted throughout the later part of his career, it is unsurprising that he should be so deeply concerned about the messages that representations of the past event con- vey. In his essay "The Origins of the Beat Generation," Kerouac relates an anecdote about the misuse of photographs to distort the past: "On the third day *Mademoiselle* magazine wanted to take pictures of us all so I posed just like that, wild hair, crucifix, and all . . . and the only publication which later did not erase the crucifix from my breast . . . was the *New York Times*" (*Good Blonde* 55). Just what is the truth of the past if it can be so easily distorted in the present? Discussing a honeymoon photograph of Cody and his new bride, Kerouac ponders, "How can the tragic children tell what it is their fathers killed, enjoyed and joyed in and killed them to make them crop open like vegetable windfalls in a bin" (*Visions of Cody* 390). It is not that the photograph is incapable of eliciting a response—magazines such as *Mademoiselle* erased the crucifix because it sent the wrong message to their subscribers. Photos are always being described as "sad" or "lost" by Kerouac. The problem is that photographs do not tell the entire story. Not only are they open to outright manipulation but they also are only the start, the beginning of a feeling that it is the writer's job to prolong and expand. Photographs, and by extensions any molar representations of the past, cannot become. They may provide the occasion for such a becoming, but by themselves are helpless to evoke the sort of movements and affects that are capable of producing change. The photographic image is, by itself, a dead memory. That is precisely what makes it so sad. Only through reenactment can memory be revived in the present, only by engaging the photograph with the truth as it unfolds in the moment can the gap between the present and the past ever be filled.

Bringing the Photograph into the Social

For the Beats, there is a "Real," and the provisional center holds. In *Visions of Cody*, Kerouac attempts to negotiate the contradictions of Hollywood's media empire: "All my B-movies, all our B-movies, taught us what we know now about paranoia and crazy suspicion. Yet would you throw away a good B-movie?—get high on T, and go and see them mope and murp and muckle in a mad dream?" (251). Although they mope and murp and muckle, Kerouac will come to use the unreality of the B-movie to read the reality of his own life and Cody's. He goes on to describe his friend in terms of a bad B-actor: "He looked like that Hollywood stunt man who is fist-fighting in place of the hero and has such a remote, furious, anonymous viciousness . . . that everybody begins to be suspicious because they know the hero wouldn't act that way in real unreality" (48). Kerouac's Cody is not a Hollywood hero, and that's what makes him so real. If the A-movie has become the real "unreality," the B-film is that unreality made real again—a deflation of Hollywood's dream balloon. What is interesting here is that Kerouac refuses to get lost amongst the filmic image. Rather than ironically camping on the movie, Kerouac uses it as a filter. Thus, Cody trying on a tight-fitting suit becomes like "irascible millionaire husbands tugging before last minute mirrors in B-movies" with his arms looking "almost as

big as Popeye's" (62). As with Warhol, media becomes a means of understanding life. Yet, while Warhol remains unconcerned where the "artificial
stops and reality begins," Kerouac is deeply concerned with rendering the
reality of his friend Cody with as much precision as possible. As Kerouac
explains in his preface, he wants a "vertical, metaphysical study of Cody's
character and its relationship to the general 'America'" (ii). Unreality, then,
is of use only insofar as it sheds light on the reality that Kerouac and his
fellow Beats are constantly trying to describe.

Despite the Beat desire to use the gaps created by photography in the
service of a higher truth, such images always circulate within a wider social sphere that continually provides representations with new meanings.
In *The Burden of Representation*, John Tagg draws on the work of Michel
Foucault to discuss the various social forces that impinge on photographic
representation. Tagg discusses the Farm Security Administration's project
to document social conditions: "The 'truth' of these individual photographs
may be said to be a function of several intersecting discourses: that of
government departments, that of journalism, more especially of docu-
mentarism, and that of aesthetics" (173). Thus, when FSA photographer
Walker Evans captures the face of a migrant worker on film, the truth of
this representation does not reside in the image itself. The truth, if that word
even applies, is deeply embedded in forces of power that run throughout
the various discourses that seek to contain it. In his article "Looking at
Photographs," Victor Burgin admonishes that photography is merely "one
signifying system among others in society which produces the ideological subject," and thus photographic theory needs to "take account of the
production of this subject as the complex totality of its determinations are
nuanced and constrained in their passage through and across photographs"
(153). This is a far cry from the sort of desire that prodded Barthes to place a
captionless photograph of his mother at the beginning of his book *Roland
Barthes* or the impulse that drove Ginsberg to record his friends with the
"sacramental presence" that would preserve them against the ravages of
time. For postmodernists, the desire to record presence in all its fullness
is itself a drive for truth that must be contextualized in the framework of
discourse, society, and power that frames it.

The postmodern insistence on the use value of the photo challenges
the Beat deployment of the photographic image in the service of the gap.
In *Trace and Transformation*, Eisinger discusses the difference between
modern and postmodern conceptions of the photo:

One of the consequences of postmodernism for photographic theory is that the paradox of trace and transformation, so central to modernist theory, has been rendered peripheral. . . . Does one see in a photograph an automatic trace of reality or a transformation of reality through which one detects the creative vision of the photographer? . . . Postmodernism, however, treats the photograph less as an image than as an object and is less concerned with what one sees in it than with the relationships into which it enters. (247)

Beat thinking on the photograph generally takes place within the modernist paradigm of trace and transformation. For Ginsberg, the photograph not only captures the sacramental quality of the world, but through a judicious use of captions, it serves to jolt the viewer into a transcendental understanding of time itself. Of course, Ginsberg was media savvy as well—his photos, which adorn dorm walls, coffee tables, and book jackets, keep handsome writers like Kerouac in a perpetual 1947, slaking America's collective thirst for wistful images of the postwar years and furthering the Beat mythos. Kerouac is worried about the transformative power of the lens, the ability of the camera to delimit the plenitude of the event through a selective framing of one affect over another. This is unsurprising, as the history of Kerouac's fame is a history of media manipulation and a battle over his own image. Even recently, a picture of Kerouac taken outside the Kettle of Fish bar in New York (with the image of Joyce Johnson airbrushed out) was used in an advertisement for Gap Khakis. But for postmodern theorists, the social value of photography becomes of paramount concern. The photograph's meaning is derived not from the image that it portrays but from the relationships into which it enters. Representation is not measured by verisimilitude, either to object or affect. Rather, representations of past events are measured by their constantly changing functions. How an image engages the social thus becomes more important than the image itself.

Of all the Beat writers, Burroughs is perhaps the most aware of the social role that images play in crafting perception. It should come as no surprise, then, that Burroughs is considered the most postmodern of the Beats as well. In *The Job*, Burroughs discusses his cut-up method, explaining, "Take a talking picture of you walking out in the morning to buy cigarettes and the papers. Run it back, you remember everything that happened, there it is on screen and muttering off the sound track. . . . Now I can make you remember something that didn't happen by splicing it in" (36). The relationship between memory and record is shifting and dubious. The visual image does not guarantee authenticity—it shapes public thinking. Burroughs realized that to alter memory, all that was required was to alter the image upon which it depends. The postmodernism of Burroughs's technique lies in its willingness to see representation not as a sacred depiction of the event but as a record that constantly changes meaning through time. Change the object, change the effects. Thus, Burroughs's cut-up method is result orientated, a technique meant to alter consciousness in an effort to evade space-time limitations that Burroughs sees as a key to repression but that could trick its maker as easily as it does its marks.

So what form should representation take in order to avoid complicity with the forms of power around it? In his novel *The Electric Kool-Aid Acid Test*, Wolfe describes how Neal Cassady would flip a hammer, over and over, with his head down. According to "the Chief" Ken Kesey, "when Cassady misses, it's never an accident. He's saying something. There's something going on in the room, something's getting up tight, there's bad vibrations and he wants to break it up" (17). Cassady's hammer-flipping is indeed a form of representation—when he misses, he is "saying something." But what he says has the forceful impact of present-tense action. It is itself an event that enters directly into the Prankster's social sphere. The dropped hammer does not need to represent anything but instead immediately "synchs" with their existence in such a way that they are brought to an understanding of the situation around them. By plunging into the present moment with unmediated intensity, Cassady is able to offer the kind of impact that Beat writings continually seek—a presentation of the real that builds an immediate and unmistakable rapport.

5. Getting Together
Heterotopia and the Moment as a Social Site

The Beat desire to "capture immediacy" is political as well as personal. This point is often overshadowed by the intense focus on the mythos that has built up around Beat personalities. Of course, the personal is already political, and the Beats' insistence on spontaneous expression within the moment carries with it a host of assumptions that challenge the postwar status quo. But Beat writings provide models for turning the passing moment into a site for collective action. Consider the famous passage from *On the Road*, where Dean invokes the memory of a jazz set in order to explain to Sal the meaning of "IT":

> All of a sudden somewhere in the middle of the chorus he *gets it*—everybody looks up and knows; they listen; he picks it up and carries. Time stops. He's filling empty space with the substance of our lives, confessions of his bellybottom strain, remembrance of ideas, rehashes of old blowing. He has to blow across bridges and come back and do it with such infinite feeling soul-exploratory for the tune of the moment that everybody knows it's not the tune that counts but IT. (206)

The jazz set and the indescribable feeling of IT that the music produces is a celebrated Beat trope where the effervescent joy of Dean's IT, the social camaraderie among black tenormen and white hipsters in an era of racial segregation, and the undeniable Beat desire for transcendence figure prominently. But what receives less attention is the notion of the social that is being constructed. This empty space where time stops brings together individuals to form a collective—even if this group measures its existence by the tune of the moment. The dynamics of such a moment warrant closer attention. What role does the tune play in producing the IT of the performance? How is it that individual members of the crowd sitting at separate tables immediately look up and know the bellybottom strain and the rehashes of old blowing of a black tenorman distanced from them by both professional training and social custom? What exactly is Dean's enigmatic IT, and how can everybody experience IT both collectively and individually?

The key to the jazz moment resides in its ability to turn individual transcendence into social cohesion. Although the tenorman may produce the IT of the event, it quickly spreads amongst the listeners, closing the gap between the musicians on stage and the audience at their respective tables. Both transcend—the tenorman in the act of musical composition and the audience as its members are caught up in the performance. But eventually, a point is reached where dichotomies collapse, and the group becomes one, even as each participant continues to experience the IT of the performance. Although personal expression may spark the feeling of IT, what stokes this fire is the construction of a collective that propels IT forward and allows each member to gain insight from the experience. Without the tenorman, IT might not be achieved, but without an audience to get caught up in the performance, this collective moment could not even begin.

This jazz moment situates Kerouac's work squarely within a utopian frame. Using the moment as a social site, Kerouac constructs a space where individuals unite for a limited temporal duration. And Kerouac is not alone in this impulse. Various Beat writers posit versions of Kerouac's jazz set, each reflecting his or her own concerns and assumptions. Beat thinking about the moment does not end with the individual but continues to address the dynamics of intersubjectivity that are necessarily created when multiple individuals convene in a particular location for a specific time. The Beats' utopianism lies in their belief that such moments, when properly constructed, can provide a social space that both enlivens its participants and poses challenges to the rigid social structures that they oppose. The Beats are often attacked as apolitical, but in reality their theories of self-expression all contain an intersubjective component. The argument follows thusly: spontaneity reveals truths hidden within the individual; every person has such truths; therefore, heightened moments of subjectivity can activate not only the individual but also others collected around that person. While no two Beats develop exactly the same theorizations of the social moment, they are united in their attempts to formulate a notion of collectivity that both avoids the pitfalls of earlier systems and offers a novel way to experience life with their fellow human.

Of course, to invoke the concept of utopia is to risk the charge of totalization that postmodernism had been leveling at such projects for the last half of the twentieth century. In his essay "Utopia and Anti-Utopia in the Twentieth Century," Krishan Kumar observes, "When philosophers announce the 'end of grand narratives,' when it is said that there is no philosophical basis for Enlightenment beliefs in Truth, Reason, Science, and Progress, it is hard to see how utopia, which tends to believe in most of those things, can survive" (265). Here, modernism, the heir to such Enlightenment beliefs in Truth, Reason, Science, and Progress, is inextricably bound up in utopian schemes. Utopia is perhaps the ultimate totalization, seeking to posit an ideal society at the end of time in which perfection is attained, and nothing new ever need occur. As such, it forms yet another "grand narrative" that postmodernism decries as not only epistemologically unsound but also dangerously naïve. As Kumar remarks in *Utopianism*, "It must lead, so the claim goes, to tyranny and totalitarianism" (90). Given the unprecedented historical atrocities of the twentieth century, postmodernism's skepticism about grand narratives that subsume everyone under the same rubric is not without merit. This point was certainly not lost on the Beats themselves, who were disdainful of not only the homegrown brand of homogenized American culture to which they so vehemently reacted but who likewise found little to celebrate in a stifling and repressive Soviet regime.

Against the tendency of modernism to totalize, postmodernism opts instead for the fragmentary, the isolated, and the discrete. Fighting homogeneity with heterogeneity, postmodernism does not seek a perfect society at the end of time. Rather, postmodernism views social formulations in terms of deferment. In his introduction to *Heterotopia: Postmodern Utopia and the Body Politic*, Tobin Siebers claims that "what distinguishes postmodernism ultimately is the extremity of its belief that neither utopia nor desire can exist in the here and now" (3). Consider marxism, perhaps the defining utopian conception of the nineteenth and twentieth centuries. According to its own tenets, the marxist society represents the inevitable culmination of historical processes. Unlike marxism, which is continually striving for *the* social formation that will express the ultimate truth of social interaction, postmodernism realizes that all such forms are necessarily contingent. As Siebers goes on to claim, for postmodernists, "equality is always the product not of sameness but of differences, and they are confident that all differences are equal" (7). The social consists of an ever-changing matrix of desires, conditions, and interactions, none of which can be elevated to dominion over the whole. What we get with postmodernism, then, is not a teleological development of society that will end with perfection or totality but instead an infinite series of social formulations, each with its own specificity and none guaranteeing its own existence over time.

The attack postmodernism wages on the notion of totality carries with it a critique of modernity's principal means of constructing such wholeness—rationality. The rational is indicted on two counts. First, it falsely assumes an epistemological ground for its reasoning, which postmodernism claims is severely lacking. More important, however, the modern insistence on rationality keeps other voices and viewpoints from being heard. Thus, postmodernism comes to champion the irrational as a means of fostering the new and opening up a space for alternatives.[1] Joel Whitebook uses the split between the rational and irrational to organize his book *Perversion and Utopia*. Looking at the role of psychoanalysis in critical theory, Whitebook observes that "after the Second World War, two major works on Freud emerged in Critical Theory—Herbert Marcuse's *Eros and Civilization* and Jürgen Habermas's *Knowledge and Human Interests*" (3). Marcuse embodies the irrational, drawing on Freud to posit a domain free from the taint of a highly rationalized society:

> Marcuse enlists Freud's early theory of perversions (later revised) in order to construe sexual perversions as the relatively direct expression of unconscious id impulses that have circumvented socialization and the reality principle. As such, they can be viewed as the preserve of an uncontaminated inner nature that could be investigated as a way of deciphering a utopian form of life. (3–4)

The irrationality of this uncontaminated inner nature becomes a means of surpassing a repressive, rationalized ego in order to posit a utopian form of life. Irrationality, for Marcuse, is the play, joy, and resistance to closure so characteristic of the postmodern position.[2] Yet, this utopia is not constrained by an organizing principle—to do that would mean reducing every idiosyncratic "perversion" into one common desire. Rather, the Marcusean utopia is more concerned with constructing a space where each individual can explore his or her unique possibility.

Compare this to Habermas. According to Whitebook, "The recognition of certain universal normative principles in modernity, [Habermas] argued, makes it unnecessary to look outside the structure of the world for the standards of critique" (6). While Marcuse needs the irrational in order to get beyond the social, Habermas is content to remain within "the structure of the world" based on rational, Enlightenment principles. The

Habermasian project of intersubjective communication is predicated on the ability of individuals to come together as rational subjects within a public sphere in order to reach agreement. The difference between the rational and the irrational is the difference between a group of subjects moving toward totalization and a differentiated collective heading toward heterogeneity. While modernity tends to draw others together under the social conception of the rational, postmodernism allows individuals the freedom to explore their own drives and desires, no matter their degree of irrationality.

This tension between the rational and the irrational, between the need for group cohesion and the demands of individual subjects, finds its best critical explication in the works of feminist thinkers. Negotiating between a universalism that threatens to subsume gender concerns under the auspices of "mankind" and an individualization that runs the risk of a fragmenting essentialism, feminist conceptions of the social shed light on what it means to construct a viable collective. Take, for instance, the discussion between Seyla Benhabib and Iris Marion Young. In *Situating the Self*, Benhabib outlines her objective: "My goal is to situate reason and the moral self more decisively in the context of gender and community, while insisting upon the discursive power of individuals to challenge such situatedness in the name of universalistic principles, future identities and as yet undiscovered communities" (8). Like Habermas, Benhabib retains a faith in the rational that is central to the functioning of modernity. While she acknowledges problems with such a conception, Benhabib remains positive that solutions can be discovered that lie within the sphere of the universalist approach.

Iris Marion Young, in *Intersecting Voices*, takes issue with Benhabib's assertion that individuals can adopt the standpoint of others: "Identifying moral respect and reciprocity with symmetry and reversibility of perspectives tends to close off the differentiation among subjects that Benhabib wants to keep open" (41). Young instead opts for a sense of "wonder" between subjects defined as "openness across, awaiting new insight about their needs, interests, perceptions, or values" (56). As with Marcuse and Habermas, the point here is not to simply choose one position over the other, since both have merits and shortcomings. Benhabib's universalism is rightly attacked by Young, since the ultimate lesson of feminism is that each person's idiosyncratic existence needs to be dutifully acknowledged by the system. At the same time, however, Young fails to achieve a system that would adequately address the inevitable conflicts that must arise in any social situation. What happens when wonder is not enough and two (or more) people cannot achieve such easy reconciliation? Here, the advantages of Benhabib become apparent—a universalistic approach at least offers a means of negotiating dissent. Only by taking stock of all positions—rational, irrational, universalistic, and individualistic—can we discover a meaningful approach to the social.

Examples of modernity's rationally ordered utopias are easy to spot and easy to attack. But what would a postmodern utopia look like, if such an entity is even possible? Michel Foucault provides a glimpse of such social formations in his essay "Different Spaces." In typical postmodern fashion, Foucault elevates questions of space over the issues of temporality, claiming, "Today's anxiety concerns space in a fundamental way. . . . Time probably only appears as one of the possible games of distribution between the elements that are spread out in space" (*Aesthetics* 177). The emphasis on elements distributed out in space leads Foucault to focus on the concept of "emplacement," defined as "the relations of proximity between points or elements" (176). Emplacement is important because it highlights the localized, embodied nature of existence. In keeping with postmodernism's insistence on the discrete, emplacement posits an actual body in an actual place doing actual work on other bodies. Of course, replacing abstract space with localized place is not inherently liberatory. But emplacements do have the possibility to countermand the current social situation: "But what interests me among all these emplacements are certain ones that have the curious property of being connected to all the other emplacements, but in such a way that they suspend, neutralize, or reverse the set of relations that are designed, reflected, or represented by them" (178). Emplacements need not simply reproduce the social structures that surround them—in certain cases, they have the ability to challenge existing conditions to produce something new.

There are two types of such liberatory spaces for Foucault. The first are utopias, but since they are "fundamentally and essentially unreal," they hold little interest for Foucault (*Aesthetics* 178). The others Foucault calls "heterotopias": "places that are designed into the very institution of society, which are sorts of actually realized utopias in which the real emplacements, all the other real emplacements that can be found within the culture are, at the same time, represented, contested, and reversed, sorts of places outside all places" (178). Here we come the closest to a version of postmodern utopia. Unlike many modern utopias, heterotopias are actualizable—they are "actual places" that challenge the "real emplacements" that contain them. Heterotopias are also numerous and various. Rather than one utopian vision that seeks to unite society, heterotopias exist in many places throughout the social sphere, each working to countermand prevailing localized conditions. And as Foucault makes clear in a later taxonomy of heterotopian types, these places outside all places likewise have an ambivalent relationship to temporality, constantly changing across time as well as space: "Heterotopias are connected with temporal discontinuities" (182). Not only can the function of heterotopias change over time but they also can achieve a break from chronological time, stepping outside temporality to achieve a timeless existence.

When juxtaposing the concept of heterotopia to Kerouac's jazz moment, the implications of Foucault's formulation become clear. The jazz set is "emplaced" within a space that is real, if ambiguous. The nightclub, although admittedly a site for the licentiousness associated with drinking, drug taking, and locating sexual partners, is nevertheless a capitalist enterprise existing within the bounds of sanction. Such rebelliousness is likewise not contained solely in Kerouac's club—it is obvious that the same type of heterotopia gets established in other nightclubs and in other cities, as well as on other Saturday nights. The empty space that the tenorman fills, then, is the gap between the standard, actual club as it gets emptied of its capitalist contents in order to be filled with a heterotopian assemblage of bellybottom strain, remembrance of ideas, rehashes of old blowing that serve no economic purpose. This is why Dean insists that the tenorman must find the tune of the moment—the heterotopia that is created in the jazz club is fleeting. The musicians must find the music for *that* particular club on *that* particular evening. Like a traveling carnival, nondescript space gets transmuted into the place of heterotopia for a limited duration, and then the tents are folded, and the show moves on to the next town, the next club, the next Saturday night.

The Beat desire to form collectives out of individual experience helps to elucidate the possible form of a viable social alternative. Beat writers were certainly aware of the dangers in crafting oppressive regimes. After all, they were reacting to one at home and held little hope in the communist social structures that were available abroad. Beat scholarship has long pointed to this dilemma as one of the major reasons for their apolitical stance—in a world without viable options, the best thing one could do was to carve out a space for personal freedom.[3] Yet, what this theory misses is that the Beats were indeed social. The difficulty of recognizing Beat contributions to the social sphere is that these formulations seldom seemed overtly political. Writing about a jazz club does not appear to be proffering a new conception of the social, at least on the surface. It is only when the implications of such formulations are teased out that Beat writing can take its rightful place in the pantheon of social philosophy. Again, it is the Beats' liminal early-postmodern position that gives their social constructions weight and force. The Beats looked to the unconscious, to desire, and to the irrational in order to find meaning in the world. But while the Beats are often aligned with the anything-goes antics of postmodern irrationality, a closer look at their thinking reveals that their conceptions of the social are oftentimes highly rational and ordered. They may be wary of the dangers that totalization poses, but they are not beyond crafting conceptions of the social that are held together by various plans and schemes. Thus, what emerges in Beat writing is an insistence on the social that seeks to learn the lesson of totality from modernism while curbing its excesses through an anticipation of what was, in the late 1950s and early 1960s, a nascent postmodernism. Although Beat heterotopias are certainly not completely or consistently successful, they do provide a new way of thinking about the moment as a social site.

William S. Burroughs and the Law

The best place to begin an inquiry into Beat heterotopia is through the work of William S. Burroughs. Incessantly concerned with resisting the ubiquitous systems of "control," Burroughs's corpus represents a working through of the possible responses to power. In his earlier works, Burroughs creates a utopian structure based on fantasy collectives structured around what lies "outside" authoritarian structures. Homosexuality, drug use, and other supposedly abnormal behavior provide the scaffolding for collectives that challenge the status quo. It must be noted here that these formulations are imaginary and reactive—mental creations whose sole function is to break free from the straightjacket of control. With his cut-up novels, Burroughs begins to explore methods that allow for the physical emancipation of subjects under tyrannical rule. Tape recordings, film splices, and hypertext now have the ability to alter surroundings, sundering the word-locks built into the nervous system that keep humans from achieving independence. Although this stage in Burroughs's oeuvre begins to move into the practical, it is still reactive, responding to control systems already in place rather than positing an entirely new conception of society. Burroughs's last turn marks a departure. While he still draws on the unconscious and desire, his final trilogy attempts to create a viable social alternative. Although Burroughs's earlier fantasy structures might be difficult to measure from a perspective that seeks to gauge their real-world efficacy, by these final novels Burroughs offers social formulations worthy of dissection and evaluation.

Burroughs's early work is best understood through one of his favorite quotes from Hassan I Sabbah: "Nothing is True, Everything is Permitted" (*Job* 97). Burroughs is quick to point out that this does not mean pure chaos, but, rather, everything is permitted *because* nothing is true. Since everything is illusion, writing has the power to enter reality with actualizing force. This is crucial for Burroughs if his aberrant formulations are going to do meaningful work in the social field. Thus in *Junky*, the drug addict is not simply a criminal or a rebel but a challenge to anyone who wants to close off the possibility of consciousness exploration—this is why the addict remains unrepentant at the end of the novel. The same rationale applies to *Queer*, where homosexuality becomes a form of desire that challenges moral constraint and custom. Such attacks culminate in *Naked Lunch*, in which all such deviant groups end up posing a challenge to fixed notions of society and subjectivity. Here, Burroughs sounds much like the Marquis de Sade's character Madame de Saint-Ange, who explains to her charge, "One fucks . . . because by fucking we obey and fulfill Nature's ordinations, and because all man-made laws which would contravene Nature's are made for naught but our contempt" (226). As with the marquis, it is a mistake to read Burroughs too literally—they both present fantasy conceptions of desire that while not always implementable as practice, nevertheless provide a way of thinking that challenges what is currently available.

While earlier novels might decry a society that forces deviant behavior to the periphery, Burroughs's novel *The Wild Boys* marks a turning point in his corpus. *Naked Lunch* might begin to posit fantasy scenes in which oppressors are attacked, and authoritarian structure collapses, but by *The Wild Boys*, revolutionary force becomes an organized challenge to established order. As the title itself suggests, the wild boys are a closely knit gang of youths who fall outside the purview of society. Normative descriptions are difficult here, as the functioning of this gang in never fully elaborated, but revolve around episodes of myth creation and violence. Jennie Skerl, in *William S. Burroughs*, remarks that "the satanic immortality of the cult, the savagery of the tribe, the perverse gratification of instinctual desire, and the naked male body define the wild boys as embodiments of demonic energy. . . . They are utopian as a *force*" (83). This force is at its best when confronting the overfed, bourgeois government troops that are chasing them. The wild boys are the perfect foil, and their lean, quick, hit-and-run tactics are no match for the cumbersome inefficiency of the traditionally hierarchical military unit. The key to the wild boys' success is that they have no strict program at all. As Timothy S. Murphy claims in *Wising Up the Marks*, while the wild boys have rituals, "[t]hese forms may resemble myth, but they are, at most, joke myths that mock the very structure of myth, or throwaway myths to be used like condoms as protection against the infection of power, binarism, and hierarchy" (167).[4] Basing their group on a desire that exceeds possible forms for its realization, the wild boys are constantly changing, moving, and adapting. A society based on ossified and rigid structures simply cannot compete.

The Wild Boys, with its presentation of the boy gang, is certainly a revolutionary program with teeth. However, it offers no viable social formation to counter the one it so violently deposes. Without an antagonist to define it, the boy gang is left standing on a ruined field and looking helpless. The gang needs an adversary since it has no internal structure to maintain itself when the fighting is over. Rather than equipping themselves with a positive content, they are instead merely a negation of the system that they challenge and thus fail to offer anything beyond the simple destruction of that system. As Burroughs himself realizes, "He who opposes force with counterforce alone forms that which he opposes and is formed by it" (*Job* 101). In order to avoid this impasse, Burroughs embarks upon a new type of project in his final trilogy. Constructing social formations that are self-consciously utopian, Burroughs attempts to create a new form of collectivity that can both challenge the dominant order while constructing its own version of society in the process. These latter texts, while they still draw on fantasy structures found throughout the Burroughs corpus, deserve closer scrutiny because they represent an attempt by Burroughs to imagine a practical utopian scheme.[5]

At the end of his essay "Different Spaces," Foucault observes that the "sailing vessel is the heterotopia par excellence. In civilizations without ships the dreams dry up, espionage takes the place of adventure, and the police that of the corsairs" (*Aesthetics* 185). This point would not be lost on Burroughs, who turns to the conception of a pirate commune as the model for his utopian vision in the first novel of his final trilogy, *Cities of the Red Night.* Quoting *Under the Black Flag* by Don C. Seitz, Burroughs writes, "The ship's money was put in a chest to be used as common property. Clothes were now distributed to all in need and the republic of the sea was in full operation. Mission bespoke them to live in strict harmony among themselves" (*Cities* xi–xii). Shunned by the rest of the world, the pirate commune lives its egalitarian existence outside the strictures of standard society. Burroughs argues for a "retroactive Utopia," claiming that had the world been reorganized on such principles of equality, present-day problems would have been avoided (xiv). Sharing common property and clothes is conceivable, but the real question is how to get a group of pirates to live in strict harmony among themselves.

To answer this question, Burroughs looks to a set of rules entitled "The Articles." Among its tenets are rules against imprisonment for debt, enslavement, torture, and interference with sexual practices, as well as the right to vote on matters affecting the commune. These "Articles" look much like the sort of legislation drafted by the French and American revolutions, and Burroughs in fact envisions them as a sort of jeremiad, forcing the French and Americans to "stand by their words" (xiv). The difference between the egalitarian mission of the commune and the rules codified in "The Articles" is the tension between a heterogeneous openness that allows for differentiation and a cohesive totality that calls for some measure of structure. While it is true that "The Articles" are mainly written to preserve heterogeneity, they still function as a type of law that governs an otherwise ungovernable colony. Burroughs may view America as a law-infested land overrun by the police and other agents of control, but his utopian vision demands that a minimum number of rules be adopted.

If *Cities of the Red Night* demonstrates the tension between egalitarian heterogeneity and the need for at least a basic organizing principle, Burroughs's second novel in his trilogy, *The Place of Dead Roads*, highlights the problems of developing a strategic plan to reach a specific goal. Taking issue with the utopians of the past, Burroughs observes that "happiness is a by-product of function. Those who seek happiness for itself seek victory without war. This is the flaw in all utopias. A society, like the individuals who compose it, is an artifact designed for a purpose" (238). For Burroughs, the attainment of the ideal state would be disastrous. Without struggle, without a purpose, the society would simply atrophy, and happiness would be impossible to achieve. There must always be a goal to strive for if the collective is to continue.

It necessarily follows, then, that a change in the purpose must correspond to a constant change in the social artifact as well. Thus, the heroes of *The Place of Dead Roads*, the Johnson Family, operate as "a cooperative structure. There isn't any boss man. People know what they are supposed to do and they do it. We're all actors and we change roles. Today's millionaire is tomorrow's busboy" (114–15). Like the pirates in Burroughs's earlier commune, the Johnsons still possess a code of conduct that cements their outlaw band. But what is important here is that flexibility in roles and procedures allows this group to quickly adapt to the particular struggle at hand. Such adaptability is a hallmark of the Burroughs project. In *The Job*, Burroughs posits his "Academy 23," a worldwide network of differing training facilities whose aim is "*decontrol* of opinion, the students being conditioned to *look* at the facts *before* formulating any verbal patterns" (138). Preparation involves the ability to react to any situation without recourse to preestablished thought patterns, developing a plan of attack that fulfills a specific need at a specific time. While plans are made to reach certain goals, as outcomes are uncertain, the method of obtaining them must be able to accommodate contingency and necessity. To stick to a plan too closely is to err on the side of rational planning that Burroughs claims plagues utopian thought. But entering battle without a plan is tantamount to suicide—one needs to have some preparation if one is to have a chance for success. Only through a careful negotiation with a goal that is ever-changing can a social collective hope to reach a desirable outcome.

The model of heterotopia that Burroughs proposes blends the need for heterogeneity and totality, for planning as well as objective, in such a way that a viable social alternative appears to emerge. But what are the implications of sexuality on this model? In *Queer Burroughs*, Jamie Russell cites another historical influence that Murphy misses—the "raid on the Stonewall Inn on Greenwich Village's Christopher Street, on Friday, June 1969" (88). While Murphy takes Burroughs's homosexuality as a given, Russell interrogates it in order to reveal the flaw of exclusion that plagues Burroughs's work. Burroughs may speak frankly in an era of tabooed homosexuality, but according to Russell, his conception of the queer is one-sided and limited. Russell writes, "The overriding problem with which Burroughs' masculine queer fantasy presents the reader is its unfaltering reliance on a definition of the masculine based upon heterosexual models. . . . Many of the desires voiced in Burroughs' texts replicate the exclusion, denial, or rejection of the feminine" (135). For Russell, Burroughs's work ironically mimics the heterosexual masculinity that it challenges, closing off possibilities for the queer and the feminine alike.

Obviously, such exclusion is at odds with the openness required for a heterogeneous social enterprise. Murphy attempts to mitigate the damages caused by Burroughs's misogyny. In his introduction, he offers rebuttals to the myriad charges of misogyny that have appeared in Burroughs scholarship. He then cites "two of the most significant scenes in Burroughs's entire body of work," which occur in *Cities of the Red Night,* as evidence that Burroughs retains a space for the feminine in his utopian schemes (183). However, this defense is of the too-little, too-late variety—as Russell makes abundantly clear, Burroughs's degradation of the effeminate, in both men and women, is so pervasive and widespread that it overshadows Burroughs's conciliatory gestures towards the feminine in his later novels. Although the exclusion of effeminate homosexuals, women, and anyone else who cannot or will not measure up to Burroughs's conception of hypermasculinity helps him to retain his outsider status, it likewise keeps his heterotopian social constructions from reaching the point of efficacy.

The exclusionary nature of Burroughs's project is not the only obstacle to his reconstruction of the social sphere. A flaw is within the logic of his heterotopia as well. As shown previously, Burroughs relies on a set of foundational principles that work to organize the functioning of his social constructions. This is as it should be—without some form of cohesion, the group risks disintegrating into a chaotic collection of individual desires and schemes. But in an effort to give these rules more prescriptive force, Burroughs oftentimes overcompensates, running the risk of the type of totalitarian regimes that he abhors. Take, for instance, the Articles. Meant as a series of stripped-down laws to govern the commune, one article deserves special attention: "Article Six: No man may be put to death except for violation of the Articles" (188). This sort of tautological doublespeak is reminiscent of such dystopias as George Orwell's *1984.* Here, the articles, crafted under the rallying cry of freedom from tyranny, themselves become the mechanism for policing the deviant behavior that they were constructed to uphold. Nor is *Cities of the Red Night* the only novel in Burroughs's last trilogy in which such contradictions occur. In the preface to *The Place of Dead Roads,* Burroughs states that the "original title of this book was The Johnson Family. 'The Johnson Family' was a turn-of-the-century expression to designate good bums and thieves. It was elaborated into a code of conduct." Like the Articles, this code of conduct governs the actions of the characters throughout the novel. Now consider what happens when this code is broken. Burroughs got the idea for "The Johnson Family" from a 1926 book entitled *You Can't Win*, by Jack Black. In a foreword to the reissue of Black's book, Burroughs explains, "This young gay cat starts bad-mouthing Salt Chunk Mary and old George—a railriding safecracker . . . says to him: 'You were a good bum, but you're dog meat now' and shot him four times" (11). Although it may be granted that Salt Chunk Mary was the "Mother of the Johnson Family," and, thus, this young gay cat had it coming, this anecdote still displays the threat of violence that stands behind modes of organization like the Articles and the "Johnson code" (11). Opting for fewer laws instead of more, Burroughs nevertheless packs these fewer laws with more terror, as if making up for quantity with quality. The excessive use of force to guarantee compliance with the social contract blunts the effectiveness of Burroughs's formulations. Not only does the specter of totalitarianism reemerge in such a situation, but if physical threats are necessary to ensure their functioning, can these articles and codes really be that desirable and effective?

Burroughs attempts to solve what he sees as the impasse between the individual and the social in the last novel of his trilogy by sidestepping the question altogether. In *The Western Lands*, Burroughs self-consciously constructs a "Book of the Dead" intended to guide souls toward the afterlife: "Consider the Egyptian concept of the seven souls, with different and incompatible interests. They must be welded into one. Otherwise, the organism remains wide open to parasitic attack" (27). The notion of collectivity that Burroughs develops in his earlier works becomes mapped onto the individual—the seven souls each with their different and incompatible interests must be reconciled into the one. Where such welding was previously undertaken by codes and articles, now the individual is charged with literally collecting his selves for the journey to the western lands.[6] Murphy characteristically reads this shift into a positive valence: "Burroughs's refrains throughout *The Western Lands*, '*every man for himself*' . . . might appear to mark the end of his revolutionary reconstitutional project, but since 'every man' is already a conglomeration of conflicting souls, they merely mark that project's metamorphosis" (192). But what type of metamorphosis is occurring here? Despite Murphy's optimism, it is difficult to see how Burroughs's shift from the social to the individual is going to avoid charges of solipsism that plague his work. Rather than opening up a space for utopian possibilities, the ascription of collectivity to an individual soul that Burroughs undertakes in *The Western Lands* closes off the possibilities for meaningful intersubjective relationship and leaves subjects stranded in a solipsistic universe of fear and mistrust.

Burroughs's utopian works occupy a paradoxical position. Burroughs wants the differentiation that goes along with postmodernism and, thus, is continually drawn towards a concept of openness that will allow expression full range. Yet, Burroughs is repeatedly called back to the modern in order to establish some sort of norm that will govern his collective enterprises. He may not lapse into a modernist utopia where rationality is exalted, but he clearly sees the need for a principle around which to organize his conceptions. While Murphy believes that Burroughs's utopian formulations leave the problems of the dominant order behind, Burroughs in actuality simply intensifies the normative principles he is supposedly against—for all his reliance on fantasy and desire, Burroughs remains within existing binaries. Without the Articles, the ship would be nothing but a loose band of pirates, bereft of purpose or direction. And without the code, the Johnsons would be merely a bunch of outlaws, under constant fear of attack from without the group as well as from within. Articles and codes are necessary forms of cohesive totalization, but when applied dogmatically, they threaten to subvert the very heterogeneity that they were designed to uphold. Burroughs's exclusionary practices run a similar risk. Crafting heterotopias that are too strict in their admittance requirements leaves a wide swath of people outside the collective, cutting off the very heterogeneity that such a group is trying to foster. Burroughs highlights the ways in which consensus and totality are obtained, but he simultaneously demonstrates the dangers in constructing a heterotopia that relies too heavily on normative principles of inclusion.

1960s Heterotopian Practice

At first glance, it seems odd that as rebellious a figure as Burroughs could be accused of resorting to an overly prescriptive notion of utopia. Yet, this surprising fact becomes more understandable when one considers that Burroughs's later trilogy stems in large part from his reaction to the sort of countercultural politics he witnessed (and to certain extent participated in) during the 1960s. The youth movement that constituted the countercultural sixties was the direct heir to a Beat social critique that inspired and informed their revolutionary politics. *On the Road*, "Howl," and *Naked Lunch* were hippie bibles. An examination of their cultural practice helps to explain not only Burroughs's reaction but also how 1950s' Beat heterotopia became 1960s' political praxis. Following the lead of Marcuse, the sixties placed irrationality and desire at the center of a critique of American political and economic policies. But sixties' countercultural practice, as Burroughs's overcompensation makes clear, was not without its own problematic elements. By rejecting any sort of governing principle as a curb on individual expression, sixties' heterotopias were oftentimes unable to create social collectives cohesive enough to accomplish their objectives.

Rather than attempt to formulate normative principles to govern collective action, the sixties' counterculture opted instead for a loose heterogeneity that adopted an anything-goes attitude.[7] Consider, for example, the auspicious beginnings of a political "party" organized by Berkeley, California, activists Jerry Rubin and Abbie Hoffman:

> We got very stoned so we could look at the problem *logically*:
> It's a *youth* revolution.
> *Gimme* a "Y."
> It's an *international* revolution.
> *Gimme* a "I."
> It's people trying to have meaning, fun, and ecstasy in their lives—a *party*.
> *Gimme* a "P."
> Whattaya got?
> *Youth International Party.*
> Paul Krassner jumped to his feet and shouted: *"YIPpie! We're yippies!"*
> (Rubin 16)

The stoned logic that produced this party was rampant in the sixties' counterculture. The hippies loved puns. From a political party that parties to the creation of public nuisances that produce "Public NewSense," the desire to play on words epitomizes the counterculture's attempts to combat their rational inheritance with an irrational joy and verve (Digger Archives). Turning the act of naming things into a game rebukes society for the inauthentic games that it forces its members to constantly play in order to survive. Although this insistence on play shares much with what a latter postmodernism will see as a corrective to the homogenizing logic of modernism, the sixties' counterculture saw an overtly political possibility in punning. The pun works much like a surrealistic jolt—once one grasps the irony in the gap between opposing meanings, the reality of the present situation that produced the incongruity becomes clear. Play is important but not only for itself. It is a means to reconnect with the present moment, to get back to the now where an authentic life can be lived. Of course, the "squares" were quick to ridicule this aestheticization of the social. To them, it was merely hippy zaniness to place such political emphasis on what seemed to be chance congruence in meanings. But as subsequent events would demonstrate, such tomfoolery was not merely fun and games. Getting masses of people back into the present moment can have serious consequences.

The thinker who best epitomizes the counterculture's insistence on the irrational as the means to a better society is Herbert Marcuse. *Eros and Civilization* made him, according to Kumar in *Utopia and Anti-Utopia*, a "hero of the counter-culture of the 1960s" (396). Marcuse, blending Freud and Marx, argued for a utopia predicated on the release of libidinal energy and a re-attention to the importance of play: "With the establishment of the reality principle, the human being which, under the pleasure principle, has been hardly more than a bundle of animal drives, has become an organized ego. . . . Under the reality principle, the human being develops the function of *reason*" (13). While the reality principle replaces basic, animal drives with an ego based on reason, the solution to this impasse is not to simply allow pleasure full reign. Marcuse's point is that while some repression is indeed necessary for the functioning of both the individual and the social, society by the sixties had gone beyond necessary repression into what he termed "surplus repression." Marcuse writes, "In the history of civilization, basic repression and surplus-repression have been inextricably intertwined, and the normal progress to genitality has been organized in such a way that the partial impulses and their 'zones' were all but desexualized" (35). Referring to the oral, anal, and genital phases of Freud's theory of sexuality, Marcuse argues that "civilization" has "desexualized" these "partial impulses" such that sexuality is now considered in its purely literal manifestation as intercourse. Sexuality does not become a facet of everyday existence but something to be experienced on select occasions only. Marcuse thus champions not a wholesale return to the libido but a reemphasis on rationality's other—a return to play, the irrational, the aesthetic, and a full-body sexuality. As Kumar explains, "Work becomes play, 'leisure' becomes no longer just relief from alienated labour but the sphere of all the 'eroticized' cultural and artistic activities of society" (395). The sixties' counterculture strove to realize this ideal, infusing every moment with play and eros in an attempt to achieve personal and social growth.

No other group better epitomized the fusion of irrational play and revolutionary practice than the Diggers. Taking their name from "the original English Diggers" of the seventeenth century, this loose affiliation practiced a combination of street theater and community outreach (Digger Archives).[8] The San Francisco collective followed the English Diggers' desire for "the establishment of communal ownership and the eradication of commercial values" (Davis 112). However, unlike their British counterparts, the Diggers rejected the "sixty-two laws" that Gerrard Winstanley proposed should be "rigidly enforced" on his group (Davis 111). On the contrary, the Diggers hoped to create inclusiveness through difference, prompting each member of society to fully activate him- or herself in order to question the existing system of social control. As Charles Perry observes in *The Haight-Ashbury*, "They became famous for free food and free crash pads, but most of their activities were strongly theatrical. . . . The Diggers had a political or supra-political purpose in all this, the creation of 'life-actors' who would be uninhibited wild cards, freely acting out their feelings at every moment" (252). The interest in the theatrical was a hallmark of the sixties' counterculture. If politics itself was a pageant of unreality foisted on the people, why not fight theater with theater?[9]

The hippies aestheticized the social, turning to art as a means for revolutionary struggle. The Diggers were no exception—their use of theater was meant to create life-actors whose uninhibitedness would challenge others to question their own desires and the extent to which they had to remain unrealized in the present social situation. The Diggers saw theater as a means of reaching an untapped irrationality that offered the possibility for freedom. In a series of free pamphlets, they laid out their manifesto: "Theater is territory. A space for existing outside padded walls. Setting down a stage declares a universal pardon for imagination" (Digger Archives). While the irrational is normally seen as occupying the space inside padded walls, here the dichotomy is reversed. The imagination is what frees the individual from the straightjacket of society, allowing life-actors to be created who know exactly who they are and what they are doing. Theater as territory is not an idle analogy. Perry describes one such performance that took place at a San Francisco intersection:

> Leaflets gave instructions to walk across the intersection in different directions to form various polygons, relying on the pedestrian's right of way over automobiles: 'Don't wait don't walk (umbrella step, stroll,

cake walk, somersault, finger-crawl, squat-jump, pilgrimage, Phylly dog, etc.).' It was a translation of the civil rights sit-in technique directed against automobiles, and at the same time a terrific goof. (104)

The most obvious gloss of this passage would be to contrast the rationalized space of the commodified automobile with the fluid, idiosyncratic movements of the corporeal body. And this is correct—the Diggers insisted on the personal as a challenge to the social. Only by discovering one's own matrix of fears and desires could one hope to become a "real" person. But it is also important to note the coupling of the irrational with political praxis contained in this passage. For the casual passerby, this theatrical scene would probably be registered either as a nuisance or an amusement. For the Diggers, however, the terrific goof is only one aspect of the performance. It is the vehicle through which one attains the life-actor. Personal expression within the ever-changing moment, no matter how crazy it might seem, is the only way to break free from social strictures. As the Diggers emphatically emphasize, "No frozen moments re-enacted for tomorrow's fantasy revolution. Life-acting is freeing eternity in *now!*" (Digger Archives).

The inclusiveness of Digger theater results from its basic tenet—everybody is acting all the time. The implied corollary to this position is that nobody is in charge. Perry notes that "participatory theater," derived primarily from Antonin Artaud and Bertolt Brecht, was "ever-present in the Haight-Ashbury" (251–52). The idea was to break down the barrier between the performers and the audience so that each could share in the possibilities that such theater offered. The Diggers took this a step further. At their "Free Stores" was a sign that read, "If Someone Asks to See the Manager Tell Him He's the Manager" (Digger Archives). On numerous occasions, Diggers would respond to the query "Who's in Charge?" with an emphatic "You Are!" Of course, this proved particularly helpful when the police arrived, since nobody was "in charge" of the quasi-legal operation. Such antics fuel the lore about hippie disorganization and anything-goes practices.

The fact of the matter, however, is that the Diggers were a rationally organized unit. In a pamphlet entitled "The Post-Competitive, Comparative Game of a Free City," detailed instructions are given on setting up food storage and distribution centers: "should hit every available source of free food—produce markets, farmers' markets, meat-packing plants . . . forming liaisons and communications with delivery drivers for the leftovers.

... [B]est method is to work in two shifts: morning group picks up the foodstuffs and the afternoon shift delivers it" (Digger Archives). As much as the Diggers advocate life-acting within the moment, establishing a food center requires forethought and planning. The point here is not that the two are mutually exclusive—there is no reason why one couldn't life-act while making rounds collecting food from a meatpacking plant. But underpinning the irrational antics of the Diggers is a highly rational process that allowed their programs to actually occur. After all, street theater must be organized, props must be produced, and leaflets printed and distributed.[10] "You" might be in charge but only through a working out of where to go, when to arrive, and how to get there can any particular "you" achieve an effective life-acting experience.

Ken Kesey and his group of "Merry Pranksters" took Digger irrationality one step further. Fueled by the drug LSD and a fearless commitment to spontaneity within the present moment, the Pranksters challenged supporters and adversaries alike to confront the system head-on. As Perry remarks, "In 1964 [Kesey] had bought a 1939 International Harvester bus with the advance money from his second novel and he and his friends had painted it in splotches of a dozen different colors. . . . They'd taken acid and acted as crazy as they felt, right out in public" (12). This confrontational style pertained to their own group dynamics as well. Shocking people out of their ready-made beliefs was seen by the Pranksters to hold social, as well as therapeutic, value. Wolfe describes an incident between two Pranksters when one mimicked the stuttering of the other to bring him to the realization that he did not stutter when angry: "The Pranksters probed everybody, to make them bring their hang-ups out front to the point where they could act totally out front, live in the moment, spontaneously, and if needling was what it took to bring you that far—" (146). Prankster rhetoric relies on an implicit belief in the power of authenticity. "Hang-ups" are the internalized social barriers that keep a person from living in the moment authentically. Self-realization is still the key to combating inauthenticity, but here the Pranksters rely on irrational behavior to jolt the subject back into the proper frame of mind. Confronted with situations that exceed expectations, Prankster targets are forced to reconsider the accepted social norms that keep them locked out of life in the moment.

Just as the Diggers took their theater into the streets, the Pranksters took this confrontational style that worked in their own group into a larger social setting—the Acid Test. When Timothy Leary proposed that the appropriate "set and setting" be established for an LSD trip, the Pranksters ridiculed that advice, explaining instead, "Let the setting be as unserene and lurid as the Prankster arts can make it and let your set be only what is on your . . . *brain*" (Wolfe 207). Thus, the "Prankster arts" would turn a large hall into a multimedia event, complete with lights, speakers, music, and collaborative art projects. Add LSD, and the Acid Test would provide participants with a space that overloaded the senses and challenged their conception of what reality might be.[11] In many ways, the Acid Test epitomizes sixties' heterotopian practice—gather as many people under as strange a set of conditions as possible, and see what emerges.

The Merry Pranksters envisioned the social moment as a loose collection of individuals, each following his or her own "trip." Collectivity was a matter of banding together for mutual support and challenge, rather than establishing strict criteria for membership. Kesey's Day-Glo International Harvester was a heterotopian space above all else—people got on, people got off, but like Foucault's sailing vessel, the bus kept moving down the highway. While the Pranksters promoted a completely decentralized experience, ironically the group was held together by Ken Kesey himself. On the most literal level, he provided the funds that allowed the bus to keep moving. More important than his role of financier, however, was that his guru status quelled dissension and allowed the group to function smoothly. Wolfe admiringly quotes Joachim Wach's work on the formation of religions, comparing Kesey favorably to the notion of the "founder": "The founder, a highly charismatic person, begins enlisting disciples. These followers become an informally but closely knit association, bound together by the new experience, whose nature the founder has revealed and interpreted" (Wolfe 114–15). Kesey discovered LSD while volunteering for studies conducted in Menlo Park, California, in 1959 (Perry 12). Proselytizing to his "disciples," Kesey quickly built up a following of like-minded individuals who saw the revolutionary potential in the drug.

While pecuniary generosity and a desire to convert are not faults, the reliance on a leader to corral group support raises the specter of totalitarianism. Postmodernism has rightly attacked the insistence modernism placed on highly charismatic leaders, who could easily become tyrannical to their subjects. In fact, according to Wolfe's account of the Prankster's cross-country bus trip, there was no small amount of paranoia concerning Kesey. He preferred a nondirective style of leadership, but nevertheless there was always a suspicion about his motives and control, especially when it came to the LSD itself, which Kesey strictly rationed. The consequence of relying too heavily on a leader is that the distance necessary for reflection on the situation oftentimes collapses. This was certainly the case with the Pranksters' relationship to Timothy Leary.[12] Deciding that the experiments Leary was conducting at his Millbrook, New York, estate were "one big piece of uptight constipation," they failed to see the many similarities between Leary and Kesey himself (Wolfe 95). Strict reliance on a leader to manufacture consent and quell dissension is certainly helpful in guiding the collective project. But its risks outweigh the benefits. Not only does it make group members open to possible exploitation but also without the leader there, where is the group to turn?

Kesey's band of Merry Pranksters and the Digger theater troupe were fairly successful incarnations of heterotopian social practice. But as group size increases, so do possible problems. Giving reign to the irrational works better in smaller groups, where something of an implicit trust exists among members who have proven themselves through a construction of close social bonds. Of course, enmity was amongst the ranks—when individuals set upon a path of full expression in every moment, there is bound to be friction. Confrontation expands exponentially, however, when group membership increases, and full vent to the irrational is tested.

There is no better example of this dilemma than in the various communal projects that were undertaken in the sixties. In his introduction to *The 60s Communes*, Timothy Miller observes that while "communal societies have long been an American cultural fixture," the sixties saw an explosion in attempts at communal life: "In a period of just a few years communal fever gripped the alienated youth of the United States—indeed, of the developed world—and thousands upon thousands of new communities were established" (xiii). Most of these communes did not last very long, and viewed in terms of longevity, they were failures. However, as Philip Abrams and Andrew McCulloch note in *Communes, Sociology, and Society*, "[t]he constant disintegration of communes, their very failure as societies, is itself evidence of their success as settings for the conquest of personal identity. . . . Communes are temporary refuges from society in which the individual can piece together a sufficiently integrated self to allow him to reenter society" (95). The commune as temporary refuge was a heterotopian space where individuals could attempt to live life in a fundamentally new manner. While their society may not have lasted forever, the gains made by the individuals within that society were carried with them into their future lives. As Miller notes, "[t]hose who lived the communal life have largely fond memories of it all, whether they still live communally or not" (233). The sixties' communal project was predicated on creating an open space where individuals could come and live their lives outside the confining social practices of dominant American society. The emphasis on free expression and self-discovery, in itself laudable, nevertheless embroiled many communes in the question of whether there should be a limit placed on an individual's right to his or her own behavior.

Beat and hippie heterotopias turn to the irrational in order to encourage the heterogeneity and playfulness that lead to a fuller conception of the individual. Irrationality's obverse, however, is less bright. While the Beats praised criminals like Herbert Huncke, New York hipster, as the epitomization of outsider status, in many communes such antisocial behavior ironically brought about the downfall of the society that sought to foster it. Miller notes that "communes found themselves with members or visitors who were unstable or threatening. . . . In several cases bad behavior on the part of the members—or, probably more frequently, of transient droppers-in at open communes—was the direct cause of a commune's demise" (178). The sixties' communes were oftentimes too heterogeneous for their own good. Dedicated to full expression and total inclusiveness, they failed to set even the most minimum limits that would serve to keep the most disturbed criminals and mental patients under control. Miller lists several instances when commune members ended up threatened, attacked, abused, raped, and, in some cases, even killed. Although these cases were admittedly both extreme and rare, they nevertheless point to a problem in fostering the free reign of irrational tendencies.[13]

In lesser cases, the focus on personal desire as a means to guide individual behavior oftentimes meant that commune members would avoid the necessary tasks that kept the commune functioning. Some communes had a leader who could get idlers working, others resorted to guilt and public pressure, but, Miller notes, "[a] great many communes that began without rules adopted, at a minimum, a work-rotation schedule, often with some kind of wheeled chart for assigning duties. Even the most anarchist commune could adopt an occasional rule that made inescapable common sense" (169). The goal of communal life in the sixties might have been complete heterogeneity and full expression of individuality, but the realities of social life demand that some structure be imposed. As increases in group size decreased the familiarity among members, the implementation of a rational plan could mean the difference between a functioning heterotopia and a chaotic assortment of recalcitrants.

Yet, even when the sixties' counterculture ran smoothly, basic inconsistencies within their program of heterogeneous openness still cast doubt on their enterprise. As with Burroughs, exclusionary practices plagued their movement. With respect to communes, Miller quotes Kit Leder, a former commune member: "Even though we had complete freedom to determine the division of labor for ourselves, a well-known pattern emerged immediately. Women did most of the cooking, all of the cleaning up, and, of course, the washing" (213). Miller goes on to admit that such gender-role bias was no worse than in larger society and that women were generally better off within the communal structure, but the fact remains that although communes might preach equality, their functioning was still predicated on gender-based models.

This assumption of gender roles likewise seeps into the counterculture's thinking about sexuality. Although an aura of transgressive permissiveness has built up around the sixties, the fact was that sexuality in this period was based on models imported from American society in general. William Gedney, a photographer who spent time among the crash pads of the San Francisco scene, notes, "Yet the scene is mostly straight boy-girl sex, the women fit more in the traditional mode of femininity, the men more masculine" (92). Basic gender distinctions are not challenged, and homosexuality, while not strictly forbidden, is conspicuously absent. Miller comments on this as well: "Even though the alternative culture certainly embraced tolerance of same-sex activity . . . it still took hippies and other cultural dissenters some time to cope with the change. Most of the communes of the time seem to have had a predominantly heterosexual orientation" (205). Homosexuals may have won advances in their fight for recognition and respect during the sixties, but the counterculture was only a distant ally in this fight.

The same can be said in regards to hippie relationships with African Americans. The gains made by Black Power in the sixties and early seventies had little to do with countercultural involvement. In fact, these two groups often engaged in adversarial relationships. The only time the unshakeable Merry Pranksters lose their "cool" in Wolfe's account is when they attempt to swim at a segregated beach outside of New Orleans and become surrounded by African Americans, dancing around their bus: "Even Kesey, who isn't afraid of anything, looks worried. 'We better get out of here,' Kesey says" (81). Ironically, they are saved by "white cops" who arrive to "break up the crowd" (81). The African Americans take over the Prankster "Movie," using their own tactics against them to "freak out" the Pranksters. Gedney traces this animosity to their difference in intentions: "Present day youth disenchantment with the middle-class hang-ups toward which the mass of Negroes are still striving" (91). The hippies wanted out of an established society strangling them with consumer goods and inauthentic lives; the "mass of Negroes," denied a share in America's postwar abundance, wanted to share in those comfortable lives.[14] Timothy Miller agrees: "African Americans were not for the most part attracted to the communal scene.... It may be that a group long familiar with poverty due to racism would not likely embrace voluntary poverty" (154). Despite their embrace of heterogeneous diversity, the counterculture was paradoxically not all that diverse. They may have advocated a policy of openness towards all individuals trying to fully explore their existential possibilities, but in reality, this exploration took place among the children of those already in power—the white, the straight, and the middle class.

Despite these problems, the counterculture's move to the heterogeneous signals a step in the right direction. Care must still be taken, however, to avoid falling into the abyss of irrationality that would create a heterogeneity incapable of doing meaningful social work. The hippies themselves were aware of this. As the rational underpinnings of the more-successful countercultural projects indicate, there must be more than a modicum of order if the collective is going to function usefully. But, sixties' heterotopian projects oftentimes overlooked this requirement of rationality to their detriment. What the collective experiments of the sixties' counterculture teach is that although the irrational may open up expressive possibilities, it is only through rational planning that such possibilities will continue to remain open at future dates for future members. The sixties lacked a practice. Of course, the moment itself may be sufficient for communality, and a heterotopia need not exist more than once. But for such group experiments to be repeatable, they must have a structure—otherwise, heterotopias are merely serendipitous, and social practice must simply hope that they appear instead of forcibly causing them to occur.

Miserable Picnic, Police State, Garden of Eden?

In the fall of 1965, Allen Ginsberg was in Berkeley, California, trying to organize a march to protest the war in Vietnam. The October march was halted at the Oakland border by police officers, and Ginsberg, along with Jerry Rubin, decided to plan another march in November. Unfortunately, the Hells Angels vowed to attack any protestors that got in their way. In response to this impasse, Ginsberg scheduled a public debate between the Vietnam Day Committee and the Angels that was held at San Jose State College. The results, according to Michael Schumacher, were less than encouraging: "The two-hour forum offered no solution to the dilemma. The people who turned out for the debate . . . jeered Ginsberg and other VDC members and egged on the motorcycle gang members" (454). This rational debate having failed, Ginsberg and Kesey tried to convince Sonny Barger, the leader of the Oakland chapter. Again, talks broke down. According to Ginsberg in "Coming to Terms with the Hell's Angels," everybody dropped acid, and then he started "chanting the *Prajnaparamita Sutra*, which was not an argument, simply a tone of voice from the abdomen. . . . Pretty soon we had a gang of about twenty people and then Neal and I think Kesey joined in—pretty soon the whole room was chanting" (*Deliberate Prose* 16). The Angels did not join the marchers, but they did not oppose them either, and the march went off as planned.

Ginsberg's ability to shift from the rational discourse of the public-debate format to the highly irrational form of LSD-inspired mantra in this anecdote is telling. The chanting of the *Prajnaparamita Sutra* wins over his adversaries and points to a new means of achieving collectivity. But it is equally important to note that Ginsberg remains flexible. He is not above using rational approaches to solve problems, and his strategies always include a planning stage that seeks to outline goals, even when these objectives are constantly open to negotiation as the moment unfolds. Although Ginsberg relies heavily on the irrational to underpin his social projects, he fuses them with enough rationality to construct a moment that has useful political consequences.

The mantra stand at the center of Ginsberg's social practice. The party with the Hells Angels not only allowed the Vietnam Day March to proceed as planned but also introduced Ginsberg to a technique that he would employ throughout his career as a social activist. Ginsberg writes, "I knew it was history being made. It was the first time in a tense, tight situation that I relied totally on pure mantric vocalization, breath-chant, to alleviate my own paranoia and anxiety, resolve it through breathing out long breaths" (*Deliberate Prose* 17). Ginsberg had discovered breath before—his poem "Howl" likewise relies on the human breath for its measure. As seen in chapter 3, Ginsberg's insistence on crafting poetry through an authentic body provides the basis for a deeper communication between reader and writer to be established. But here, Ginsberg takes bodily intersubjectivity even further by exploring the social possibilities that getting back to the body allows. In "Reflections on the Mantra," Ginsberg defines this practice: "Mantram (singular), mantra (plural) is a short verbal formula . . . which is repeated as a form of prayer meditation over and over until the thin-conscious association with meaning disappears and the words become pure physical sounds" (*Deliberate Prose* 148). Mantra go beyond rational discourse. For Ginsberg, getting back to the body means replacing a rationally based discourse, centered in the mind, with a mantric practice that utilizes the entire body to produce meaning.[15]

Ginsberg's return to the body has profound social consequences. Although mantric breathing is indeed a personal act, Ginsberg makes it clear that this technique quickly extends beyond the individual. As chapter 3 shows, Ginsberg believes that the physicality that mantra introduce into the breather can be transported to another. Ginsberg's text, infused with breath rhythms, literally alters the reader's body as the work unfolds. What Ginsberg has discovered is a means of totalization—mantra bind individuals together to form a group. Ginsberg discusses the social implications of mantra in his "CBC Broadcast on Mantra":

> Since there is so much fragmentation of my mind and everybody else's mind, I'm finding the body vibrations projected or articulated by soulful yogic devotional tearful chanting to be a communication that sometimes surpasses argumentative language, especially in public political circumstances like mass meetings, because that kind of chanting articulates the mutuality of soul and feeling. (*Deliberate Prose* 151)

Again is shown the dichotomy between a rationalized argumentative language that resides in fragmented minds and the body vibrations that exceed rational discourse. Common language distances individuals, while soulful yogic devotional tearful chanting has the ability to bring them together in a mutuality of soul and feeling. Ginsberg's mantric moment is composed of individuals finding each other through the investigation of mutually existing bodies—a heterotopia of breath.

The use of breath as the binding force for social collectivity helps Ginsberg to avoid the excesses that plague other heterotopian projects. Burroughs's attempts at totalization were fraught with either an exclusionary practice that limited access to his project or the threat of violence that stood behind the law. Mantra have neither. Since everyone breathes, access to social collectivity remains open to all. Totalization can thus occur without recourse to an othering that creates scapegoats and marginalized groups—no threat stands behind mantric practice. The only criterion for acceptance is a good faith desire to participate. Mantra allow for a heterogeneity essential for openness and inclusion that nevertheless relies on a system to support it. Everybody breathes differently, each with his or her own body, but everyone is united in his or her use of the mantra. Thus, Ginsberg's practice avoids the anarchic individualism characteristic of other sixties' social formations. Breath, as a function all share, can be brought together. But that does not mean that individuality is lost. Rather, the mantra chanter becomes simultaneously aware of both the world around his or her individual being and a larger connection to the group as a whole. The synchronization of breath that mantra create makes possible a collection of individuals who nevertheless occupy a unified collective. Mantra thus combine a universalism of breath that is necessary to achieve totality with the retention of heterogeneous, idiosyncratic experience that keeps individuals within the group open to the possibilities of the moment.

Mantra get bodies back to the present. In a 1969 *Playboy* interview, Ginsberg comments with regard to the Hare Krishna mantram that "you can use it as a vehicle for any emotion you're feeling, and also as a method to regulate breathing and point your consciousness to one place where your body is" (*Spontaneous Mind* 177). The importance of mantra as a body-based technique is that it situates the chanter in actual physical space. Directing consciousness to the one place where one's body is, mantra focus attention to the state of the moment, either as the emotion one is feeling, the literal position of the body, or both. The insistence on the Foucauldian "emplaced" body was an integral part of Beat and counterculture collectivist technique. As Ginsberg explains in an interview regarding the 1967 Gathering of the Tribes for a Human Be-In, "The whole notion of the Be-in was a Snyderesque meditation: be-in rather than a sit-in, to merely be there, like 'be here now.'" (*Spontaneous Mind* 453–54). A sit-in might gather support for a cause, but a be-in helped individuals to meditate on their own relationship to friends, emotions, and physical surroundings. Getting back to the body through mantric breathing has the curious result of planting the practitioner even more firmly within the world around them. The return to the moment that Ginsberg's mantric practice enacts sends it in two directions simultaneously—towards a sociality both previously unrealized and an intensification of the connection to surroundings already established.

Despite his insistence on mantra, Ginsberg does not entirely abandon the rational. In addition to calling a public forum to discuss issues with the Hells Angels, Ginsberg also wrote "Demonstration or Spectacle as Example, as Communication or How to Make a March/Spectacle" and distributed it as a handbill. "How to Make a March/Spectacle" was Ginsberg's attempt to organize the marchers beforehand so as to avoid direct confrontation with the police or the Angels—a "'pro-attestation,' testimony *in favor* of something" (*Deliberate Prose* 15). Ginsberg's advice leans heavily on the irrational, as the term "spectacle" in the title demonstrates. One suggestion calls for "small floats or replicas" made to resemble "Thoreau behind bars" or a "Dixieland Band float dressed as Hitler Stalin Mussolini" (12). But alongside such "theater," Ginsberg also places tactical recommendations designed to ensure the success of the march itself: "Front lines should be the psychologically less vulnerable groups. The Women for Peace or any other respectable organization, perhaps a line of poets and artists, mothers, families, professors" (11). Placing Women for Peace, mothers, and families in the front lines is not only good theater but good strategy because they are less likely to be provoked and less likely to be directly attacked. Ginsberg also advocates taping the march with several cameras in order to "combine for documentary film which could be used in court in case of legal hassles later, and also to circulate for propaganda and profits" (12). Here, Ginsberg not only plans for the event itself but anticipates possible outcomes and how they might be achieved. Camera footage might not only make a police officer think twice about using a club but also if violence does occur, it is documented for both propaganda and legal hassle purposes, as well as to financially support other demonstrations in the future. Only through judicious planning that leaves space for contingency and flux can a group hope to achieve ends that are themselves continually open to negotiation.

A paradigmatic example of Ginsberg-inspired collectivity occurs in the demonstration that took place outside the Chicago Democratic Convention in August 1968. Initially, Ginsberg conceived of the demonstration as a "Festival of Life" that would be a "continuation of the Human Be-in" (*Spontaneous Mind* 180). By bringing together various strands of the counterculture, Ginsberg hoped to create "a grass-roots planet academy festival where teeny-bopper poet-revolutionaries and technological prophets could be let loose to sing naked and exercise the great humane arts free—and blueprint a new nation" (180). Ginsberg viewed the event in terms of a Burroughsian academy, where the youth of the nation would have a chance to meet with elders in order to form a blueprint for a new nation. The demonstration would contrast a new means of social organization with the older, more ineffective variety of politics occurring within the walls of the convention. To achieve this goal, Ginsberg made several trips to Chicago in order to work with fellow organizers on planning the festival (Schumacher 507). Once he arrived in Chicago, however, Ginsberg quickly realized that such an event was impossible to stage in a city ready and eager to boil over into violence: "Few people realized what a locked-up police state Chicago was, just like Prague. . . . Police and City Hall break laws and lie. . . . Inside the convention hall it was rigged like an old Mussolini strong-arm scene" (*Spontaneous Mind* 181). In a situation in which the political machine was corrupt, and the police knew no bounds, Ginsberg's plans went from creating a utopian academy that would challenge the tenets of existing society to simply ensuring the safety of all those who attended the demonstration. Although Ginsberg himself admits in the *Playboy* interview that the festival "didn't come anywhere near its goal," remaining flexible in both means and ends allowed him to ensure a safer event that nevertheless retained a positive political impact (*Spontaneous Mind* 181).

As with any armed conflict, the Chicago demonstration was a battle over space. The Yippies envisioned holding the demonstration in Lincoln Park, since the space of the park represented free access and the right to assemble. Still, they worked within legitimate channels to secure this right. Hoffman declares in *The Realist*, "A permit is a definite contradiction in philosophy since we do not recognize the authority of the old order, but tactically it is a necessity" (Mailer, *Miami* 136). Ginsberg, too, tried to persuade the city to allow the gathering but "had no more luck than had Hoffman" (Schumacher 508). The permits were not granted. Protestors nevertheless kept arriving, and a showdown was inevitable. Ginsberg traces the ensuing violence to the city's refusal to allow people to sleep in the park: "'The streets belong to the people,' as Abbie Hoffman kept saying. 'The streets belong to whoever we say can have them,' the cops replied" (*Spontaneous Mind* 181–82). The park is highly charged space—whoever holds this symbol of the people has control over access to the public sphere. Such confrontations over what is considered the common space of the park were rampant in the sixties.

Ginsberg learned this lesson firsthand in Prague when university students crowned him King of May. His coronation took place in the public space of the park amidst laughter and celebration, but the party secretary for cultural affairs found the election of a homosexual foreigner unseemly and ordered him deposed (Schumacher 440). While park space may appear to belong to the people, the right to use these spaces must nevertheless be won from governments that have a vested interest in controlling their access. The park has all the makings of a "different space" that Foucault describes. It is an oasis within the city that has the potential to challenge the space around it. But whether the park will erupt into a heterotopia or remain circumscribed by the prevailing social forces is a difficult question. As Ginsberg himself rhetorically queries in his poem about the convention, "Grant Park: August 28, 1968": "Miserable picnic, Police State or Garden of Eden?" (*Collected Poems* 507).

Unsurprisingly, Ginsberg again relies on mantra to turn the confrontational space of the public park into a collective Garden of Eden. Mailer, relying on an account by Steven Lerner of the *Village Voice*, provides a glimpse into one such confrontation in a series of violent episodes that occurred over several days and nights: "Gas was everywhere. People were running, screaming, tearing through the trees. Something hit the tree next to me, I was on the ground again, someone was pulling me to my feet, two boys were lifting a big branch off a girl who lay squirming hysterically" (*Miami* 152). And this violence was only the beginning. By the end of the convention, police would run amok, beating reporters, hippies, and even elderly passersby alike. Amidst this violence, Ginsberg employs his mantra technique to calm himself and others, allowing for safe passage through the chaos:

> Clubbing would have seemed a curiously impertinent intrusion from skeleton phantoms—unreal compared with the natural omnipresent electric universe I was in; the cops would have been hitting only one form of electric. . . . I was in a dimension of feeling other than the normal one of save-your-own-skin. I was so amazed and gratified that I don't think I would have minded any experiment, including death. (*Spontaneous Mind* 179)

Here, mantra work on the personal level—removing the fear of death, they allow a physically threatened Ginsberg to remain poised and collected in a tense situation that threatened to explode into violence at any moment.

Once the fear of losing the ego-laden self is destroyed, the body becomes resilient, since attack from without only encounters one form of the electric. Extended to the level of the collective, mantra technique allows others to come together to form a space free from fear. Each protestor becomes empowered with the feeling Ginsberg describes, drawing from the collective to reinforce feelings of strength and well-being.

But Ginsberg's mantra technique works on another level as well. Not only does it calm its user during periods of stress but it can also have the same liberating effect on nonpractitioners. In response to interviewer Paul Carroll's objection that "the chanting, of course, didn't stop the violence," Ginsberg responds, "As a matter of fact, it did stop a lot of violence; it really calmed several scenes where police didn't have remote-control orders to attack" (*Spontaneous Mind* 183). Ginsberg's point is that if police have specific orders to attack, they will carry out those orders. But if they simply happen upon chanting protestors, the sound of OM turns the situation into a human-to-human encounter that leads to nonviolence. Yet, one thing is for certain, according to Ginsberg in his "Statement on 1968 Chicago Democratic National Convention": "When the arms of the police were filled with flowers and their mouths filled with AUM there was civic order" (*Deliberate Prose* 50). Ginsberg's mantra technique was successful. Schumacher relates an anecdote in which Ginsberg and fellow poet Ed Sanders "picked up fifteen to twenty others along the way, everyone humming 'OM,' Allen and Ed walking in the center of the line. They walked without incident to the Lincoln Park Hotel" (509). Here, mantra, far from being simply another antic of the countercultural left, demonstrate their pragmatic political effects.

The Festival of Life demonstration at the Chicago Democratic Convention was an ambiguous site of confrontation. The authorities did their best to turn Chicago into a police state, ensuring that Ginsberg's dream of a Burroughsian academy could only become a miserable picnic. But through a flexibility constantly adapted to meet the ever-changing demands of the moment, Ginsberg and his comrades were able to meet these challenges and to even profit through their adversity. On a personal level, Ginsberg's mantra technique was given new inspiration and reached new heights of understanding during this trying experience. Collective consciousness was also raised. Ginsberg explains that "what happened in Chicago is only one local example. Suddenly a lot of people have awakened and asked: What in hell am I doing on this poisoned planet, where everybody else is running around waving flags and shooting guns?" (*Spontaneous Mind* 188). Chicago stripped the government bare, revealing the brute force and coercion that lies behind supposedly democratic rule. This point was not lost on the "average," middle-class American as well. Viewing the spectacle through their televisions, many must have paused to consider why a government "by the people" must beat those very people into submission. And anybody who rode Ginsberg's om to safety would have realized that consciousness could be infinitely expanded. Judged from a reporter's account, a line or a circle of om chanters amongst a bevy of tear gas and mace hardly seems to qualify as a Garden of Eden. But from inside the group, mantra have the power capable of transforming violent chaos into an idyllic community of bodies breathing together the liberating sound of the universe om.

Conclusion
Making the Most of the Moment

The Beat message is simple—focus on the moment. Capturing that elusive moment, however, is a bit more complicated. We view the Beats through our nostalgia for a simpler time when right and wrong seemed much easier to define. The Beat quest for the moment becomes a marker that we use to gauge our own culture and actions. The Beats are no longer merely writers but cultural icons held up as models to emulate. This is why discussions about the Beats can so easily devolve into a type of hero worship that ceases to engage their ideas critically. Rather than succumbing to the mythos of the Beats as the standard for authenticity, this volume has instead tried to critique this assumption in order to reveal Beat concepts in all their complexity. Throughout their careers, the Beats grappled with questions of truth, meaning, and the relationship to the passing moment. An analysis of this struggle, with all of its inconsistencies and problems, provides a clearer picture of the Beats and their place in postwar America.

Given the intense media focus the Beats have received, it is easy to see how their lessons have become lost. Originally derided as dangerous and obscene, the Beats are now considered countercultural forebears. The Beats themselves were instrumental in this change. Tireless self-promoters, Beats like Burroughs and Ginsberg appeared on television shows, at benefits and readings, and even in advertisements in order to gain a larger share of media exposure. And their effort has not gone unrewarded. More Beat anthologies, biographies, and histories are in publication than ever before, and even their more obscure works have found their way into print. An academe that was generally hostile to the Beats has now imported many of their texts into the classroom, and critical studies of their works abound. If 1950s' society expressed shock and outrage at the Beats, today many view them as quintessential hipsters.

This change in attitude, however, does not mean that messages propagated by the Beats are finding more attentive ears. Many have argued that the commodification of the Beat ethos has left the style while removing the substance. Certainly, the early reception of the Beats bears this out—in the late fifties and early sixties being "Beat" oftentimes simply meant adopting a clichéd style and slang. Time may have tempered such overt misrepresentations, but even today, a knowledge and appreciation of who the Beats were does not necessarily translate into an understanding of what they said or why they said it. More exposure does not always equal a broader dissemination of Beat thinking. Rather than trying to relive the Beat moment in an uncritical way, we need to challenge it. If the Beats are to become more than just a lifestyle choice, we must critique the commonplaces that have built up around them by placing their work into larger social, theoretical, and historical contexts. Only then can an accurate picture of their contributions emerge.

For the Beats, the moment is where truth and authenticity reside. Getting back to this present means leaving the comforting assumptions of the world behind to embrace the unpredictability that arrives with each new instant. The questions that the Beats faced (and that drive this book) are, how much to control and how much to let go? To arrive at each new present without some sort of preparation risks getting subsumed in the maelstrom. But arriving fully prepared leaves no room for growth or change. The fundamental difficulty the Beats encounter is a hermeneutical one—how do we make the part relate to the whole? As the Beats experimented with new experiences, they were faced with the task of reconciling discrete moments with their desire that their project have a larger meaning. As shown in this volume, the Beats are at their most modern when they attempt to ground their experience in the stability of the past and most postmodern when they push themselves and their writing to the limit. The early postmodernism of the Beats lies somewhere between, in their almost paradoxical desire for new experience that still "makes sense" across space and time. When they do achieve this, it is because they find a means of judiciously blending past, present, and future in such a manner that distinctions among these temporalities evaporate, and new possibilities are revealed.

But we have also seen that the use of the moment is never uninterested. The instant is not sufficient to ensure freedom since the moment is itself subject to material constraints, as Baraka's vexed relationship to American social space and Beat women's difficulties in finding "free time" to write their experience make clear. And we must keep in mind that Beat formulations are not immune to their own prejudices and shortcomings, many of which were actually imported from the very society they criticized. We cannot accept the Beats at face value. Fortunately, a broadened Beat canon acts as a corrective by offering fresh perspectives on the established ways we have come to see the Beats. What women and African American Beats demonstrate is that conformity must be challenged on the material as well as mental levels. Rethinking how to live the moment does no good if those conceptions cannot be actualized in the real world. The moment of white male transcendence was actually informed—in very direct ways—by African American and feminist concerns, which cannot be dissociated in the reception of the Beats.

Ultimately, it is the Beat's position in American cultural history that makes their work so valuable. The Beats, as early postmodernists, are important transitional figures, providing a way of thinking how the modern became the postmodern in both cultural and literary-historical terms. In their attempt to span the divide between these two periodizing concepts, they reveal the strengths and weaknesses of both moments. Their attempts at synthesis, of course, do not always yield balanced results. Nevertheless, the Beat desire to live in the moment while trying to capture it for posterity reveals the tensions between a desire for the novelty experience brings and the need to retain some stability in an instable world. Capturing the change from the modern to the postmodern, the Beats provide a new conception of the moment.

Now that the period of "high" postmodernism witnessed in the 1980s and 1990s has itself become historical, we can look back in an attempt to understand the relationship among the modern, the postmodern, and the current cultural situation. The Beats offer more than just a reconsideration of the past. They also provide a lens through which to view our own cultural moment. The Beats' early postmodernism not only helps us to understand the development and climax of postmodernism at the end of the twentieth century but also the main question that the Beats faced—how much control and how much openness—is very much our own. Leaving the excesses of the "high" postmodern behind, we look forward into an unknown future. Like the Beats, we must struggle to retain the plurality and questioning attitude that postmodernism bequeathed us while we fight the desire to abandon ourselves to indeterminacy. For that project to succeed, we need to find a means of creating meaning. The Beat insistence that there is a contingent truth, fleeting but nonetheless total, provides such a starting point.

Notes

Introduction: Rethinking the Beats

1. The attention now paid to women Beats is long overdue. This trend started with anthologies such as Richard Peabody's *Different Beat* and Brenda Knight's *Women of the Beat Generation* that introduced readers to women Beat writers often elided from discussions of the Beats and whose works are unfortunately sometimes difficult to find. A collection of scholarly essays on Beat women has also appeared: Ronna C. Johnson and Nancy M. Grace's *Girls Who Wore Black*. Along with their collection of interviews, *Breaking the Rule of Cool*, Johnson and Grace's work forms the core of literary scholarship on women Beat writers. While I draw heavily on their work to position Beat women as precursors to a later second-wave feminism, I am more interested in what Beat women can tell us about the moment. Works that deal with race and the Beats are even scarcer. *Reconstructing the Beats*, edited by Jennie Skerl, aims to remedy this lack and includes several chapters on previously marginalized writers (including women). Manuel Luis Martinez's *Countering the Counterculture* castigates the Beats for a neoimperialistic relationship to Mexico that is "less aggressive" but "serves much the same psychic and nationalistic purposes as the Mexican-American War" (96). Amiri Baraka's literary success has meant more scholarly attention, though his period with the Beats still receives less interest. Lesser-known Beats like Bob Kaufman are not as fortunate because he is hardly recognized at all, though Maria Damon includes a chapter on Bob Kaufman in her study *The Dark End of the Street*. The omission of race is a problem for Beat studies, not only because African American Beats deserve to be heard but also because what they say illuminates issues that studies of the Beats often take for granted.

2. This trend can be seen in numerous studies. Perhaps the most noteworthy in this regard is Timothy S. Murphy's *Wising Up the Marks*. Murphy combines close readings of Burroughs's work with theoretical considerations, all the while keeping an eye open to cultural context. Oliver Harris's *William Burroughs and the Secret of Fascination* likewise uses theory to help explain Burroughs's early writing. And Skerl's *Reconstructing the Beats* sets itself the goal of "re-vision[ing] the Beats from contemporary critical perspectives" (2).

3. Here one immediately perceives a slippage in terms that plagues discussion of this topic. There is a difference between "modernity" and the "modern" on one side and "modernism" and the "modernist" texts it produces on the other. Modernity is rife with totalizing gestures—witness the appeal of the logic of marxism, which posits a complete and finalized utopian society at the end of teleological time. Yet, modernism and modernist texts that address the question of the "modern" likewise engage

in the logic of totality. While modernist texts, especially those within the rubric of the avant-garde, might appear to inhabit a postmodern world that derides meaning, the difference is one of intent. Even at their most fractured, modernist works still rely on a belief in the past greatness of grand narratives or in their possible resurrection. Postmodernism, however, sees even the nostalgia for a totalizing past as untenable.

4. Both Tony Trigilio's *"Strange Prophecies Anew"* and *Allen Ginsberg's Buddhist Poetics* argue for the importance of the postmodern in understanding Ginsberg's poetic strategies. In her article "'You're putting me on': Jack Kerouac and the Postmodern Emergence," collected in *The Beat Generation: Critical Essays*, Ronna C. Johnson characterizes Kerouac's work as *"pre*-postmodernist," positioning his work as a movement from the "ideologies of late high modernism to those of the nascent postmodern" (37). And Murphy's work subtitled *The Amodern William Burroughs*, claims that Burroughs's work lies somewhere beyond these two periodizing concepts. *Capturing Immediacy* extends this discussion in greater depth, believing that the modern-postmodern split is essential for an understanding of the Beats and their conception of the moment.

1. Being Present: Authenticity in Postwar America

1. The term "existentialism" is, of course, highly contested. The danger here is collapsing a disparate group of thinkers under one simple rubric. Unfortunately, such labels are necessary if larger trends are to be traced. Thus I follow Cooper in his assessment that what unites thinkers as diverse as Martin Heidegger, Maurice Merleau-Ponty, and Jean-Paul Sartre (and separates them from phenomenologists like Edmund Husserl) is their belief that "there is no prospect for examining 'meaning' and the 'meaning'-making activities of conscious beings unless these latter are taken to be practically and bodily engaged with the real world" (5–6). Dismissing Husserl's eidetic reduction, these philosophers believe that only through lived existence can one come to make sense of the world. Each philosopher has his or her own conception of authenticity. Heidegger conceives of it as an acknowledgment of death, Merleau-Ponty as an embodied existence in the world, and Sartre as a project freely chosen, but for all of these philosophers, what is most important is that the individual become fully aware of his or her existence within the present moment.

2. Beat scholarship is quick to echo these dismissive sentiments, when existentialism is discussed at all. In his 1990 study *The Daybreak Boys*, Gregory Stephenson claims that existentialists "share a central mood of despair and futility, a sense of repugnance with the body, an atmosphere of tragic tedium, and an emphasis upon negation and emptiness. They also share an imagery of confinement and constriction, of inertia and immobility" (11). By contrast, for Stephenson, Beat work is characterized by "vigor and energy, by sensuality and by spiritual aspiration" (11). Over a decade later, John Lardas's book *Bop Apocalypse* provides a similar binary, arguing that "the Beats' religious individualism, then, was not an existentialist opposition of the self versus society but one of self in service of society. Its focus was on somatic connection rather than intellectual exposition, apprehension and physical communion rather than abstract representations" (97). These contentions do possess some merit. Sartre, for instance, claims in *Being and Nothingness* that "conflict is the original meaning of being-for-others" (475), and Martin Heidegger struggles to come to terms with the other in *Being and Time*. Death is a concern for all of these writers, as well as the angst associated with freedom

of choice. But all of these topics are addressed throughout the Beat canon. What these critics are relying on, then, is ready-made notions of existentialism that are derived from cultural assumptions about a phenomenon divorced from the literature itself.

3. Mailer, in "The White Negro," echoes Holmes's denouncement of Sartre, claiming that "to be a real existentialist (Sartre admittedly to the contrary) one must be religious" (341). Sartre is invariably the lightning rod for such attacks on the spiritual bankruptcy of existentialism. Kerouac concurs in his essay "What Am I Thinking About," citing Heidegger as the "Founder of Existentialism, never mind your Sartre" (*Good Blonde* 188).

4. Heidegger's project is always concerned with the question of being but undergoes a shift with the publication of "On the Essence of Truth" in 1930. Before this "turn," Heidegger focuses on Dasein as a means of understanding how we know the world. Although Dasein is more of a "happening" than an object, Heidegger's work, at this point in his career, has a major impact on the sort of questions existentialism is raising. After this "turn," Heidegger examines the history of being and human existence becomes less of a focus. I am following Heidegger's earlier work here because it offers a discussion of being that sheds light on Beat attempts to live authentically in the passing moment.

5. Consider, too, the function of debt in postwar consumer society. Abstracting the consumer out of the present and into the sort of timeless future that Heidegger describes, the debtor fixates on the *marginal*—the next bill, the next installment, the next purchase. In *Time Passages*, George Lipsitz notes that "mortgage debt accounted for just under 18% of disposable income in 1946, but it grew to almost 55% by 1965. To ensure the eventual payment of current debts, the economy had to generate tremendous growth and expansion, further stimulating the need to increase consumer spending" (47). This reliance on debt had disturbing consequences. First, it limited the debtor's options. With house and car payments to meet, the consumer of the fifties was less likely to engage in the sort of rebellious activities that Kerouac and the Beats advocated. Debt keeps the worker at the machine, forcing him or her to produce if he or she is to meet payments. Even more troubling, however, is that debt creates a mindset that forces the debtor to constantly worry about tomorrow. Rather than simply fulfilling today's needs, the consumer must also fret about whether he or she will meet the financial demands of the next week, the next month, or the next year.

6. Marxism, like existentialism, has experienced a difficult reception in Beat scholarship. Although he concedes that the Beats were against "materialist values," Lardas claims that "their ranting, however, was not Marxist-inspired diatribe" (69). Not only does Lardas seek to distance Beat polemics from the taint of ideology but also his use of the term "diatribe" lends an air of pessimism and bitterness to marxist critique reminiscent of his attacks on existentialism. Such dismissals are interesting because marxist thought can be seen throughout the Beat canon. Ginsberg and Baraka both had Marxist leanings, and while Kerouac and Burroughs denounce it, their antimarxist stance owes more to a postwar suspicion of any totalizing ideology than an outright attack on marxism proper. According to Graebner, the notion of intellectual freedom was a rallying cry in postwar America: "[T]he growing attachment to freedom seemed a reasoned response to the cold, rigid, inflexible, overbearing, and dangerous ideologies that seemed to have got the world into so much trouble" (140–41). A number of reasons for marxism's demise can be pointed to in postwar America—Stalinist

purges, the Nazi-Soviet pact of 1939, the need to support America in World War II, the emergence of the cold war, and McCarthyism were all factors in the gradual rejection of the communist party in America. But by far, the leading cause was the rejection of any sort of reductively totalizing regime, with capitalism being just as open to attack as communism. The response to such programmatic thinking had to be an insistence on the personal, the novel, and the spontaneous. For a more informative account of marxism's role in Ginsberg's work, see Ben Lee's fine essay "'Howl' and Other Poems: Is There an Old Left in These New Beats?"

7. There were, of course, exceptions. Women had entered the workforce in large numbers during the war, and not all of them returned to the home when it was over. Moreover, as Leila Rupp and other historians demonstrate, for women of lower economic backgrounds and nonwhite racial identities work was often a necessity. But for white, middle-class women (including Beat women), the pressures to get married and establish a household were enormous.

8. Compare this to Ginsberg's "Mind Is Shapely Art Is Shapely" or "First Thought Best Thought" and William Carlos Williams's "No ideas but in things." These three poetic statements form a continuum, from di Prima's mantra in which the poet is determined from the outside by social necessity, to Williams's in which intervention occurs to the degree that a "thing" is culturally embedded, to Ginsberg, who wants to retain complete subjective determination of the artistic product.

9. Here, the focus is on the railroad, but this critique holds equally true for Kerouac's road travels. Whether he is driving, hitchhiking, or riding the bus, Kerouac must rely on the American highway infrastructure built by President Dwight D. Eisenhower after the war. This system is underwritten by a whole network of codes—one must pay for gas, adhere to traffic laws, and literally remain "on the road" itself. Kerouac will challenge all of these conventions in his quest for spatial freedom. But in the end, even novels like *On the Road* must be viewed with an eye towards the inherent limits of spatial and temporal rebellion in postwar America.

10. Critics debate the influence of his ancestry on Kerouac. Some believe that his French Canadian roots serve to marginalize him, and others point to his Catholicism as stigmatic. Yet, neither of these carries with them the outward signs such as skin color that mark ethnic minorities like African Americans.

11. The railroad did offer employment opportunities for African Americans, most notably as porters. Still, African Americans were relegated to service positions aboard the trains—they were seldom its engineers.

2. The Visionary State: Uniting Past, Present, and Future

1. Critics, too, have seized on this aspect of Beat literature. Regina Weinreich, in her study *The Spontaneous Poetics of Jack Kerouac*, focuses on Kerouac's epiphanies as a site for his continual remaking of myth. Ben Giamo's *Kerouac, the Word and the Way* is subtitled *Prose Artist as Spiritual Quester*. Kerouac's "spiritual quest," Giamo writes, was "for the ultimate meaning of existence and suffering and the celebration of joy in the meantime—when you can get it, and by all means get IT" (xiv). Giamo goes on to quote Kerouac's description of the alto man in *On The Road*: "The model seems clear enough: to know time is to escape its structure through improvisation, then the secret note hit and the moment enlivened. . . . One only has to think of Coltrane's method and sound. There you have it, and—once you do—IT carries you away" (35).

John Lardas's *Bop Apocalypse* discusses the visionary moment in terms of Oswald Spengler. Further examples could be cited, but these suffice to demonstrate the importance of visionary experience in understanding Beat conceptions of the moment.

2. As many commentators note, a major difficulty in discussing periodizing concepts such as modernism is deciding which texts are paradigmatic. Spanos's target here is "New Criticism, which has its source in the iconic art of symbolist modernism" (22). Thus, Spanos is willing to admit many modernist texts under his postmodern (what I am calling "early postmodern") rubric.

3. The literature of postmodernism is vast, and Ermarth is offering only one variant. Deleuze and Guattari offer another when they introduce the notion of the "schizophrenic" as a model for a new subjectivity. As Daniel W. Smith notes in his introduction to *Essays Critical and Clinical*, their aim is to "describe schizophrenia in its *positivity*, no longer as actualized in a mode of life but as the *process* of life itself" (xxi). Other examples could be adumbrated, but the point here is that despite individual differences in conceptions, the decentering of the subject that takes place in postmodern thought goes beyond that offered in the early postmodern and certainly exceeds that of the modern.

4. What is the relationship between the Black Mountain poetics of Olson and the Beat poetics of Kerouac? According to Belgrad, "The relation of beat poetry to Charles Olson's projective verse reflects the semiautonomous development of a common aesthetic" (199). While Olson and Kerouac had heard of one another, their theories of poetics developed separately. Nevertheless, their manifestoes sound eerily similar. In "Projective Verse," Olson claims, "Objectism is the getting rid of the lyrical interference of the individual as ego, of the 'subject' and his soul" (*Collected Prose* 247), while in "Essentials of Spontaneous Prose," Kerouac admonishes, "If possible write 'without consciousness in semi-trance'" and to never "afterthink except for poetic of P.S. reasons" (*Good Blonde* 70). Differences between these writers do exist, but for the purposes of theorizing the early-postmodern moment in literary and cultural history, the claims made on Olson's behalf are applicable to the Beats as well.

5. For Janine Pommy Vega, openness is earned through the body. In *Tracking the Serpent*, she presents her philosophy of trekking as a series of rules. Rule number 5: "Make much of the view from any rest stop. After the long march of stones on the ground, the opening out over distance is a benediction, and deserves your gratitude" (106). The "march of stones" becomes the penance for the "benediction" of the vista— an arduous journey gives way to a spectacular vision that is the reason for the trek. Rule number 3 provides a similar message: "Acceptance of an uphill climb" leads to a "readiness to accept whatever happens" (106). Physical exhaustion breaks down preconceived barriers, leaving the trekker receptive to new experience. The role that the body plays in Beat thinking is explored in chapter 3.

6. Heidegger's relationship to the political is a particularly thorny issue. In *The Other Heidegger*, Fred Dallmayr uses Heidegger's later works to defend Heidegger from attacks on his association with Nazism: "While opposed to political atomism or radical individualism, Heidegger at the same time is averse to any type of collectivism, particularly since the latter is basically only a disguised subjectivism" (63). Here, nationalism is involved in a "covering up" of being that keeps Dasein from discovering its true potential for selfhood. According to Dallmayr, "Heidegger refuses to identify *polis* either with state (*Staat*) or city-state (*Stadt*), preferring instead its translation

as 'place.' . . . [P]olis is not a stable habitat or a positive-empirical arrangement but rather the arena of the perennial contest between being and nothingness, life and death" (65). The "national narrative of repetition through struggle" that Osborne speaks of, then, might best be thought of not as a particular political formation but as an ongoing, collective struggle that must be continually reperformed if authenticity is to be achieved.

7. Yet, at the same time that Ginsberg speaks of "cosmic consciousness," he likewise dons an American hat in his celebrated "Uncle Sam" poster. Like Dallmayr's Heidegger, the Beats locate "nation" not in an ossified political form but in an ever-repeated interaction among time, space, and human beings. For the Beats, America resides in a tradition of poets, thinkers, and revolutionaries whose conceptions of America never really attained national acceptance. What, then, is America's place in the visionary? On the narrative level, it is everywhere—the Beats are Americans, so it makes sense that their visions contain elements that are American by default. But America remains a privileged site for cosmic consciousness to occur, despite repressive social formations that must constantly be combated.

8. This raises the question of whether jazz is truly available to white Beats such as Kerouac. If the jazz experience is fundamentally racially determined, then what Kerouac is experiencing is a desire for a transcendence that only African Americans can truly achieve. As Baraka queries in *Black Music*, "What is a white person who walks into a James Brown or Sam and Dave song? How would he function? What would be the social metaphor for his existence in that world? What would he be doing?" (187). For Baraka, black music builds an atemporal space dependent on racial considerations. Such an edifice is designed to house black people, and the best that a white person such as Kerouac can hope for is to be invited in as a temporary guest.

9. In "'All things are different appearances of the same emptiness': Buddhism and Jack Kerouac's Nature Writings," Deshae E. Lott argues that "the meaning he derives [from nature] returns again and again to the Buddhist supra rational void where everything is everything and where everything is empty" (183). Lott argues that Kerouac's view of sunyata "gives him new eyes when there's nowhere new in America to go," but such a declaration sounds more like escapism than exploration (183). David Sterritt, in his book *Screening the Beats: Media Culture and the Beat Sensibility*, provides a rather terse chapter in which he draws some simple parallels among Kerouac's Buddhist sunyata, cinema, and dreams. For a discussion of sunyata in Ginsberg's work, see Tony Trigilio's "'Will You Please Stop Playing with the Mantra?' The Embodied Poetics of Ginsberg's Later Career," collected (along with Lott's article) in editor Jennie Skerl's *Reconstructing the Beats*.

3. Immanence and Transcendence: Reich, Orgasm, and the Body

1. Are we talking about literal or figurative bodies here? For the Beats, these two levels are intertwined. Their writing was very much derived from their lives, and they expected lives to be changed through an encounter with their works. Consider di Prima's disclaimer to an admonition she made in her *Memoirs of a Beatnik*. In this 1969 novel, Di Prima advises women to "get welfare, quit working, stay home, stay stoned, and fuck" (76). Yet, in a footnote written in 1988, she goes on to declare, "Please, folks, this is not, repeat is not an encouragement to avoid condoms now. Flirting with pregnancy is one thing: having a kid can be a great celebration of life; flirting with

AIDS is something else: is simply courting a quick and ugly death" (74). Di Prima's discussion of the orgasmic moment is not simply representational but enters into the social (or at least attempts to do so) with political force. Thus the disclaimer—di Prima realizes that Beat works are not read simply as stories but as accounts of lived experience that provide readers with recipes for living.

2. The debate over how to view sexuality in the Victorian period is vexed. In his introduction to *The History of Sexuality*, Michel Foucault takes issue with the belief that sexuality was repressed in the Victorian era, instead claiming that the "nineteenth century and our own have been rather the age of multiplication: a dispersion of sexualities, a strengthening of their disparate forms, a multiple implantation of 'perversions.'" (37). Paul Robinson, however, challenges Foucault by making a distinction between discourse and practice: "There is a difference between talking and doing, at least when it comes to sex. Moreover, even at the level of talk, surely it matters what exactly is being said, and the Victorian discursive explosion propounded such notions as that masturbation led to insanity, that women were asexual, and that sodomites ought to be hanged" (*Modernization of Sex* xi). In fact, all of the sources used in this chapter on the history of sexuality acknowledge their debt to Foucault, then continue to equate the Victorian period with sexual repression.

3. However, "orgasmic potency" is not always easy to achieve in practice. Michel Cattier notes in *The Life and Work of Wilhelm Reich* that Reich had to defend his theory from the simple observation that many neurotics were capable of orgasm. Thus, Reich distinguished between good orgasms and bad. As Cattier explains, "In none of his patients was there any hint of involuntary behaviour or loss of alertness during the sexual act. . . . This is what Reich called 'orgastic impotency'" (29–30). It is not enough to have an orgasm—the orgasm must involve a complete surrender for the act to have its full consequence. As Reich himself explains, "People confuse 'fucking' with the loving embrace" (*Selected Writings* 27).

4. Deleuze and Guattari are most interested in Reich's "middle period" when the thinker was attempting a synthesis of Freud and Marx, since their own project is an attempt to understand the link between desire and the social. Interestingly, this is exactly the period that the anti-marxist Burroughs deplores: "Reich's social and political theories, and his polemics, bore me" (Lardas 278). As for the other major Freud-Marx synthesizer, Herbert Marcuse, Deleuze and Guattari have this to say: "Reich was the first to raise the problem of the relationship between desire and the social field (and went further than Marcuse, who treats the problem lightly)" (*Anti-Oedipus* 118).

5. Nor is he the only Beat writer to address this question. In *Gay Sunshine Interview*, Ginsberg relates that "basically the bias, if any, in yoga is toward chastity, retention of sperm. Sperm is art, poetry, music, yoga. Sperm is *Kundalini,* serpent power. . . . Retention of sperm is apparently one of the basic understandings of some forms of yoga" (37). Again, once sperm is yoked to a vitalist essence, the excretion of semen is rendered as loss. If Ginsberg is correct, the art of maintaining this sperm is yoga itself. Ginsberg also explores the opposite extreme: "It's an important human experience to relate to yourself and others as a hunk of meat sometimes. That's one way of losing ego, one holy divine yoga of losing ego: getting involved in an orgy and being reduced to an anonymous piece of meat, coming, and recognizing your own orgiastic anonymity" (34). Catapulting flesh into the mass, the orgy decentralizes individuality and disembodies the orgiast.

6. Numerous examples of Beat misogyny from various authors could be adumbrated, but one example will suffice. In *The Subterraneans*, Kerouac works out a "schedule" that allows him to have sex with Mardou while attending to his writing. Kerouac muses, "'This is the cleverest arrangement I ever made, why with this thing I can live a full love-life,' conscious of Mardou's Reichian worth, and at the same time write those three novels" (105). Mardou's Reichian worth makes her a valuable asset—she allows Kerouac his weekly transcendence while allowing him to continue his more intellectual novel-writing. Thus, he arrives at her home "carrying again my big forward-looking healthybook Reich and ready at least to 'throw a good one in her' in case its all bound to end this very night" (105). One wonders if Kerouac has read Reich at all. Of course, *The Subterraneans* is intended as a confessional novel where Kerouac bares the less-than-flattering details of his life. But Kerouac's treatment of Mardou is indicative of a general Beat trend towards viewing women as an instrument rather than an end. Mardou is there for Kerouac to achieve his transcendent orgasmic moment. The only difficulty for him is how to sustain her orgasmic possibility with the least amount of entanglements possible.

4. Recording the Moment: The Role of the Photograph in Beat Representation

1. Several commentators on Beat literature have noted the disjunction between participation and recording. Michael Davidson, in *The San Francisco Renaissance*, uses it as a guide for thinking about Beat literature: "This disparity between participation and reflection animates much Beat writing. . . . I see this tension as both a limitation and a generative element of Beat writing" (66). Through an analysis of Kerouac, Ginsberg, and poet Michael McClure, Davidson arrives at the conclusion that such writing works only when authors are aware of the gap itself. Davidson believes "the desire to make the poem transparent before the world often leaves the poet without grounds for adequate self-reflection. In their best work, the Beat writers were aware of the dangers of such participation and made that a generative element of their work" (93). Tim Hunt has a slightly different view. In *Kerouac's Crooked Road*, he draws on Kerouac's discussion of his "sketching" technique to declare that "value or analysis is no longer that which the writer holds and then sets out to embody, but rather that for which the writer is searching in the mediation which is the act of writing" (124). Here, writing is not a means of recording the present but of disclosing it—writing makes meaning in the present. Hunt, however, remains reticent on the ultimate implications of such fiction. He observes that "the self remains finally in part unknowable, an experience of uncertainty, but Duluoz and Kerouac come to accept this as the necessary price of the inner world's vitality" (250). Kerouac uses his imagination to build a new self in every new present, but this continual repetition leaves him groundless. The act of imagination supplants life lived in the present, and Kerouac must become a constant producer of a myth to provide meaning to his life. The critic Maria Damon also addressed this split in an unpublished talk given at Wayne State University. Damon read Bob Kaufman's poem "Bagel Shop Jazz" into this very register, noting that Kaufman's personality is divided in the poem—he is both the participant in the scene as well as its commentator. Damon traced this duality to the psychological alienation fostered by cold-war mentalities that presaged the movement to full-scale schizophrenia in the later-postmodern period, as well as to Kaufman's dual racial identity as both Jewish and African American.

2. The processes used to attain the moment are as varied as the photographers that employ them. Cartier-Bresson argues for a definition of photography as "the simultaneous recognition, in a fraction of a second, of the significance of an event as well as of a precise organization of forms which give the event its proper expression" (42). Alfred Stieglitz is equally enigmatic. He counsels patience, waiting for "the moment in which everything is in balance; that is, satisfies your eye" (Newhall 153). Interestingly enough, Robert Frank has a slightly different approach. According to Sontag, Frank looks for what he terms the "in-between moments" when the world is in disequilibrium and off-guard (121). And here is Andy Warhol's philosophy, which despite its characteristic style sounds eerily like Frank: "My idea of a good picture is one that's in focus and of a famous person doing something unfamous. It's being in the right place at the wrong time" (*Photography* 33). While moments may be countless, they are not all created equal.

3. This is likewise seen in Kerouac's description of his trip to Florida with Robert Frank. In his essay "On the Road to Florida," Kerouac praises Frank's photographic ability, then comments, "I wished I'd have had a camera of my own, a mad mental camera that could register pictorial shots, of the photographic artist himself prowling about for his ultimate shot" (*Good Blonde* 26). Kerouac's desire to capture Frank is not in the service of a metacomment on photography, as can be seen in Sherrie Levine's postmodern photographic appropriations of earlier Edward Weston prints. Rather, Kerouac is interested in gaining a better hold on Frank himself and the ineffable quality that makes his photography so compelling.

4. This desire for an endpoint aligns the Beats with many avant-garde filmmakers of the postwar period. In *Visionary Film*, P. Adams Sitney points out that Warhol deflated many of the assumptions held by filmmakers of the time. Warhol's "*Sleep* was no trance film or mythic dream but six hours of a man sleeping" (371). This insistence on surface content ran counter to theorists like Stan Brakhage and Kenneth Anger, who, like the Beats, were more concerned with the interiority of experience. Thus, as Sitney makes clear, "The great challenge, then, of the structural film became how to orchestrate duration; how to permit the wandering attention that triggered ontological awareness while watching Warhol films and at the same time guide that awareness to a goal" (374). By focusing on end results rather than simple process, these filmmakers sought to shift attention from the flatness of the filmic image to the subjectivity of viewer response.

5. Kerouac would have been familiar with Baudelaire through William S. Burroughs, who kept a copy of the poet's work in the apartment that Kerouac frequented (Charters, *Kerouac* 56). Proust was an even more direct influence on Kerouac. In a letter to his friend Neal Cassady, he describes his writing as "a kind of special stylized Proust-like but American private monotone, modern Proust indeed" (*Selected Letters* 473). Bergson was most likely unknown to Kerouac.

6. In a translator's note, Brian Massumi cautions that the term "affect" as deployed by Deleuze and Guattari does not denote "a personal feeling" but rather "is an ability to affect and be affected. It is a prepersonal intensity corresponding to the passage from one experiential state of the body to another and implying an augmentation or diminution in that body's capacity to act" (xvi). What we are witnessing here, then, is less a personal sentiment than an interaction between bodies, both mental and physical.

7. This difference is likewise seen in Kerouac's attempt to retrace his bloodline back to Europe. Thus, in his 1965 novel *Satori in Paris*, Kerouac explains, "I had come to

France and Brittany just to look up this old name of mine which is just about three thousand years old and was never changed in all that time" (72). This insistence on genealogy and the truth of the past in the present engages in just the sort of "skeletonization" that Cassady warns against. Deleuze and Guattari also find this aspect of Kerouac the least praiseworthy, commenting in *A Thousand Plateaus* that Kerouac's quest for ancestry embodies the sort of arborescent structure that their rhizomatic method is dead set against: "America is a special case. Of course it is not immune from domination by trees or the search for roots. This is evident even in the literature, in the quest for a national identity and even for a European ancestry or genealogy (Kerouac going off in search of his ancestors)" (19). Becoming does not seek to anchor being in the past but to send it off into a new trajectory in the present.

5. Getting Together: Heterotopia and the Moment as a Social Site

1. Perhaps the terms "unreason" or "unrational" might be better employed here, since "irrational" has pejorative medical connotations that are by no means to be associated with the postmodern.

2. While Marcuse's insistence on irrationality marks a postmodern trend in his thinking, his corpus should not be considered postmodern in its entirety. In the text of most concern here, *Eros and Civilization*, Marcuse attempts a fusion of Karl Marx and Freud, two thinkers whose works both epitomize the modernist drive towards totality. Marcuse's search for an uncontaminated, "authentic" inner nature is likewise at odds with postmodernism's skepticism about untainted origins.

3. The trend in more-recent Beat scholarship is to view the aesthetic as inextricably bound up in questions of the social. As Belgrad makes clear, "The social significance of spontaneity can be appreciated only if this aesthetic practice is understood as a crucial site of social work: that is, as a set of activities and texts engaged in the struggle over meanings and values within American society" (1). Beat writing, so the argument goes, does cultural work—once the text begins to circulate in society, its impact quickly exceeds its original reception. While this conception of the centrality of the aesthetic is indeed both correct and relevant, here the focus is on more-direct acts and formulations of the social. It is not simply that Beat texts contribute to the "struggle over meanings and values" but that they offer distinct ways of reenvisioning the social that deserve closer scrutiny.

4. The idea of a throwaway myth helps in understanding the early postmodernism of Burroughs's project. While the wild boys craft grand narratives to guide their functioning as a social unit, these myths are only temporary. Consistent with heterotopian social practice, the wild boys retain an organizing principle only long enough to achieve their goal, then the myth is abandoned, lest it become tyrannical. Murphy himself describes this process in terms of "amodernity":

> Amodernism, like the reflexive postmodernism we already recognize, accepts the failure of its modernist ends (for instance, the resolution of gender, class, and ethnic conflicts and the concomitant spiritual unification of society) and means (for instance, the regeneration of myth as a centering structure), without taking the additional step of homogenizing all remaining difference. (2)

The point here is that while amodernity rightly rejects appeals to any unifying grand narrative, it still believes, unlike postmodernism, that possibilities do exist for social amelioration. Murphy's term is congruent with our use of the rubric "early postmodernism," both describing a situation in which two periodizing concepts are each mined for their possibilities—modernism for its ability to unify and direct and postmodernism for its ability to incorporate difference.

5. The cut-ups of Burroughs's Nova trilogy likewise represent an attempt to break free from the straightjacket of control. But as with his earlier works, Burroughs fails in this trilogy to reach notions of collectivity that have affirmative content. Following Count Alfred Korbyzki, Burroughs sees such "linguistic control" as residing at the physical, bodily level, and, thus, freedom from "syntax" becomes tantamount to freedom from an oppressive corporeality. But such a conception is more in line with the discussions of authenticity presented in the first chapter of this work. The Nova trilogy is not creating a utopian scheme that can attain real-world efficacy but is instead offering a range of techniques useful in countermanding the inauthenticities of a language-plagued world.

6. The masculine is used here because Burroughs conceives of the Western Lands in a purely male register: "The Western Lands is the natural, uncorrupted state of all male humans. We have been seduced from our biologic and spiritual destiny by the Sex Enemy" (75). Again, women are locked out of the Burroughs utopian scheme, denigrated as sex enemies who are in direct conflict with the attainment of the Western Lands seen as the goal of every male human.

7. This blanket statement fails to do justice to the myriad groups that formed during this tumultuous period in American cultural history. Student groups, for instance, were often involved in serious political demonstrations organized around rational principles of rebellion. Nevertheless, the characterization of the sixties as a time when free vent was given to a wide range of behavior is still apt.

8. Besides being a tribute to their forebears, the name "Diggers" is also a play on the vernacular of the time. "To Dig," according to Burroughs's introduction to the original version of *Junkie*, means "to size up." Kerouac, Ginsberg, and Neal Cassady use the verb in a less-invidious manner as a means of describing a certain type of understanding that gets developed when one individual attempts to place themselves in the position of another. "Digging" can also involve a moment of comprehension, as when one fully realizes the implications or relevance (usually cosmic) of a given situation. "Digging," in all its facets, was integral to the Diggers' project, and it is difficult to imagine the double meaning of the term being lost on them.

9. In "Coming to Terms with the Hell's Angels," Ginsberg, too, has recourse to the image of theater: "Our march had to get its theater together, just as the police and the government did. I think that was the beginning of our realization that national politics was theater on a vast scale, with scripts, timing, sound systems. Whose theater would attract the most customers, whose was a theater of ideas that could be gotten across?" (*Deliberate Prose* 18). With the advent of mass media, revolution was not simply a matter of empowering the disenfranchised but making the idea of rebellion marketable for public consumption.

10. The Diggers were ferocious in their attacks on the flightiness and backsliding they saw occurring around them. The LSD-abusing "tripsters" came in for special attack as unwelcome distractions from the tasks at hand. Discussing the creation of a "Free City Garage and Mechanics," one pamphlet cautions that "the garage should be large enough and free of tripsters who only create more work for the earnest me-

chanics" (Digger Archives). Such dismissals illustrate that although they believed in the life-activating potentials of LSD, the Diggers could still focus on the routine jobs that needed to be done. According to Perry, the Diggers also had a "distaste for the grandstanding habits of the Berkeley left" and were "generally hostile to the *Oracle*," a San Francisco-based counterculture publication (103, 111). Such attacks earned the Diggers a deserved reputation as the conscience of Haight-Ashbury.

11. The Acid Test also highlights the counterculture's reliance on technology as a means to attain the utopian state. A poster for the 1966 "Trips Festival" declares that this culmination of previous Acid Tests will include, among other things, "members of the s.f. tape music center. big brother & the holding company rock'n'roll. the don buchla sound-light console. overhead projection . . . roy's audiooptics. movies. ron boise & his electric thunder sculpture" ("Hipstory"). The hippies went beyond the simplicity of the Beat jazz band, incorporating the newest and most-expensive electronic equipment that America had to offer. As Kumar remarks in *Utopia and Anti-Utopia in Modern Times*, "The utopian current of the 1960s flowed largely within a tide of technological optimism. . . . Technology—especially the electronic technology of television and hi-fi—was an essential part of the counter-culture; and it was also the essential basis of the utopian vision of Brown and Marcuse, as of the May 1968 radicals in France" (402). In Marcusean terms, technology needed to be liberated from its role in producing "surplus repression" and channeled into uses that were more playful and more life-sustaining.

12. Another is an amusing anecdote relating to a commune in Tennessee known as "The Farm." Stephen Gaskin, a faculty member at San Francisco State College, was the leader of a group of hippies who decided to set up a collective in 1971. According to Timothy Miller, "Some communes, especially religious ones, had charismatic leaders whose authority was the basis of all structure. At the Farm the charismatic authority of Stephen Gaskin was for a time nearly absolute" (167). This dominance was so complete that a former member relates that he became reluctant to confront Stephen with his lack of musical ability: "Stephen became the second drummer in our band. I saw that he wasn't a fully enlightened drummer. . . . I couldn't find ways in the most simple musical terms to explain to him how to correct it. . . . I would just get choked up" (167). Gaskin was not a poor leader, but the aura that had built up around him made it difficult for his followers to view matters objectively at times. For an account of countercultural terrorism in the Buddhist community, see Trigilio's *Allen Ginsberg's Buddhist Poetics*. Trigilio discusses an incident that occurred at a seminary retreat in Snowmass, Colorado, where the poet W. S. Merwin and his companion Dana Naone were forcibly "stripped of their clothing to teach a lesson on the naked vulnerability of mind" (157).

13. The poster child for such irrational antics was and is Charles Manson. For the "square" world, Manson encapsulated the dangers that irrationality held for society. Here, irrationality meant the lawless state of anarchy where every desire, no matter how immoral or dangerous, finds satisfaction. Needless to say, Manson was seized upon by the media to discredit a movement that was highly ambivalent regarding his antics in the first place.

14. Consider the case of Amiri Baraka in this regard. In his black-nationalist period, Baraka leaves the white world behind and takes the uptown train to Harlem. While he eschews white support, his tactics and goals remain similar to the counterculture. Baraka may be less concerned with fostering the irrational, but he likewise sees art

as a means to political liberation, as he makes clear in his poem "Black Art": "We want 'poems that kill.' / Assassin poems, Poems that shoot / guns. Poems that wrestle cops into alleys" (*LeRoi Jones / Amiri Baraka Reader* 219). Like the Diggers, Baraka brought this poetry into the street. In his *Autobiography*, Baraka claims, "We brought street-corner poetry readings, moving the poets by truck from site to site" (212). And like the counterculture, Baraka had a knack for word play, his most famous being the substitution of "Error Farce" for his time spent in the "Air Force." Baraka did not end with personal empowerment, however. He saw expression as a means to reconnect with race, and from there, he sought to build a force that would challenge white oppression.

15. Compare the function of breath in mantra with Burroughs's use of it in *The Western Lands*. While for Ginsberg breath is equated with bodily regulation and inter-subjective rapport, in Burroughs's novel, breath is allied to death and disease. "Breathers" are entities "whose breath is the stench of death" (162). For Burroughs, breath is a movement outward meant as an attack and not a means for intersubjective rapport.

Works Cited and Consulted

Abrams, Philip, and Andrew McCulloch. *Communes, Sociology, and Society.* Cambridge, Eng.: Cambridge UP, 1976.

Aitken, Robert. *Encouraging Words: Zen Buddhist Teachings for Western Students.* New York: Pantheon, 1993.

Baker, Houston A. *Modernism and the Harlem Renaissance.* Chicago: U of Chicago P, 1987.

Baraka, Amiri. *The Autobiography of LeRoi Jones.* Chicago: Hill, 1997.

———. *Black Music.* New York: Morrow, 1968.

———. *Blues People: Negro Music in White America.* New York: Morrow, 1963.

———. *Home: Social Essays.* New York: Morrow, 1966.

———. *The LeRoi Jones / Amiri Baraka Reader.* Ed. William J. Harris. New York: Thunder's Mouth, 1995.

———. "The Screamers." *Tales.* New York: Grove, 1967. 71–80.

———. "Suppose Sorrow Was a Time Machine." *The Fiction of LeRoi Jones/Amiri Baraka.* Chicago: Hill, 2000. 1–4.

Barrett, William. *Irrational Man: A Study in Existential Philosophy.* New York: Doubleday, 1962.

Barthes, Roland. *Camera Lucida: Reflections on Photography.* Trans. Richard Howard. New York: Hill, 1981.

Bataille, Georges. *Eroticism: Death and Sensuality.* Trans. Mary Dalwood. San Francisco: City Lights, 1986.

Baudelaire, Charles. *My Heart Laid Bare.* Trans. Norman Cameron. New York: Haskell, 1975.

Belgrad, Daniel. *The Culture of Spontaneity: Improvisation and the Arts in Postwar America.* Chicago: U of Chicago P, 1998.

Benhabib, Seyla. *Situating the Self: Gender, Community, and Postmodernism in Contemporary Ethics.* Cambridge, Eng.: Polity, 1992.

Benjamin, Walter. "Theses on the Philosophy of History." *Illuminations.* Trans. Harry Zohn. Ed. and intro. Hannah Arendt. New York: Schocken, 1968. 253–64.

Bergson, Henri. *The Creative Mind.* Trans. Mabelle L. Andison. New York: Greenwood, 1968.

Berman, Marshall. *All That Is Solid Melts into Air: The Experience of Modernity.* New York: Simon, 1982.

Bersani, Leo. *The Culture of Redemption.* Cambridge: Harvard UP, 1990.

Bertens, Hans. *The Idea of the Postmodern: A History.* London: Routledge, 1995.

Birt, Robert. "Existence, Identity, and Liberation." *Existence in Black: An Anthology of Black Existential Philosophy.* Ed. Lewis R. Gordon. New York: Routledge, 1997. 203–14.

Bové, Paul. Preface. *Early Postmodernism: Foundational Essays*. Durham: Duke UP, 1995. 1–16.

Burgin, Victor. "Looking at Photographs." *Thinking Photography*. Ed. Victor Burgin. London: Macmillan, 1982. 142–53.

Burke, Edmund. *A Philosophical Enquiry into the Origin of Our Ideas of the Sublime and Beautiful*. London: Blackwell, 1987.

Burroughs, William S. *Cities of the Red Night*. New York: Holt, 1995.

———. Foreword. *You Can't Win*. By Jack Black. Edinburgh: AK, 2000. 11–13.

———. *The Job: Interviews with William S. Burroughs*. New York: Penguin, 1989.

———. *Junky*. New York: Penguin, 2002.

———. *The Last Words of Dutch Schultz*. New York: Arcade, 1975.

———. *Naked Lunch*. New York: Grove, 1992.

———. *The Place of Dead Roads*. New York: Holt, 1995.

———. *Queer*. New York: Viking, 1985.

———. *The Soft Machine*. New York: Grove, 1988.

———. *The Western Lands*. New York: Penguin, 1988.

———. *The Wild Boys: A Book of the Dead*. New York: Grove, 1992.

Calinescu, Matei. *Five Faces of Modernity: Modernism, Avant-garde, Decadence, Kitsch, Postmodernism*. Durham: Duke UP, 1987.

Cartier-Bresson, Henri. *The Mind's Eye: Writings on Photography and Photographers*. New York: Aperture, 1999.

Casey, Edward S. *The Fate of Place: A Philosophical History*. Berkeley: U of California P, 1997.

Cattier, Michel. *The Life and Work of Wilhelm Reich*. Trans. Ghislaine Boulanger. New York: Horizon, 1971.

Charters, Ann, ed. *Beat Down to Your Soul: What Was the Beat Generation?* New York: Penguin, 2001.

———. *Kerouac: A Biography*. New York: St. Martin's, 1994.

Coontz, Stephanie. *The Way We Never Were: American Families and the Nostalgia Trap*. New York: Basic, 1992.

Cooper, David E. *Existentialism*. Oxford: Blackwell, 1999.

Corso, Gregory. *Long Live Man*. New York: NewDirections, 1959.

———. *Mindfield: New and Selected Poems*. New York: Thunder's Mouth, 1998.

Dallmayr, Fred. *The Other Heidegger*. Ithaca: Cornell UP, 1993.

Damon, Maria. *The Dark End of the Street: Margins in American Vanguard Poetry*. Minneapolis: U of Minnesota P, 1993.

Davidson, Michael. *The San Francisco Renaissance: Poetics and Community at Mid-Century*. Cambridge: Cambridge UP, 1989.

Davis, J. C. "Utopia and the New World, 1500–1700." *Utopia*. Ed. Roland Schaer, Gregory Claeys, and Lyman Tower Sargent. New York: New York Public Library, 2000. 95–118.

Deleuze, Gilles. *The Fold*. Trans. Tom Conley. Minneapolis: U of Minnesota P, 1993.

———. *Masochism: Coldness and Cruelty, Venus in Furs*. 1967. Trans. Jean McNeil. New York: Zone, 1991.

Deleuze, Gilles, and Felix Guattari. *Anti-Oedipus: Capitalism and Schizophrenia*. Trans. Robert Hurley, Mark Seem, and Helen R. Lane. New York: Viking, 1977.

———. *A Thousand Plateaus: Capitalism and Schizophrenia*. Trans. Brian Massumi. Minneapolis: U of Minnesota P, 1998.

———. *What Is Philosophy?* Trans. Hugh Tomlinson and Graham Burchell. New York: Columbia UP, 1994.

Derrida, Jacques. *Of Grammatology.* Trans. Gayatri Chakravorty Spivak. Baltimore: John Hopkins UP, 1976.

Digger Archives, The. March 26, 2002. <http://www.diggers.org/overview.htm>.

di Prima, Diane. *Dinners and Nightmares.* San Francisco: Last Gasp, 1998.

———. *Memoirs of a Beatnik.* San Francisco: Last Gasp, 1969.

———. *Recollections of My Life as a Woman.* New York: Viking, 2001.

———. *Revolutionary Letters Etc.* San Francisco: City Lights, 1971.

Edwards, Richard. *Contested Terrain: The Transformation of the Workplace in the Twentieth Century. United States.* New York: Basic, 1979.

Ehrenreich, Barbara. *The Hearts of Men: American Dreams and the Flight from Commitment.* New York: Anchor, 1983.

Eisinger, Joel. *Trace and Transformation: American Criticism of Photography in the Modernist Period.* Albuquerque: U of New Mexico P, 1995.

Eliot, T. S. "Tradition and the Individual Talent." *The Norton Anthology of Theory and Criticism.* Ed. Vincent B. Leitch. New York: Norton, 2001. 1092–97.

Ermarth, Elizabeth Deeds. *Sequel to History: Postmodernism and the Crisis of Representational Time.* Princeton: Princeton UP, 1992.

Eysteinsson, Astradur. *The Concept of Modernism.* Ithaca: Cornell UP, 1990.

Fanon, Frantz. *Black Skin, White Masks.* Trans. Charles Lam Markmann. New York: Grove, 1967.

Felski, Rita. *Doing Time: Feminist Theory and Postmodern Culture.* New York: New York UP, 2000.

Fields, Rick. *How the Swans Came to the Lake: A Narrative History of Buddhism in America.* Boston: Shambhala, 1992.

Foucault, Michel. *Aesthetics, Methods, and Epistemology.* Trans. Robert Hurley and others. Ed. James D. Faubion. *Essential Works of Foucault.* Vol. 2. New York: New, 1998.

———. *The History of Sexuality: Volume I: An Introduction.* Trans. Robert Hurley. New York: Vintage, 1990.

———. *The Use of Pleasure: Volume 2 of The History of Sexuality.* Trans. Robert Hurley. New York: Vintage, 1990.

Fox, Meg. "Unreliable Allies: Subjective and Objective Time in Childbirth." *Taking Our Time: Feminist Perspectives on Temporality.* Ed. Frieda Johles Forman, with Caoran Sowton. Oxford: Pergamon, 1989. 123–34.

Freud, Sigmund. *The Freud Reader.* Ed. Peter Gay. New York: Norton, 1989.

Fulton, Ann. *Apostles of Sartre: Existentialism in America, 1945–1963.* Evanston: Northwestern UP, 1999.

Gedney, William. *What Was True: The Photographs and Notebooks of William Gedney.* Ed. Margaret Sartor. New York: Lyndhurst, 2000.

Gerhard, Jane. *Desiring Revolution: Second-wave Feminism and the Rewriting of American Sexual Thought 1920 to 1982.* New York: Columbia UP, 2001.

Giamo, Ben. *Kerouac, the Word and the Way: Prose Artist as Spiritual Quester.* Carbondale: Southern Illinois UP, 2000.

Gilroy, Paul. *The Black Atlantic: Modernity and Double Consciousness.* Cambridge: Harvard UP, 1992.

Ginsberg, Allen. *Allen Verbatim: Lectures on Poetry, Politics, Consciousness.* Ed. Gordon Ball. New York: McGraw, 1975.

——. *Bixby Canyon Ocean Path Word Breeze.* New York: Gotham, 1972.

——. *Chicago Trial Testimony.* San Francisco: City Lights, 1975.

——. *Collected Poems: 1947–1980.* New York: Harper, 1984.

——. *Death & Fame: Poems 1993–1997.* New York: Harper, 1999.

——. *Deliberate Prose: Selected Essays 1952–1995.* New York: Harper, 2000.

——. *Gay Sunshine Interview.* Ed. Allen Young. Bolinas: Grey Fox, 1974.

——. *Howl.* Ed. Barry Miles. New York: Harper, 1986.

——. *Howl and Other Poems.* San Francisco: City Lights, 1996.

——. "Improvised Poetics." *Composed on the Tongue.* Ed. Donald Allen. Bolinas: Grey Fox, 1980. 18–62.

——. *Indian Journals.* New York: Grove, 1996.

——. Interview with Ekbert Faas. *Towards a New American Poetics: Essays and Interviews.* By Ekbert Faas. Santa Barbara: Black Sparrow, 1978. 269–88.

——. *Iron Horse.* San Francisco: City Lights, 1978.

——. *Journals Mid-Fifties.* New York: Harper, 1995.

——. "Negative Capability: Kerouac's Buddhist Ethic." *Disembodied Poetics: Annals of the Jack Kerouac School.* Ed. Anne Waldman and Andrew Schelling. Albuquerque: U of New Mexico P, 1994. 364–75.

——. "The New Consciousness." *Composed on the Tongue: Literary Conversations, 1967–77.* Ed. Donald Allen. San Francisco: Grey Fox, 1980. 63–93.

——. *On the Poetry of Allen Ginsberg.* Ed. Lewis Hyde. Ann Arbor: U of Michigan P, 1984.

——. *Photographs.* Altadena: Twelvetrees, 1990.

——. *Snapshot Poetics.* San Francisco: Chronicle, 1993.

——. *Spontaneous Mind: Selected Interviews 1958–1996.* New York: Harper, 2001.

——. *Writers at Work: The Paris Review Interviews.* New York: Viking, 1967.

Glassman, Joyce. *Come and Join the Dance.* New York: Wolff, 1961.

Goodman, Paul, Frederick Perls, and Ralph E. Hefferline. *Gestalt Therapy: Excitement and Growth in the Human Personality.* New York: Dell, 1951.

Gordon, Lewis R. *Existentia Africana: Understanding Africana Existential Thought.* New York: Routledge, 2000.

Grace, Nancy M., and Ronna C. Johnson. *Breaking the Rule of Cool: Interviewing and Reading Women Beat Writers.* Jackson: UP of Mississippi, 2004.

Graebner, William. *The Age of Doubt: American Thought and Culture in the 1940s.* Boston: Twayne, 1991.

Green, Jonathan, and James Friedman. *American Photography.* New York: Abrams, 1984.

Harris, Oliver. *William Burroughs and the Secret of Fascination.* Carbondale: Southern Illinois UP, 2003.

Harvey, David. *The Condition of Postmodernity: An Enquiry into the Origins of Cultural Change.* Cambridge: Blackwell, 1990.

Heidegger, Martin. *Being and Time.* Trans. John Macquarrie and Edward Robinson. London: SCM, 1962.

"Hipstory: Trips Festival January 1966." *The Trips Festival,* 2003. <http://www.digthatcrazyfarout.com/trips/trips_festival_history.html>.

Holmes, John Clellon. "The Philosophy of the Beat Generation." Charters, *Beat Down* 228–37.

Hunt, Tim. *Kerouac's Crooked Road: The Development of a Fiction.* Hamden: Archon, 1981.

Hutcheon, Linda. *A Poetics of Postmodernism: History, Theory, Fiction.* New York: Routledge, 2004.

———. *The Politics of Postmodernism.* New York: Routledge, 2000.

Irigaray, Luce. *An Ethics of Sexual Difference.* Trans. Carolyn Burke and Gillian C. Gill. Ithaca: Cornell UP, 1995.

———. *The Irigaray Reader.* Ed. Margaret Whitford. Oxford: Blackwell, 1991.

Jameson, Fredric. Foreword. Lyotard, *Postmodern Condition* vii–xxii.

———. "Postmodernism and Consumer Society." *The Anti-Aesthetic: Essays on Postmodern Culture.* Ed. Hal Foster. Port Townsend: Bay, 1983. 111–25.

———. *A Singular Modernity.* London: Verso, 2002.

Jay, Martin. *Downcast Eyes: The Denigration of Vision in Twentieth-Century French Thought.* Berkeley: U of California P, 1994.

Johnson, Ronna C. "'And Then She Went': Beat Departures and Feminine Transgressions in Joyce Johnson's *Come and Join the Dance.*" Johnson and Grace, *Girls* 69–95.

———. "'You're putting me on': Jack Kerouac and the Postmodern Emergence." *The Beat Generation: Critical Essays.* Ed. Kostas Myrsiades. New York: Lang, 2002. 37–56.

Johnson, Ronna C., and Nancy M. Grace, eds. *Girls Who Wore Black: Women Writing the Beat Generation.* New Brunswick: Rutgers UP, 2002.

———. "Visions and Revisions of the Beat Generation." Johnson and Grace, *Girls* 1–24.

Jones, Hettie. *How I Became Hettie Jones.* New York: Grove, 1990.

Kandel, Lenore. *The Love Book.* San Francisco: Stolen Paper, 1966.

Kaufman, Bob. "Second April." Broadside. San Francisco: City Lights, 1959.

Kerouac, Jack. *Atop an Underwood.* Ed. Paul Marion. New York: Viking, 1999.

———. *Dharma Bums.* New York: Penguin, 1986.

———. *Dr. Sax.* New York: Grove, 1987.

———. *Good Blonde & Others.* San Francisco: Grey Fox, 1996.

———. Introduction. *The Americans.* By Robert Frank. New York: Aperture, 1978. 5–9.

———. "Letters from Jack Kerouac to Ed White, 1947–68." *Missouri Review* 17.3 (1994): 107–60.

———. *Maggie Cassady.* New York: Penguin, 1993.

———. *On the Road.* New York: Penguin, 1976.

———. "The Railroad Earth." *Lonesome Traveler.* New York: Grove, 1988. 37–83.

———. *Satori in Paris.* New York: Grove, 1988.

———. *Scripture of the Golden Eternity.* San Francisco: City Lights, 1994.

———. *Selected Letters 1940–1956.* New York: Penguin, 1996.

———. *Some of the Dharma.* New York: Viking, 1997.

———. *The Subterraneans.* New York: Grove, 1981.

———. *The Town and the City.* San Diego: Harcourt Brace, 1983.

———. *Tristessa.* New York: Penguin, 1992.

———. *Vanity of Duluoz.* New York: Penguin, 1994.

———. *Visions of Cody.* New York: Penguin, 1993.

Knight, Brenda, ed. *Women of the Beat Generation. The Writers, Artists, and Muses at the Heart of a Revolution.* Berkeley: Conari, 1996.

Kristeva, Julia. *The Kristeva Reader*. Ed. Toril Moi. New York: Columbia UP, 1986.

Kumar, Krishan. *Utopia and Anti-Utopia in Modern Times*. Oxford: Blackwell, 1987.

——. "Utopia and Anti-Utopia in the Twentieth Century." *Utopia*. Ed. Roland Schaer, Gregory Claeys, and Lyman Tower Sargent. New York: New York Public Library, 2000. 251–67.

——. *Utopianism*. Minneapolis: U of Minnesota P, 1991.

Kyger, Joanne. *Going On: Selected Poems 1958–1980*. New York: Dutton, 1983.

Lardas, John. *The Bop Apocalypse: The Religious Visions of Kerouac, Ginsberg, and Burroughs*. Urbana: U of Illinois P, 2001.

Lee, Ben. "'Howl' and Other Poems: Is There Old Left in These New Beats?" *American Literature* 76.2 (2004): 367–89.

Lhamon, W. T. *Deliberate Speed: The Origins of a Cultural Style in the American 1950s*. Washington, DC: Smithsonian Institute P, 1990.

Lipsitz, George. *Time Passages: Collective Memory and American Popular Culture*. Minneapolis: U of Minnesota P, 1990.

Lott, Deshae E. "'All things are different appearances of the same emptiness': Buddhism and Jack Kerouac's Nature Writings." Skerl, *Reconstructing the Beats* 169–86.

Lukács, Georg. *History and Class Consciousness: Studies in Marxist Dialectics*. Trans. Rodney Livingstone. Cambridge: MIT P, 1968.

——. "Reification and the Consciousness of the Proletariat." *History and Class Consciousness: Studies in Marxist Dialectics*. Trans. Rodney Livingstone. Cambridge: MIT P, 1968. 83–222.

Lyotard, Jean-François. *The Inhuman: Reflections on Time*. Trans. Geoffrey Bennington and Rachel Bowlby. Stanford: Stanford UP, 1991.

——. *The Postmodern Condition: A Report on Knowledge*. Trans. Geoffrey Bennington and Brian Massumi. Minneapolis: U of Minnesota P, 1984.

Mackey, Nathaniel. *Discrepant Engagement: Dissonance, Cross-culturality, and Experimental Writing*. Tuscaloosa: U of Alabama P, 1993.

Mailer, Norman. *Miami and the Siege of Chicago*. Cleveland: World, 1969.

——. "The White Negro." *Advertisements for Myself*. New York: Putnam's, 1959. 337–71.

Marcuse, Herbert. *Eros and Civilization: A Philosophical Inquiry into Freud*. Boston: Beacon, 1966.

Martinez, Manuel Luis. *Countering the Counterculture: Rereading Postwar American Dissent from Jack Kerouac to Tomas Rivera*. Madison: U of Wisconsin P, 2003.

Massumi, Brian. Foreword. *A Thousand Plateaus: Capitalism and Schizophrenia*. By Gilles Deleuze and Felix Guattari. Trans. Brian Massumi. Minneapolis: U of Minnesota P, 1998. ix–xv.

McPherson, James Alan. *Railroad: Trains and Train People in American Culture*. New York: Random, 1976.

Merleau-Ponty, Maurice. *Phenomenology of Perception*. Trans. Colin Smith. London: Routledge, 1962.

Miller, Timothy. *The 60s Communes: Hippies and Beyond*. Syracuse: Syracuse UP, 1999.

Mitchell, Juliet. *Psychoanalysis and Feminism: Freud, Reich, Laing, and Women*. New York: Vintage, 1975.

Mohr, Michael. "Emerging from Nonduality: Koan Practice in the Rinzai Tradition since Hakuin." *The Koan: Texts and Contexts in Zen Buddhism*. Ed. Steven Heine and Dale S. Wright. New York: Oxford UP, 2000. 244–79.

Murphy, Timothy S. *Wising Up the Marks: The Amodern William Burroughs*. Berkeley: U of California P, 1997.

Nadel, Alan. *Containment Culture: American Narratives, Postmodernism, and the Atomic Age*. Durham: Duke UP, 1995.

Nealon, Jeffrey T. "Refraining, Becoming-Black: Repetition and Difference in Amiri Baraka's *Blues People*." *Symploke* 6 (1998): 83–95.

Newhall, Beaumont. *The History of Photography*. New York: Museum of Modern Art, 1982.

Nicosia, Gerald. *Memory Babe: A Critical Biography of Jack Kerouac*. New York: Grove, 1983.

Olson, Charles. *Collected Prose*. Ed. Donald Allen and Benjamin Friedlander. Berkeley: U of California P, 1997.

O'Malley, Michael. *Keeping Watch: A History of American Time*. New York: Viking, 1990.

Osborne, Peter. *The Politics of Time: Modernity and the Avant-Garde*. London: Verso, 1995.

Osofsky, Gilbert. *Harlem: The Making of a Ghetto*. New York: Harper, 1966.

Panish, Jon. *The Color of Jazz: Race and Representation in Postwar American Culture*. Jackson: UP of Mississippi, 1997.

Peabody, Richard, ed. *A Different Beat: Writings by Women of the Beat Generation*. New York: High Risk, 1997.

Perry, Charles. *The Haight-Ashbury: A History*. New York: Rolling Stone, 1984.

Polsky, Ned. "2. Ned Polsky." In Mailer, "White Negro," 365–69.

Prebish, Charles S. *American Buddhism*. North Scituate: Duxbury, 1979.

Proust, Marcel. *Remembrance of Things Past*. Trans. Frederick A. Blossom. New York: Random, 1932.

Reich, Wilhelm. *The Cancer Biopathy: Volume II of the Discovery of the Orgone*. Trans. Andrew White with Mary Higgins and Chester M. Raphael. New York: Farrar, 1973.

———. *Character Analysis*. 1933. Trans. Vincent R. Carfagno. New York: Touchstone, 1972.

———. *The Function of the Orgasm: Sex-Economic Problems of Biological Energy*. Trans. Theodore P. Wolfe. New York: Orgone Institute P, 1942.

———. *Selected Writings: An Introduction to Orgonomy*. New York: Farrar, 1973.

Reumann, Miriam G. *American Sexual Character: Sex, Gender, and National Identity in the Kinsey Reports*. Berkeley: U of California P, 2005.

Robinson, Paul A. *The Freudian Left: Wilhelm Reich, Geza Roheim, Herbert Marcuse*. New York: Harper, 1969.

———. *The Modernization of Sex: Havelock Ellis, Alfred Kinsey, William Masters, and Virginia Johnson*. Ithaca: Cornell UP, 1989.

Rubin, Jerry. "Selections from 'Yippie' and 'Chicago.'" *Counterculture and Revolution*. Ed. David Horowitz, Michael P. Lerner, and Craig Pyes. New York: Random, 1972. 15–26.

Rupp, Leila J., and Verta Taylor. *Survival in the Doldrums: The American Women's Rights Movement, 1945 to the 1960s*. New York: Oxford UP, 1987.

Russell, Jamie. *Queer Burroughs*. New York: Palgrave, 2001.

Sade, Marquis de. *Justine, Philosophy in the Bedroom, and Other Writings*. Trans. Richard Seaver and Austryn Wainhouse. New York: Grove, 1965.

Sargeant, Jack. *The Naked Lens: Beat Cinema*. London: Creation, 1997.

Sartre, Jean-Paul. *Being and Nothingness*. Trans. Hazel E. Barnes. New York: Washington Square, 1992.

Savran, David. *Taking It like a Man: White Masculinity, Masochism, and Contemporary American Culture*. Princeton: Princeton UP, 1998.

Schumacher, Michael. *Dharma Lion: A Biography of Allen Ginsberg*. New York: St. Martin's, 1992.

Seager, Richard Hughes. *Buddhism in America*. New York: Columbia UP, 1999.

Siebers, Tobin. Introduction. *Heterotopia: Postmodern Utopia and the Body Politic*. Ed. Siebers. Ann Arbor: U of Michigan P, 1997. 1–38.

Sitney, P. Adams. *Visionary Film: The American Avant-Garde*. New York: Oxford UP, 1979.

Skerl, Jennie, ed. *Reconstructing the Beats*. New York: Palgrave, 2004.

———. *William S. Burroughs*. Boston: Twayne, 1985.

Smith, Daniel W. "'A Life of Pure Immanence': Deleuze's 'Critique et Clinique' Project." Introduction. *Essays Critical and Clinical*. By Gilles Deleuze. Trans. Daniel W. Smith and Michael A. Greco. Minneapolis: U of Minnesota P, 1997. xi–liv.

Sontag, Susan. *On Photography*. New York: Anchor, 1990.

Spanos, William V. "The Detective and the Boundary: Some Notes on the Postmodern Literary Imagination." Bové 17–39.

Stephenson, Gregory. *The Daybreak Boys: Essays on the Literature of the Beat Generation*. Carbondale: Southern Illinois UP, 1990.

———. *Exiled Angel: A Study of the Work of Gregory Corso*. London: Aldgate, 1989.

Sterritt, David. *Screening the Beats: Media Culture and the Beat Sensibility*. Carbondale: Southern Illinois UP, 2004.

Sullivan, James D. *On the Walls and in the Streets: American Poetry Broadsides from the 1960s*. Urbana: U of Illinois P, 1997.

Suzuki, Shunryu. *Zen Mind, Beginner's Mind*. New York: Weatherhill, 1981.

Tagg, John. *The Burden of Representation: Essays on Photographies and Histories*. Minneapolis: U of Minnesota P, 1993.

Trigilio, Tony. *Allen Ginsberg's Buddhist Poetics*. Carbondale: Southern Illinois UP, 2007.

———. *"Strange Prophecies Anew": Rereading Apocalypse in Blake, H.D., and Ginsberg*. Madison: Fairleigh Dickinson UP, 2000.

United States. National Park Service. *Lowell: The Story of an Industrial City*. Washington, DC: Div. of Pub., Natl. Park Service, 1992.

Vega, Janine Pommy. *Tracking the Serpent: Journeys to Four Continents*. San Francisco: City Lights, 1997.

Warhol, Andy. *Photography*. Pittsburgh: Andy Warhol Museum, 1999.

Watten, Barrett. "Turn to Language." *Critical Inquiry* 29.1 (2002): 139–83.

Watts, Alan W. *Beat Zen, Square Zen, and Zen*. San Francisco: City Lights, 1959.

———. "Beat Zen, Square Zen, and Zen." *The Portable Beat Reader*. Ed. Ann Charters. New York: Penguin, 1992. 607–14.

———. *Zen and the Beat Way*. Boston: Tuttle, 1997.

Weinreich, Regina. *The Spontaneous Poetics of Jack Kerouac: A Study of the Fiction*. Carbondale: Southern Illinois UP, 1987.

Whitebook, Joel. *Perversion and Utopia: A Study in Psychoanalysis and Critical Theory.*
     Cambridge: MIT P, 1995.
Whitford, Margaret. Introduction. Irigaray, *Irigaray Reader* 1–15.
Wolfe, Tom. *The Electric Kool-Aid Acid Test.* New York: Bantam, 1989.
Young, Iris Marion. *Intersecting Voices: Dilemmas of Gender, Political Philosophy, and
     Policy.* Princeton: Princeton UP, 1997.

Index

Page numbers in italics denote illustrations.

Erik Mortenson is an assistant professor in the Department of English and Comparative Literature at Koç University in Istanbul, Turkey. He has published extensively on the Beats in journals such as *Chicago Review, Janus Head,* and *College Literature.* He is working on a book that examines the image of the "shadow" in postwar America.